Sir Thomas Beecham

A Centenary Tribute

Sir THOMAS BEECHAM

Alan Jefferson

Foreword by Sir Robert Mayer, CH

MACDONALD AND JANE'S · LONDON

For Antonia:

inspirer
persuader
prompter
sternest critic
Beloved Wife

Copyright © Alan Jefferson 1979
First published 1979 by
Macdonald and Jane's Publishers Ltd
Paulton House
8 Shepherdess Walk
London N1 7LW
ISBN 0 354 04205 X

Filmset in Great Britain by
Northumberland Press Ltd, Gateshead, Tyne and Wear
Printed and bound by
Richard Clay (The Chaucer Press) Ltd, Bungay, Suffolk

Contents

'All sorts of things are said about my "flair", my "genius", my "temperament", but I seldom get credit for my main virtue and attribute – *inexhaustible industry*.'
                                        Sir Thomas Beecham

LIST OF ILLUSTRATIONS

Beecham at Delius's grave in Limpsfield, 1935 (*Christopher Redwood/ Norman Cameron*)
Beecham rehearsing the LPO (*London Philharmonic Orchestra*)
Beecham in a family play at Lympne Castle in Kent
With Ludmilla Tchernicheva and Leonid Massine, 1935 (*Dancing Times, and London News Agency*)

Between pages 176 and 177
Beecham with Eva Turner, 1935 (*London News Agency*), and with Wilhelm Furtwängler, 1936 (*Hamish Hamilton Ltd*)
Beecham as guest-conductor of the Berlin Philharmonic Orchestra, 1935 (*Denham Ford*)
The fake German press photograph of Beecham with Hitler (*Hamish Hamilton Ltd*)
Dinner at the Savoy Hotel for the Berlin Philharmonic Orchestra, 1937 (*Raywood Ltd and Royal Opera House Archive*)
Beecham at a rehearsal of *Das Rheingold* at Covent Garden, 1934
Betty Thomas and her son Jeremy, c. 1933 (*Jeremy Thomas*)
Betty-Humby Beecham and Sir Thomas in duet, c. 1949

Between pages 192 and 193
Beecham in 1942 at the time he became an associate conductor at the Met (*Metropolitan Opera Archives*)
Beecham in Seattle, 1942 (*Seattle Times, and J. D. Gilmour*)
On the film set of *The Red Shoes*, 1947 (*Denham Ford*)
With Dennis Brain, 1950
Anthony Pini and Beecham in action
Beecham with Sibelius, 1955, and with Carl Ebert at Glyndebourne in 1960

Between pages 224 and 225
Beecham playing cricket, and being greeted by a gendarme in Nice (*Edward Quinn*)
Lady Shirley Beecham and Sir Thomas
Beecham's 80th birthday dinner, 1959 (*Central Press*)
The RPO luncheon at Portsmouth on the day of Beecham's last concert, 7 May 1960 (*J. A. Hewes, Photographers, Southsea*)
Beecham in about 1960

Foreword

One day, when the definitive history of music in Britain in the twentieth century comes to be written, the year 1945 will be seen as a turning point. For that was the year in which, for the first time in British history, the State undertook a measure of responsibility for the support of the arts, including, of course, music. This decision caused an immediate leap forward into the era of the new musical Britain. The primary concrete result was the emergence of London as the musical capital of the world. Then came regional development, with the creation of opera companies in Glasgow, Cardiff and Leeds, and with less ambitious music societies springing up all over the country. During the final decades of the century the expansion will continue, I feel sure, with opera and symphony concerts flourishing throughout the land to vie with the perennial popularity of oratorio. The stage is all set, and fortunately the resulting incalculable enrichment of our cultural life may be achieved at a cost which is negligible in comparison with its value to the nation.

But if the post-war development owes much to government support, this happy state of affairs would never have been possible without the dedication and determination in pre-1945 days of people like Henry Wood, John Christie, and – foremost among them – Thomas Beecham. Beecham was unique. Others were patrons, innovators, conductors, impresarios. He combined all these functions in himself, but he was endowed in addition with the rare quality of genius.

My first meeting with him was in 1931. The impresario Lionel Powell had just engaged Furtwängler to conduct the Berlin Philharmonic on a tour of Britain. In the midst of the negotiations Powell died, and the tour was put in jeopardy. I was in close contact at the time with those concerned in the organisation of the tour, as also was Beecham, and together we were able to step in and save the situation.

The visit of the Berlin Philharmonic was an inspiration to Beecham. For a long time London had had several orchestras, but the players were mostly the same in each; they merely changed their hats. Beecham, always a perfectionist, dreamed of an orchestra of his own like those of Berlin or Vienna. He consulted me about the possibility of sponsorship, and together with Malcolm Sargent, the first conductor of the 'Robert Mayer Concerts for Children', I tapped a number of likely sources, especially the industrialist and philanthropist Samuel Courtauld. The upshot of our joint efforts was the creation of the London Philharmonic Orchestra (of which the reader will find the fascinating details in this book).

Beecham, as Artistic Director, selected the players. Courtauld and to some extent I myself were responsible for the finances; and Beecham got the orchestra he wanted. When, four years later, the orchestra's Board was dissolved, Beecham insisted, as a final gesture, on offering the services of the LPO to my children's concerts; and the children had the unforgettable experience of having this legendary figure in their midst. Indeed, I myself have good reason to be thankful to Beecham's persistence, far ahead of his time, in trying in vain to launch opera in Britain in 1922. It was partly as a belated outcome of his efforts then that I was able to launch my 'opera nights' for young people fifty years later.

It is a pleasure to add this personal word of appreciation to Mr Jefferson's excellent account of one of the outstanding figures of English life in any century.

Sir Robert Mayer

Preface

WHENEVER I TALK to people who knew Beecham their faces light up and they ask: 'Well, what can I tell you about him?' It is as though he still shines through them, making them delight in having known him, in having been part of his life. For I never met him.

Thomas Beecham was passionately interested in everything. A new score, an old score, an old friend or a new one – each was scrutinised, then taken up or rejected. He had an eye for quality, yet certain trivia amused him. He made fun of silly people, who sometimes felt honoured by the fact that he had noticed them.

He gave to every one of his dear friends a unique piece of himself, letting all of them believe they held the key to his great being. Not so. Were they all to be put together, missing pieces would still leave gaps in the picture.

By nature he was a philosopher but he went to various extremes to conceal this lest he were branded an intellectual. He had to be free. He created the image of 'T.B.', man of the world, critic and humorist, as a defence against invasion of his real self. Only once, towards the end of his life, when he stood on the stage of the Sheldonian Theatre in Oxford and propounded his original ideas on the Jacobean dramatist John Fletcher, did he publicly step from one field of expertise into another. Most of his 'lectures' were off-the-cuff chats, like the bulk of *A Mingled Chime*, a connoisseurs' book rather than a straight autobiography. But what prose!

His inspiration was continuous and his achievements magical, whether on the concert platform, in the opera house or in the boardroom. His love of detective novels, football, cricket and wrestling was all an extension of his continuous interest in people and what they are capable of doing: one professional's examination of others.

Beecham has often been called an Edwardian, but I see him rather as one who possessed the conservatism, grand manner and personal attributes of a Victorian; for although he lived in changing times, he retained all that was about him when he was born. Only when he made music did his personality become timeless. Then, too, his 'shell' disappeared.

It is still too early for the definitive biography of Sir Thomas Beecham, but here I have sought the essence of the man from his background and his work. He was uncomfortably aware of the camera and it was extremely difficult to catch him off his guard. Nevertheless, the pictures reproduced within these pages help to set him in his period.

Alan Jefferson
Liskeard, Cornwall

Acknowledgments

I AM INDEBTED to a great number of individuals and corporate bodies for helping me throughout the course of researching and writing this book.

I am especially grateful to Shirley, Lady Beecham, who has helped and advised me and who has been most generous in lending material. Other members of Sir Thomas Beecham's family to whom I am indebted are: Mrs E. O. Betts, sister; Miss Anne Francis, niece; and Thomas Beecham, son. Jeremy Thomas, stepson, has also been generous in relating events and lending material. Mr Thomas, Felix Aprahamian and Walter Legge have all read the draft text and have made invaluable suggestions. Miss Olive Chadwick of St Helens has provided me with much important data and has tirelessly answered questions. I am grateful to them all.

The following have also helped me, and I want to acknowledge my gratitude to them: Peter Bennett, David Bicknell, F. W. Birchall, May Blyth, The Lord Boothby, Sir Adrian Boult, Raymond Bryant, Archie Camden, The Earl of Carnarvon, Miss M. M. Coxhead, Dr and Mrs Del Mar, Denham Ford, Sir Rupert Hart-Davis, Lady Grant-Lawson, Arthur Hammond, Sir Robert Mayer, Mrs Jean Melloni (British Council, Mexico City), Mrs D. Morella, Harry Mortimer, Ivor Newton, The Viscount Norwich, Mrs Claudia Ottley, Christopher Redwood, The Hon. James Smith, Paul Strang, Frau Pauline Strauss, Mrs Emmie Tillett, Virgil Thomson, Denis Vaughan, Miss Kathrine Sorley Walker.

I wish to express my gratitude to the following publishers for permission to quote from their respective books as stated: Hutchinson Publishing Group, *A Mingled Chime* by Sir Thomas Beecham, Bart.; MacGibbon & Kee/Granada Publishing, *Barbirolli* by Michael Kennedy; Routledge & Kegan Paul, *On Wings of Song* by Lotte Lehmann. Also to George Christie for his permission to reprint an extract from a letter written by his father, John Christie, which first appeared in *Glyndebourne* by Spike Hughes.

And I most cordially thank the following organisations for their help:

ASLEF
Bayrischen Staatsoper
BBC Written Archive Centre
BBC Manchester
Bedford Estates
Beecham Proprietaries Ltd
Capital Radio
Concertgebouw, Amsterdam
Covent Garden Market
  Authority
Czech Philharmonic Orchestra
Dancing Times
Dresden Staatsoper
EMI Limited
Embassy of the Federal Republic
  of Germany
Department of the Environment
Essex County Council
GLC Record Office
Glyndebourne Festival Opera
Hungarian State Opera
The British Library
Libraries of: Birmingham

Essex County
Knowsley
Leeds
Liverpool
Manchester
Norfolk County
Plymouth
St Helens
San Francisco
London Philharmonic Orchestra
Metropolitan Opera, New York
Oxford University: Faculty of
  Music and Wadham College
Royal Albert Hall
Royal Archives, Windsor
Royal College of Music
Royal Liverpool Philharmonic
  Orchestra
Royal Opera, Stockholm
Royal Opera House Archive,
  Covent Garden
Royal Philharmonic Orchestra
Theatre Museum, London

Chapter One

FAMILY LIFE

THOMAS BEECHAM was the grandson of the inventor of Beechams Pills. He was born in St Helens, Lancashire, on 29 April 1879, heir to a huge fortune. Old Tom, his grandfather, and Joseph, his father, had worked unsparingly to amass this wealth and now, at last, they had someone to succeed them. Thomas's birthplace was in Arthur Street, adjoining the relatively new factory where pill-making went on at a great rate.

Old Tom had started life as a shepherd-boy in Oxfordshire in the 1830s and had once carved on his crook: 'If you will you may succeed in wonderful things. Look up! Try again.' He lived by these words and never allowed himself to bow to adversity. After giving up his sheep he had started in business as a pedlar on his own account, hawking his herbal remedies around the street markets of thriving Lancashire and resorting to any methods in order to sell the day's stock. He finally settled in Wigan, where his success was achieved by great determination, personal magnetism and an extraordinary intelligence. This brilliance was accompanied by a highly temperamental nature which his wife, Jane, had to suffer. In later life this was described as eccentricity, but Old Tom's intolerance and faithlessness were such as to blight their married life.

Jane's good singing voice was probably her only talent, yet it seems to have been the origin of musical ability in the family. Old Tom had none. He made Jane his slave, and as soon as their first son, Joseph, was old enough, he was given work to do every evening when he came home from school. In their poor dwelling behind the market in Wigan, Joseph applied his real talent for mathematics and English until he gradually became indispensable to his father. In 1858 the family moved to St Helens.

Five years later Tom bought a cottage in Westfield Street with a shed in the garden where the manufacturing went on at top speed. In 1865 the value of their output of pills had risen to £2,300; in 1867, when Joseph was nineteen, it came to more than £4,500 and some of the profits were put into property in or near Westfield Street. By 1876 Old Tom and Joseph had acquired enough ground and funds to demolish the houses and build a factory. When this was opened the turnover was £20,000 and the Beechams had a staff of four men.

Joseph loved and courted Josephine Burnett, an eligible local girl who had been born in London. Her father was a barber in St Helens who also dealt in silks. Little is known of the Burnetts except that they originally came from France. Josephine had a striking appearance and manner, and was very musical: she sang well and played the piano. Joseph courted her with painful shyness but their common interest in music helped considerably. He was now established and felt the need of a wife. His mother had died suddenly and painfully, and his father was already courting a girl of twenty-nine, almost half his age. Old Tom and Joseph strongly objected to each other's marriages, but both took place. Joseph and Josephine were married in August 1873, when he was twenty-four, and lived in Westfield Street, where their first three children were born. Emily came first, in 1874; then one who died at birth or soon after; and Laura, who was born in 1877.

In that year they moved into a larger and altogether more suitable house in Arthur Street, adjoining the factory, where Joseph could at last entertain. He was taking part in more of the local activities than before. He had been playing the organ at the Congregational Chapel for some years, and now he began to subscribe to charities, sponsored the St Helens Cycling Club, joined committees (where at first he was too withdrawn to be of much help) and gradually began to climb the local social ladder. His object was twofold: to become accepted by such families in St Helens as the Gambles and the Pilkingtons, and eventually to become Mayor. He had set his heart on that. Then one day Mr and Mrs Joseph Beecham received the invitation they had been waiting for, to a reception in the Mayor's Parlour. They had at last arrived.

Laura died at Christmas-time in 1878, but in the following April the first son, Thomas, was born. He was an unusual, advanced and intelligent child from the start, and seemed to know exactly how to get his own way. When he was only about five he was taken to his first concert, a piano recital of Grieg's music. He was stunned by its effect on him, and after he had been put to bed, unable to sleep, he decided that without doubt he, too, must learn to play the piano. So he walked downstairs in his nightshirt and interrupted a gathering of grown-ups to tell them so. Not only was this audacious behaviour for a Victorian child but surprisingly it had the desired effect, and piano lessons began soon afterwards.

One of the adults downstairs that evening was the astonished Old

Tom. He cut an unlikely figure in Josephine's drawing-room, with his working-man's clothes that he would never change and his working-class behaviour that he couldn't. He enjoyed spending quiet hours with his family in such surroundings – a far cry from those days in Wigan where the walls of his front-room were defaced by sales figures and formulae. Although he did not always get on with his dour son Joseph, he was proud of him for having inherited and developed the determination and ambition which were his own hall-mark.

Arthur Street was no longer good enough for Joseph now that he was growing richer year by year. His surroundings had to be appropriate to the man. In 1884, after two more daughters had arrived, Old Tom and Joseph talked about how they might improve their business premises and their houses. The ideal solution was for Joseph to move altogether and find another house; they would then pull down their factory and surrounding buildings and build a larger one on the site.

Thinking ahead to his ambition of one day becoming Mayor of St Helens, Joseph bought and extended an imposing residence called Ewanville in the Blacklow Brow district of Huyton, half-way between St Helens and Liverpool; and in the summer of 1885, when Young Thomas was six, the whole family moved there. So here they were, the product and promoters of industrial revolution, with newly-acquired wealth, not altogether accepted socially wherever they went, and certainly not willing to be on the same terms as the working people in Huyton. One can see Ewanville as a moated house, metaphorically speaking; for the Beechams, once inside it, kept to themselves.

In Josephine's part of the house there were two reception rooms of great splendour. The drawing-room, in particular, was beautifully furnished in the fashion of the time, with knick-knacks and *objets d'art* from all over the world which Joseph had collected on his travels for the firm. He went every year to the United States, where he not only supervised the selling of Beecham products but absorbed the harder American marketing methods. Eventually he saw such promise there that he set up a subsidiary company in New York. He attended the principal trade exhibitions there and visited Chicago, then only a town of shacks. His trips to Europe were more frequent and he also extended his tours farther afield to North Africa and the Near East. For his time, Joseph was an experienced and intrepid traveller; yet he never took Josephine with him.

The children, apart from Emily and Thomas, led a restricted life away from their parents in their nursery, the kind of existence that all children of rich families led until the beginning of the last war. The centre of

Joseph's home life was a large room in which there was a massive billiard-table, an organ and plenty of space for the other musical instruments that he was to add soon after moving in. Among these was an orchestrion which he had bought in Geneva; it was worked by electricity, and soon after being installed it managed to fuse all the lights in Huyton.

Thomas had the free run of this room when his father was not at the organ, playing his other instruments or playing billiards – a game he also taught his son. When Joseph was alone at the organ he wallowed in the music he was creating, unable to co-ordinate his hands and feet properly, and lost to the world. His efforts gave little pleasure to anybody else, least of all Thomas, who thought 'the Pater's' ability very poor indeed. Nevertheless, father and son used sometimes to sit together on the organ bench, Joseph managing the pedals while Thomas played on the manuals from opera scores.

These moments probably meant a great deal to Joseph, who was a lonely man and ill-attuned to his wife. He desperately needed somebody close, just to sit with, saying nothing but being *with* him. His shyness led him to be secretive, suspicious and easily put out of countenance by anybody better educated than himself. He never spoke on any subject which he did not completely understand, for he had a horror of being ridiculed. At this time in Thomas's life Joseph was already thinking of him as his greatest support and friend.

Joseph had another friend to whom he turned for support, a Congregational minister, the Rev. Alfred Carter. He had met him through the church, for the Beechams had been practising Congregationalists ever since they arrived at St Helens. The rest of the family heartily disliked the minister, whom they regarded as an *éminence grise*. But as Joseph lacked self-confidence and was very shy, he needed an adviser – not on business matters, in which he was incisive, but because otherwise he would try to avoid unpleasant circumstances by dodging them and simply not dealing with them – tactics that generally made things even worse.

So, to place responsibility for decision elsewhere, Joseph generally sought Carter's advice on matters which he considered to be of prime importance, among which was the education of his children. Carter was old-fashioned and bigoted; he was also a prig. Once Joseph asked him whether he thought it would be good for Emily and Thomas to accompany him to the opera. Anything to do with the theatre seemed to Carter to be sinful. The mere mention of *La Traviata,* that disgraceful opera by Verdi with a courtesan as its heroine, was enough to make his point, and Thomas's initiation to the opera was therefore delayed.

Joseph never seems to have consulted his wife over the children's welfare or upbringing. The two were already unhappy together. Josephine did not want to have so many children so quickly; Joseph, like his father, was a lusty man, and felt that neither his wife nor his children understood him. He began to seek his private pleasures elsewhere. Later he had another house in London, Hill Brow, in Arkwright Road, Hampstead, built for him in 1903 at a cost of £40,000. It had a concert hall and a splendid organ. So with this alternative ménage and his many trips abroad, Joseph was able to go away for months on end and never see his wife.

Thomas was sent to a local school run by a Mr Norris, in a house just beyond the end of the Ewanville garden. A Mr Unsworth came over from St Helens once or twice a week to give him piano lessons. Literature was the only academic subject which interested Thomas: he didn't put his back into any of the others. Unsworth, though, was persuaded by Thomas to stop giving him piano exercises by pre-classical composers, which didn't interest him in the least, but to tell him as much as possible about operas and their libretti. Unsworth was impressed, did as he was bid, and told Joseph that his son possessed an unusual talent.

There came the day when Joseph, having somehow got round his Richelieu, took the family over to Liverpool where the Carl Rosa Opera Company was appearing for an eight-week season from early January 1890. His first performance seems to have had physical as well as mental repercussions on Thomas on the following day. It is a pity that we do not know what the opera was. The boy behaved very strangely, with all his emotions sharpened – like someone in love. He tells us in *A Mingled Chime* that he later preferred going to *Aida* above all, that he cared very much for *Figaro* and preferred Gounod's *Romeo and Juliet* to *Faust*. As yet *Tannhäuser* and *Lohengrin* were too slow-moving. Joseph's favourite opera was *Lohengrin*, which he was said to have heard more than a hundred times in opera houses all over the world. Joseph had a great fondness for the opera, but Thomas had an absolute passion for it which, once roused, remained for ever.

With music and opera predominant in his mind, Thomas did not do very well under Mr Norris's guidance at the local school. He felt, too, that he was only kicking his heels there. Joseph had come to the same conclusion, and in September 1892 Thomas was sent westwards across the flat, green Lancastrian countryside to Rossall, the nearest public school for boys. In sending his son to a public school, Joseph was doing what he felt was expected of him, although he had only the vaguest idea of the effect it might have on the fortunate boy who was receiving a far better education than he had ever had himself.

Rossall stood in isolation, away from the town of Fleetwood, on the edge of the Irish Sea. Sometimes tall waves broke through the school's sea-wall into the grounds, while a wind, laced with sea and rain, stung the boys' faces as they ran across the quadrangle between lessons – a wind so forceful that one of Thomas's contemporaries swears that the boys used to lie on it, 'balanced, half-way up!' This strong climate continues to inject rude health into Rossalians and may account for the longevity of so many of them.

With a sandy shore, part of the ten miles to Blackpool, and occasional glimpses of the Isle of Man when the weather allows, the school has great charm, even if its buildings reflect some of the ruggedness of the prevailing weather. But at first Thomas hated it.

He found himself, to his amazement, pitched among 360 other boys who were entirely unable to share his pleasures and delights. He realised for the first time that things worked differently outside Ewanville. For a while he was unhappy, mainly homesick, and abhorred this new world to which his father had condemned him. But soon he discovered compensations.

Thomas went into Batson's House (now called Fleur de Lys) which occupied those rooms around the school's main archway. His housemaster, Thomas Batson (with whom he shared initials), has been described thus: 'T.B. had a fine character, a fine presence, vast strength and fitness, a scholar's brain and a grand voice.' He certainly had the greatest influence for Thomas's good at this stage of his life.

The music master at Rossall was Dr Sweeting, another man whom Thomas admired. He believed in a strong musical curriculum in the school, and also provided the occasional concert for the boys with outside singers or instrumentalists. At one such concert, while Thomas was in a state of ecstasy at being able to hear singing again, a boy behind told him to stop praying, and kicked him. This developed into a fight and the two boys were sent out of the hall. Reprimanded by Batson, Thomas suffered under the chill reproof: 'And I understood, Beecham, that you were fond of music.'

The rare delight of a live concert served all the more to highlight the unhappiness in between, for there were no open music rooms at Rossall, nor was he – yet – allowed to play on the Father Willis organ in Chapel. But his music lessons with Dr Sweeting were periods of great satisfaction. Thomas could play any Beethoven sonata at sight, and this astonished his master. One or two boys, his friends or admirers, used to listen outside the door during break when he was having a piano lesson.

From the moment of his arrival at Rossall, Thomas made a dramatic impact on his contemporaries. 'There's a new boy with a moustache,' ran the rumour. And there was, sure enough. Very soon they found that he had the most marvellous sweets sent from home. And he really could play the piano far better than any boy there.

After his first term Thomas enjoyed a particularly varied Carl Rosa Opera Season in Liverpool. Eugène Goossens senior was the principal conductor, and among the operas Thomas heard were *Otello*, *Tannhäuser*, *Lohengrin*, Meyerbeer's *The Prophet*, and the relatively new *Cavalleria Rusticana* (called *Rustic Chivalry* in English).

Thomas was first noticed in the school magazine during the Lent term of 1894, while playing for his House, as 'a member of a bully' in Rossall's unique version of hockey. In the summer of that year he distinguished himself in the Jubilee Concert. In the Lent term of 1896 he was a monitor in the lower-sixth form, and in the same year he was made captain of his House. When he reached this eminence he was allowed to have a piano in his study, a privilege never before accorded to a boy at Rossall, and never known since. School tradition has it that his study was the room above and to the right of the archway, viewed from the quadrangle.

Thomas sang first bass in a madrigal quartet made up of boys and masters. C. L. Stocks sang second bass and together they explored the old English masters – Weelkes, Wilbye and Byrd. This practical knowledge and the purity of the works which he sang were to be vitally important to Thomas Beecham later, though nobody who heard him 'singing' in the second half of his life would ever believe that he was once first bass in the Oriana Madrigal Society.

The photographs of Thomas at Rossall always show him doing something different from any of the other boys. He has, too, by far the most interesting face in these pictures. In 1896 he is the only boy to sport a moustache; in the three 1897 pictures his pose is extravagant (the moustache has gone): a Stetson hat among the cricket team, or a carnation in hand as he sits next to the other T.B. as captain of his House, looking moderately serious and rather pleased with himself. Then there are the hands: always active – placed patronisingly on the shoulders of two boys in front of him; folded a trifle defiantly to match the curling lip below the Stetson hat; or twirling the flower almost subconsciously.

The Stetson was a souvenir of Thomas's visit to the USA with his father at Easter 1893. Returning late, after the summer term had begun, he was an object of great curiosity and admiration to the whole school. He had a lot to tell his friends.

Sir Thomas Beecham

The Beechams, father and son, sailed on the largest ship afloat, the *Campania,* and on board were many celebrated people all bound for the same place, the Chicago Exhibition. The tenor Ben Davies was on board, and Thomas accompanied him at the piano. He found New York exceedingly hot and was glad to make the acquaintance of the ice-cream soda, but even this delicacy did not compensate for the mosquitoes which he detested then and ever after. The Chicago Exhibition exceeded all expectations and from there the two travelled to Albany and thence to Boston. Joseph was unable to complete his business and was forced to send Thomas home alone, which of course did not trouble the boy at all.

He volunteered to help organise 'the inevitable concert' on the ship and was introduced to an exceedingly large passenger, the Swedish baritone, Carl Frederick Lundquist. He was suffering from an incurable glandular disease which made him grotesquely oversize and which forbade him any further appearances on the opera stage. Lundquist was 52 at the time, and his voice was of exceptional quality, production, control and condition. Beecham accompanied him on the piano from memory in arias and songs: a strange spectacle to have witnessed, and a glorious opportunity for the schoolboy.

By the summer of 1897 Thomas had been at school for five years and was already feeling that he and Rossall had seen the best of one another. His interest in games had fallen off, though if he were selected to play in a house (or infrequently) school match, he would do so with great abandon and showmanship. His passion for music continued unabated and he now frequently played the Rossall organ. He hoped, above all, that his father would agree to send him to a German university.

Germany was then the most interesting and important country in the world for young people, especially if they were musical. Thomas had already visited the USA and had been thrilled at the adventurous spirit of the New World. This was the land for scientists and businessmen, the land of get-rich-quick. Everything that was happening there was done at great speed and, it seemed, with much noise. Exciting as it was, there was seldom the opportunity or the conditions for mental relaxation. Thomas needed time to give to prolonged thought and to reading in creative surroundings, and in any case he was far more interested in music than in commerce. Europe could give him this peace of mind, as well as its rich inheritance of architecture, painting and music.

The leaders of the two prevailing musical cults were Richard Wagner and Johannes Brahms, both German. In 1897 Wagner had been dead for only fifteen years, and his operas were not yet fully understood. To hear them meant going to opera houses – ideally to Bayreuth itself. The only alternative to live opera was in selections of 'bleeding chunks' at concerts, for, of course, there were no mechanical means of vocal reproduction at that time. Bayreuth was indeed the centre of all things Wagnerian, while at Dresden one could hear the finest performances of all kinds of opera. So if Thomas had been able to establish himself in Germany, how splendid life would have been, and how much more easily could he have absorbed the huge pulse of music that was beating inside that country.

Joseph was in two minds about it but, on consulting his adviser, received sternly negative advice about Germany. Why should the boy wish to go there, of all places, when there were the two best universities in the world at Oxford and Cambridge? Far better send him to one of these, where he would be among wholesome Englishmen rather than a pack of foreigners.

Thomas argued and pleaded, but to no avail. He was given the choice and opted for Oxford because he had friends there already and others about to go up. So in September 1897 he arrived at Wadham College to read Classics.

Wadham dates from 1613, the institution of Nicholas and Dorothy Wadham, at that time existing outside the city walls. C. B. Fry describes it as 'that gem of Jacobean simplicity... built with enthusiasm, grey Cumnor stone, and the advice of no architect.' In Thomas's time the Warden was G. E. Thorley, a sensitive and understanding man, yet one who stood no nonsense, as his portrait reveals.

In 1897 Wadham's undergraduate strength was no more than ninety-seven, of whom twenty-seven went up at the same time as Thomas. His name is entered in the register as a 'Dissenter'; he said he did not profess the standard mode of worship of the Church of England, and thus was under no obligation to attend chapel. He had been brought up in the family as a Congregationalist, had behaved like an Anglican at Rossall, and had now decided that such time as was saved by not going to chapel would be better spent at the piano or reading. Only one subsequent remark is known in which he acknowledges any acceptance of a Divine Being, and that was in 1935, over Delius's grave.

Thomas lived out of college in an undistinguished red-brick Victorian house in Walton Street, to the west of Wadham and about ten minutes' walk away. Living out of college meant that he was far more independent, and also that he could have a piano in his rooms.

There is an article in the *Wadham Gazette* for Thomas's first term about a 'very good Smoker' in which the freshmen excelled. The two singled out for mention by name were 'Beecham (piano) and H. M. Tennent (song)', and the *Gazette* went on to state that 'Things became afterwards rather irregular.' H. M. Tennent was to become one of London's most celebrated impresarios of straight plays and to found the theatrical management which still bears his name.

Thomas had adopted a lukewarm attitude to sport in his last year at Rossall, and was both delighted and surprised to be invited to join his college football XI as a regular member. In the following summer he also played cricket for Wadham. His picture among the football team makes him appear less composed than before, and certainly far less so than thereafter. In spite of the cut and buttoning of his jacket, he seems already to be a little portly.

In his first term he worked well and attended a fair quota of lectures; he was enjoying himself and all was going well. He was spending too much, though. Joseph came to visit him and, knowing how his father must always be caught at the right moment when a favour was to be asked, Thomas took him out in a boat on the river. But his inexperience as a sailor resulted in the boat's capsizing, and a furious Joseph left Oxford the same afternoon. Hopes for an increase in allowance were lost.

In the Christmas vacation 'the Pater' seems to have forgotten the incident, for he allowed Thomas to go to Germany with a friend instead of to the Carl Rosa at Liverpool. Dresden immediately opened up a new world. It took the shine off life at Wadham, and on his return Thomas planned how he might find the chance to go back to Germany as soon as possible. In the new term his attendances fell off, his work declined, and at last he could resist the call no longer and committed the heinous University crime of absenting himself in term-time. He spent another glorious week in Dresden and came back to find that his absence had gone unnoticed. Living out was a help, and in 1898 there was nothing like a roll-call or the system of 'scouts' which later prevailed. Even so, Thomas seems to have brought into play some sort of extraordinary power which maintained a presence for him while he was away. Later on he was frequently to make use of such a gift, though in reverse, by disappearing almost before people's eyes.

Now Thomas was fully determined to go to Germany and enjoy the operatic and social delights which he had already twice tasted there, and again he asked his father whether it would not be very much in the interest of the firm for him to learn another language and other people's ways, rather than remain at Oxford. Joseph did not give this permission, but it seems that he consented to his son going down from Oxford.

His manner of exodus from Wadham was amusing. The Warden, Thorley, seemed sorry to see him go and said: 'Your untimely departure has, perhaps, spared us the necessity of asking you to go.' So perhaps the

Dresden adventure had come to light after all, coupled with inattention in the third and last term. College records reveal that three other first-year undergraduates went down at the same time, so Thomas's was not an isolated case. By now he had to a large extent eradicated his Lancashire accent, just as F. E. Smith smoothed out his own while up at Oxford. (Joseph Beecham had a less good ear than his son and never got rid of his broad vowels and local expressions.)

Thomas was derogatory about his tutors, partly, no doubt, because he himself was much travelled and already possessed a worldliness which few of his tutors had acquired. In addition, his reading was broad and deep and had been implanted on his photographic memory for ever. Sixty years later he was able to describe both the page number of a particular quotation and its position on that page. His classics tutor was probably H. P. Richards, reckoned to be the best Greek scholar of his day in England as well as a first-rate teacher with a keen and pliant mind.

Music did not exist as a degree subject until 1946, but Thomas had private lessons in theory from Dr John Varley Roberts, the organist at Magdalen. Roberts was a good choral trainer but very old-fashioned, of the 'Just throw your heads back, lads, and sing' school. Thomas found time to play the Wadham organ and to continue singing bass, although there was no formal madrigal society in Oxford in 1897.

Thomas's return to St Helens was not much welcomed by anybody. 'The Pater' regarded him as a rebel and was determined that his second son, Henry (nine years younger than Thomas), would go neither to public school nor to university. He would receive a 'proper' education to equip him for the family business, untarnished by the upper and intellectual classes. It was a bit embarrassing for him when, as a millionaire in the 1920s, he could only say that he had gone to Liverpool Grammar School and a business training college.

Thomas was given some sort of a job on the publicity side of Beechams, with an office near his father's. There he whiled away the time quite profitably to himself, for there was always a music score under his blotter. He was merely waiting, he said, in Micawberish fashion for something to turn up. He knew it would, and it certainly did. But meanwhile he registered his impatience by letting his hair grow long, treating the factory and office staff in a lordly manner, and making it plain to all that he felt there were more appropriate activities in store for him elsewhere. This undignified behaviour made the Rev. Mr Carter more resolved than ever to prevent the boy from having his way.

The family life which Thomas again shared at Ewanville was less happy than ever. Joseph was at home a good deal more than usual, because in 1899 he became Mayor of St Helens, the honour upon which he had long set his heart. His relations with Josephine were very bad. He dominated and bullied her, while paying unwelcome attention to every female member of his staff. This was so distasteful to those of his children who understood it, especially to the eldest daughter Emily, who sided with her mother, that neither she nor Josephine but the next daughter, Josie, used to accompany the Mayor at functions. Josie was two years younger than Thomas; she was known as 'Holly' and was his favourite sister.

Thomas was glad to get away in the summer of 1899 for a long stay in Europe, journeying alone in easy stages through the cathedral cities of Belgium and up the Rhine to Bavaria and the Bayreuth Festival. He imagined that by steeping himself in the grandeur of Rhineland architecture he was preparing himself properly for his first *Ring*. But the four performances profoundly disappointed him. He was glad to get away from Bayreuth and to explore the glorious countryside around it. He went to Alexandersberg, a small spa ten miles from the Bohemian border, where he met some German students and young officers whose political views greatly interested him. They were all imbued with nationalistic pride and an insistence that Germany would soon take Britain's place as the foremost European nation. Beecham's conciliatory arguments got him nowhere, but as the days were spent pleasantly and the presence of some very attractive American girls added further delights to his holiday, he stayed longer and spent far more money than he had bargained for. Already his bountiful manner seemed part of his nature. He was obliged to return by the cheapest route possible.

It was not altogether surprising that he should find Americans congenial, for they and he could be reckoned as being on the same social plane in England. There was no aristocracy in the United States and Beecham was not accepted among the upper classes at home. Oscar Wilde noted the effect made in British society by American girls in the late 1880s and after: 'They have a quaint pertness, a delightful conceit, a native self-assertion. They insist on being paid compliments and have almost succeeded in making Englishmen eloquent. For our aristocracy they have an ardent admiration; they adore titles ... There is something fascinating in their funny, exaggerated gestures and their petulant way of tossing the head ... As for their voices, they soon get them in tune.' By 1909 it was calculated that over five hundred American women had acquired titled husbands in Europe and had contributed $220 million as dowries or personal fortunes.

In the previous spring a Miss Utica Welles had stayed with the

Beechams at Ewanville. Joseph and Emily, on a visit to the USA in 1898, had met her family in New York. Welles was a doctor of medicine; he also practised psychiatry and was a hypnotist. His wife had once been one of two sisters in a telepathic 'act'. Emily and Utica struck up a friendship which resulted in a reciprocal visit by the American girl to Ewanville.

Thomas first met Utica, then only sixteen years old, during his last vacation from Wadham. She was enchanted by his personality and by the way he played the piano. In 1899 she returned to Ewanville, this time with her parents. She had set her heart on Thomas Beecham and meant to pin him down to a promise of marriage while he was more or less captive in St Helens and before any other girl had the chance, for women found him extraordinarily attractive. There was something about his dark brown eyes, so dark that they sometimes seemed to be black. They could bore right into a woman and make her feel that he knew all about her at once. They dominated his features and exercised a strong power that was practically hypnotic.

The Welles family was financially independent and Dr Welles was now the staff doctor at the American Embassy in London. He bought a house in South Kensington, 9 Roland Gardens, and since he was officially accredited at the Court of St James he possessed diplomatic status. In March 1899 Utica had been presented at Court. In St Helens and Huyton this meant a great deal; and there was no objection at all to the young couple becoming engaged to be married.

It was clear to the Welles's that there was immense wealth in the Beecham family, and that was good enough for them. The doubtful family background which had for so long marred Joseph's social progress was of no account to these Americans; in any event the handicap had been virtually overcome by his becoming Mayor. Dr and Mrs Welles were, in any case, primarily interested in their daughter's happiness and wishes, for she was a strong-minded young lady, used to getting her own way.

Thomas duly proposed to Utica and was accepted. (She had her eighteenth birthday in August 1899.) Joseph imagined and fervently hoped that this development would calm down his son, and that the responsibility implicit in an engagement of marriage would make him settle down in the firm. But the very opposite happened. Thomas now had a base in London *chez* Welles. London (and to a lesser extent Manchester) meant music to him. If he were to become settled in London he would be able to go to concerts and opera and meet the artistic personalities involved in them. He was thoroughly disenchanted with Beechams as a way of life, and the domestic scene at Ewanville was fast approaching a crisis.

Josephine's repeated pregnancies, coupled with her age (she was now in her late forties), had produced a condition which Joseph and the Rev. Mr Carter considered to be dangerous. Arrangements were made for her to be committed to an asylum 'for her own safety'. Some people in middle age can become diabetic when a shock is allied to an unbalanced physical condition. Josephine Beecham now contracted the lesser form of epilepsy (known as *le petit mal*) which is usually hereditary, but she certainly did not suffer from it earlier, nor did it appear in any of her children. Love and affection and quiet nursing were all that Josephine needed from her husband, but none was forthcoming.

One day Josephine mysteriously disappeared. Emily and Thomas, who were away, rushed home to find out where she was, for they knew that their father had done something desperate. He refused to tell them what had happened; there was a terrible scene; he disinherited them both for challenging him and threw them out. It was not infrequent at the turn of the century for a person to be 'put away' for reasons of domestic convenience when there was little real medical evidence to support such drastic treatment. Both Emily and Thomas were fearful of the effects it might have on their mother's already delicate mental state.

In early 1900 Emily and Thomas went to London to begin their fight against their father in the courts, and to try to trace their mother's whereabouts. Emily did most of the work, while Thomas was called in when needed. They both lodged with the Welles's, where Utica, and his own attempts at composition, occupied a good deal of Thomas's time.

He had passed through London before but had never lived there or been able to take part in the life of the city. Certainly when he arrived he was very much the country cousin in appearance: shy, or at any rate withdrawn, dressed in a black coat, brown boots, pork-pie hat and knitted, buttoned pullover. Dr Welles generously let Thomas have a room of his own at Roland Gardens where he lived for three years, composing operas, meeting people, going to concerts and waiting for the situation between his father and mother to be unravelled before he felt he could marry Utica.

About a quarter of a mile down the Old Brompton Road from Roland Gardens towards South Kensington station was a harp shop. (It was still there in the early 1960s.) George Morley lived above it and plied his trade to harpists all over the world. He was as avid a reader as Beecham was, and very hospitable too. He used to entertain friends, acquaintances and customers until far into the night, and Beecham became such a frequent visitor that Morley's shop and the house above it seemed like an extension of Roland Gardens. He played billiards and chess with one or two of Morley's regulars; and gradually Beecham's accent, manners and dress became more like those of his new friends. He met literary as well as musical people at Morley's and began to form his own band of cronies.

Beecham was also seen to have developed a strange facial idiosyncrasy. He gyrated his nose and screwed it up, sniffing as he did so and pursing his lips. In later life the gyration expressed disgust or disapproval, while the pursed lips meant a number of things, often done while he was thinking of something else, unconnected with any observer.

We do not know what influence the Welles's had over Beecham at this stage, but they fully supported him and his sister in their efforts to rescue their mother and re-establish her. Eventually she was traced to a Northampton home. Solicitors, sent by Emily and Thomas, visited her and she began to petition for divorce against Joseph. His infidelities were too numerous and too blatant to be concealed; there was ample evidence to bring the case to court and to obtain Josephine's release.

The case was unpleasant, long-drawn-out and distinctly damaging to Joseph's reputation. Old Tom was asked by a member of the Beecham management why he did nothing to minimise the glaring newspaper reports which must have been having a bad effect on the company's image. The old man laughed and replied: 'What, me stop old Joe? Not likely. He's the best bit of free advertising I've ever had!'

Eventually the case drew to a close; the final settlement on Josephine was fixed at £4,500 a year, instead of the £2,000 which Joseph had offered. Joseph was pressed for details of his personal fortune, which he lessened considerably, although his income was thought to be in the region of £80,000 a year. He was known to keep £100,000 on current account in case he might need it suddenly. If £4,500 seems rather a small part of his fortune to pay his ex-wife, it nevertheless left her comfortably off; she was now free and in the care of Emily and the Welles's. From now on the Americans regarded themselves as Josephine's guardians, even when they were abroad. Sometimes Emily stayed with her mother, but it was not long before she went to Italy to become a well-known dancing teacher, known as 'Madame Hélène Dolli'. She never married.

Beecham's only 'job' so far, in the sense of receiving a salary for work done, was in the spring of 1902. He was taken on as accompanist to a nondescript opera company which played outer London theatres for five weeks. Since the audiences at these theatres normally enjoyed variety or musical comedies, it is not surprising that the opera company attracted very thin houses and vanished without trace. This was Beecham's first experience of opera from within a company and was of great importance to him, although there is no evidence that he conducted any of the performances.

The other directly musical enterprise in which he actively participated was the Oriana Madrigal Society, founded by Charles Kennedy Scott to revive the pure and beautiful Elizabethan compositions which had passed into neglect. Otherwise Beecham composed, and went to concerts. At about this time he invented his 'pocket orchestra' – a modified chessboard, with miniature orchestral sections instead of chessmen. When set up they were 'conducted' in a fearsome way by Beecham, who lunged and pounced and made dreadful faces at them while reading his score. They never moved. He did it all for them, and they gave him confidence in directing his gestures to the right quarters and at the right time. The 'pocket orchestra' was kept fully employed for a number of years. Beecham had it as late as 1911, when he used to prop it up in railway carriages, to the consternation of other passengers once the imaginary concert had begun. After that it was all done from memory.

In July 1903 Thomas Beecham married Utica Celestina Welles at St Mary's Church in Cranley Gardens. Josephine was one of the witnesses and Emily was the bridesmaid. Joseph did not attend. The break between him and his elder son was complete.

This meant that Thomas was cut off from any paternal allowance. Old Tom made him a wedding present of Mursley Hall, the shooting-box which he had built in Buckinghamshire in 1881 at a cost of £10,000, as well as £300 a year to assist in its upkeep. After a short honeymoon visiting English cathedrals, the young couple went abroad to France, Italy and Switzerland. It seems evident, from later financial negotiations, that Dr Welles sponsored these travels by way of a loan to Beecham. In addition, Beecham promised to settle a substantial sum on Utica in anticipation of his future inheritance from the family firm, and a legal document was drawn up, probably at Dr Welles's instigation.

Since the beginning of 1900, when Beecham had gone to live with the Welles family in London, they had all become used to a *ménage à quatre*. Now, when the two young ones had married, Dr and Mrs Welles still considered them all one family and, though they had a base in Switzerland, continued to visit them. At first it was 'We'll just come over for a week and see how you're getting on', but before long the Welles's had joined 'the children' so as to be with Utica for the birth of her baby and had brought her two elder brothers and Josephine with them.

One can argue that they knew more about children than head-in-score Thomas did, but this is scarcely the point. C. L. Stocks, one of Beecham's contemporaries at Wadham, wrote: 'Marriage is the re-birth of two people in one joint personality; a child is its proof of success.'

Thomas had, after all, as much right to be responsible for their child's upbringing as Utica had, but he was prevented from taking part in what was made out to be a highly specialised medico-female ritual. This did him a great deal of psychological harm, for he was still very uncertain of himself. So in 1904 he left his wife and young son Adrian in Florence with the Welles's for another six months, and returned to England alone, via Bologna and Paris. He had been married for only a little over a year, and now his marriage looked like breaking up unless he could persuade Utica to rely on him and not on her parents. Thomas wanted to return to Roland Gardens with his wife and son. However, Dr and Mrs Roland Welles persuaded Utica that to go back to London at the outset of winter would be bad for the baby and that Florence provided a more salubrious climate. In the spring of 1905 the party returned to Roland Gardens from Italy, and Dr Welles financed Thomas's first London concert.

It was far easier in 1905 than it is now, three-quarters of a century later, for an entirely unknown conductor to appear before a London audience. Beecham engaged forty seasoned members of the Queen's Hall Orchestra for a concert of his own choice of works at the Bechstein (now the Wigmore) Hall. He already had experience in playing a variety of musical instruments and could read a score accurately. During his honeymoon in Switzerland he had practised the trombone, to the great discomfiture of members of his *pension,* who had banished it and him to a boat in the middle of the adjacent lake. It was not as though he was about to stand in front of a totally unfamiliar ensemble; but the orchestra thought otherwise. They treated him like a new boy and played him up both at the single rehearsal and at the concert. Even so, there were those in the audience, critics included, who appreciated what he was doing and gave him credit for it. At least some of his qualities were recognised immediately, curious though he may have appeared in action.

Beecham bought a house at Boreham Wood, but when he suggested to Utica that she move there she again demurred on the grounds that it would be damp and unhealthy for the baby. They would remain at Roland Gardens until the spring. This attitude, however well-meaning of Utica, was seriously undermining her relationship with Thomas. He was engaged in serious re-study but let it be known that he was available to conduct a permanent orchestra. Early in 1906 Utica did move to Boreham Wood and took Adrian to live in the same house as his father for the first time. At last it seemed that they had been reunited, and although Beecham spent a good deal of time in London he was being the dutiful husband and father.

Beecham's next step towards musical recognition came when he was invited to become the conductor of a new enterprise – a joint gamble. This was the New Symphony Orchestra. The four concerts which they gave were highly praised by the critics and musical people, though financially they were disastrous.

Beecham now suddenly found himself the centre of interest in London musical life. Making himself look like the great Hungarian, Artur Nikisch, Beecham appeared before the public as the epitome of a conductor, and this went a long way towards helping to establish him before he had properly formed his own character and 'image'. The pose served as a useful stepping-stone between the uncertain, shy provincial and the self-assertive man-about-town he was soon to become.

The similarity to Nikisch was really rather striking and went much further than build, beard and pose alone. The veteran bassoonist, Archie Camden, who played for them both, recalls that although there was a great similarity between the two conductors, there was of course a difference of age, experience and mature personality. Even so, according to Archie Camden, one watched the eyes, always the eyes; and Beecham's eyes exercised a hypnotic influence over his players, so that they were willing to do exactly as he bid them. In Nikisch's case it was more a question of electric personality.

It was in the conductor's room at Queen's Hall after the first New Symphony Orchestra concert that Beecham first met Frederick Delius. The composer was so impressed that he went round to meet the young conductor, of whom he had never heard, to ask him whether he might hire the orchestra for a concert of his own music. 'He must be a cardinal, or at least a bishop, in mufti!' was Beecham's first reaction to the appearance of this handsome and aesthetic stranger.

The meeting was of no less importance to Delius himself. It has been suggested many times that, without Beecham's forceful support, none of Delius's major works would ever have been performed in England. It was Beecham's persistence, his belief in this music amounting to an infatuation, which made him the world's leading Delius conductor for over fifty years. In any branch of the entertainment business there is a proven theory that new personalities are made in two ways: either by becoming the star performer of an accepted work; or by introducing a new form of art. Beecham seems to have managed to do both at once, and virtually launched himself twice in that 1907–8 season.

Beecham continued to conduct the series of New Symphony Orchestra

Beecham's grandparents – the eccentric millionaire Thomas Beecham (1820–1907) and his first wife Jane. *Below* The timekeeper's lodge at the back of the first Beecham factory at St Helens, built in 1876. Young Thomas as a child lived round the corner.

Beecham's parents – Josephine, born in Lambeth of French extraction, and Joseph (seen here on one of his business trips to the USA just before the First World War), whom she married in 1873. *Below* Beecham at the age of nine, playing tennis in the garden of Ewanville. The conservatory can be seen on the right.

Right A corner of the elaborately ornamental drawing-room at Ewanville, showing the Broadwood grand piano which Beecham's mother played. *Below* Five of Beecham's sisters outside the conservatory at Ewanville: (from left) Edith (b. 1884), Jessie (b. 1886), Josie (b. 1881), Chrissie (b. 1894) and little Olive (b. 1889). The photograph was probably taken in 1900, after Emily (the eldest sister) had left home.

Beecham as head of his House at Rossall, sitting next to the headmaster, Batson (April 1897), and *below* (left, back row) as a member of the Wadham College football team during his first term at Oxford the following winter.

concerts at Queen's Hall, forcing his strengthening personality upon soloists, players and audiences and quickly building up his own prestige. This was a transitional period for him from being a keen and eccentric musical nobody to becoming a conductor of interest and promise.

Having found Delius thoroughly to his liking, Beecham began to cultivate the man and to try to discover everything about him. In 1908 they went on holiday together to Norway, and Beecham soon learned that Delius's isolation in the village of Grez-sur-Loing (near Fontainebleau), where he lived and composed, had made him inept at communicating with people. Nowhere was this more evident than in his scores, which did not state anything about dynamics, phrasing or instrumental balance. That was perhaps why they had made so little impression upon the many musical publishers all over Europe who had received them. They were as difficult for a musician to read as a book lacking punctuation and paragraphs.

The chrysalis stage in Beecham's life came to an end in 1908. Until then he had lived in what he describes as an alien mind of 'indecision, unrest and self-questioning'. He had once intended to be a great pianist. Then he had decided he would be a composer of operas. When he realised that he was not going to succeed in either of these roles he became despondent and so – with one great fling of life's dice – he chose conducting as his life's career.

Beecham was pleasantly surprised to find that he was receiving good notices, pats on the back from friends, full co-operation from his players and 'the convincing counsel and constant conviction of Frederick Delius'. Delius was twenty-seven years older than Beecham, and for a while he stood *in loco parentis*. Beecham eagerly accepted most of what he said and was more than willing to devote the rest of his life not only to conducting Delius's music, but to acting as his editor as well. Yet it would not be too cynical to suggest that Delius's conviction as to Beecham's worth was partly a selfish one. He had found his champion in London and he was not going to let him escape.

Beecham calls 1908–9 his 'happy year'. It was the first real turning-point in his life and his career. Now he had achieved self-confidence and was beginning to create a unique personality – his theme – which he manipulated like a set of variations throughout the remainder of his life, according to conditions of age, health, wealth, poverty, bankruptcy and other miseries or delights at one end or the other of the Beecham see-saw.

This self-confidence led him to believe that he would be able to take over and then rule the NSO, but he was sadly disappointed. Once prevented from doing so, however, he decided to let it be.

Sir Thomas Beecham

In February 1909 a new orchestra appeared at Queen's Hall called the Beecham Symphony Orchestra. It soon became established as the most adventurous band in London, playing many works by Delius as well as a large proportion of Mozart, Haydn and French composers. It was a colossal gamble on Beecham's part because he had no money except what Utica's father gave him.

He was now thirty and a successful mature musician, but there were several aspects of his behaviour which for ever defied a complete description of 'grown-up'. He loved practical jokes and the Beecham Symphony Orchestra enabled him to indulge in them. The Orchestra used frequently to tour from soon after its formation and success until the outbreak of the First World War. This wasn't merely a flag-showing operation in the provinces but a very real method of keeping ninety men employed. One might imagine that the owner and conductor of an orchestra would keep himself apart from his musicians and behave towards them in a formal manner, but not Beecham. He not only joined in their pranks, he invented many of them.

It is not known who first thought of letting off fireworks as the orchestral train was pulling out of a railway station, but this happened with such frequency, and always at Crewe Junction, that the BSO became known to railway passengers and staff as 'The Fireworks Orchestra'. In hotels, too, Beecham led the raids on bedrooms, changed shoes outside bedroom doors, dropped sheets-full of electric bulbs down lift shafts and generally behaved in an undergraduate manner.

The effect of all this on members of the Orchestra, except when the jokes went too far and caused actual harm, was healthy, and they loved Beecham for it. They actually looked forward to the next tour. So, too, did Beecham, for his own reasons.

Utica's second son, Thomas, was born in Boreham Wood in June 1909. Beecham was appearing there less frequently and in the autumn he let the house. Utica moved back to Roland Gardens with the two boys, having been to Eastbourne in August and then packed up the house for good. Beecham was sometimes there, sometimes not. He was devoting his whole heart and soul to music and had little time left for his wife and sons. But he seemed to have time to spare for somebody else.

One morning in October 1909 the whole of England became aware that things were not right and proper in the Beecham household; and it was Thomas's household this time, not Joseph's. A sensational divorce story occupied the front pages of the *Daily Sketch* and the *Daily Mirror*, both picture papers. A Mrs Maud Foster was being sued for divorce by her husband, and a Mr Thomas Beecham was named as co-respondent. He was said to be living at 'an Elstree cottage'. Elstree and Boreham Wood are more or less the same place. The evidence rested on three items. First, a servant had seen Mrs Foster standing with her arms round Beecham's neck while he was playing the piano (a situation which, he said later, would have made it well-nigh impossible for him to play at all). Secondly, they had been seen together through a window from outside in the garden, apparently wearing few clothes. And lastly, Beecham had persuaded a private detective to stop working for Mr Foster, and to act for him instead.

Throughout the case, which lasted for eight days, Beecham maintained the utmost calm and confidence. One newspaper reported that, when he was called, 'he strode with as much easy dignity and grace into the witness box as if he were taking his place in front of his orchestra'. On another day it was reported that when he entered the court he took up 'the attitude of a man perfectly at ease and not at all put out by being asked to talk'.

There was enormous public interest in the case. In those days before the cinema, and long before television, legal cases provided the public with the sensations it wanted. KCs were the 'stars', and so sometimes were the plaintiffs and defendants too. Since it was happening in real life it had a greater impact than the theatre. The large crowds that gathered in Temple Bar, studying the newspapers avidly to compare the photographs with the real people going in and out, completely identified themselves with the proceedings.

When Utica went into the witness box she said that she had always been on very affectionate terms with her husband since she had married him in 1903. She knew Mrs Foster and had encouraged her friendship with her husband because she felt that she would be useful to his career. The able defence for Mrs Foster and Beecham read part of a letter the former had written to Joseph Beecham's solicitor in an effort to patch up the break between father and son: 'Mr Beecham is certainly the greatest musical personage of today and will place England musically ahead of other countries given time and courage. I say courage simply because the boy has lost all interest in life, has not felt any for years and years. He longs to talk to his father. It's not the money. And he says himself: "My father does not care for me. He is what I have wanted all these years."'

This did not seem, to learned Counsel, to be the kind of letter which would have been written by a woman who was trying to take another woman's husband. But from his observation of Beecham in court and what else he had learnt about him, Mr Foster's Counsel could not accept the whining, little-boy-lost plea in Mrs Foster's letter as sounding authentic Beecham at all.

The case came to an abrupt end on 31 October, when the jury unanimously and very swiftly found Mrs Foster guilty. Costs, amounting to well over £3,000, were awarded against Beecham. Four KCs had been engaged, whose fees alone amounted to £1,200. (One has to multiply this by twelve to get some idea of its value in today's money.)

Throughout the case Utica had adopted a calm, patient and loyal attitude towards her husband. She had been at Eastbourne with her children at the time when the offence was said to have taken place, which made it easier for her to avoid awkward questions. When, after the case, a titled lady-friend telephoned her and gloatingly offered the advice: 'Sue the unfaithful man, my dear; get a divorce and a large lump of alimony!', Utica's reply froze the telephone line: 'I do not believe in divorce.' And she never did divorce him, remaining in her conviction a latterday Catherine of Aragon despite the many infidelities of her spouse, who was branded a cad by society.

Beecham would have been in an impossible financial position had it not been for the timely reconciliation with his father in the previous July. This had partly been brought about by Ethel Smyth, then a struggling composer whom Beecham knew quite well. She was a 'character' and he admired her tenacity in the face of critics and others who were opposed to the idea of a woman composer-conductor. Certainly Mrs Foster had played no significant part in the reconciliation. Joseph had been drawing nearer and nearer to his son, and was full of admiration for his musical activities. On several occasions in the early part of 1909 Beecham had spotted his father among the audience at his concerts and had pointed him out to friends and to his leader.

Beecham and his orchestra were engaged to accompany Ethel Smyth's opera *The Wreckers* at His Majesty's Theatre in June 1909 at about the time when his second son, Thomas, was born at Boreham Wood. During a rehearsal he called Ethel Smyth aside and said: 'D'you see the right-hand man of two men standing behind a pillar at the back of the stalls? Well, that's my father!' Eventually father and son were brought together after nearly ten years, when Joseph was willing to condescend by saying to Thomas: 'You dam' well annoyed me,' and his son replied, 'And you annoyed me too.' Then they shook hands and thereafter were very close until Joseph's sudden death seven years later.

Joseph Beecham settled his son's account with the divorce court and placed as much of the family fortune as he wanted at his disposal. Thomas was now all set to widen his activities from a few performances of a single opera to several seasons in London. He had decided that opera was the thing for him. He would still continue to give concerts, but would concentrate upon the lyric stage.

In 1910 the Beechams took over Covent Garden for an early winter season; moved to His Majesty's for ten weeks during the summer with a season of opéra-comique; and returned to Covent Garden in the autumn. Not only did Beecham meet a number of first-class singers, but society, which had previously shunned him, began to take an interest in this extraordinary young man, likening him to Halley's comet, which had been seen that year.

Beecham began to receive invitations to big London houses, for his attractive personality and ready wit were a constant source of delight at parties. He would also play the piano elegantly and often wittily to illustrate a point he was making. 'The English don't understand music,' he declared, 'but they seem to like the noise it makes.'

Utica was determined not to let him go, and in order to be even nearer her husband's sphere of activities, musical and now social, she persuaded him to move again. Shortly before Christmas 1910 they moved into 32 Upper Hamilton Terrace, in St John's Wood. (This is now 121 Hamilton Terrace, though the actual house was demolished in the 1930s and another one built there.) Their Christmas card 'From Mr and Mrs Thomas Beecham' has a photograph of Utica and her two sons, but the father is not shown. Sir Joseph bought the house for them.

Beecham was again welcome at Ewanville whenever he wanted to visit, and also at his father's London house in Arkwright Road. Ewanville was much the same, though of course neither Josephine nor Emily was there any longer, and the youngest sister, Chrissie, was away at school. Brother Henry, whom Thomas had not seen since he was eleven, was now an extremely handsome young man of twenty-one, whose eyes possessed the same hypnotic power as his brother's. He had a passion for motor-cars and drove them in a dashing manner. He showed Thomas his paces round Huyton, and during the school holidays his sisters described how they had gone for very uncomfortable journeys with Harry, occasionally as far as Scotland.

Henry Beecham had a dark, almost saturnine complexion and a Habsburg lip; he looked the double of Alfonso XIII, last King of Spain, and was exactly his age. When Harry visited Madrid in 1909 and attended the opera, the whole audience stood up as he entered his box.

Henry's part of the Beecham fortune was not entailed, like Thomas's, and he lived the life of a millionaire when he came into his inheritance. Shortly after the First World War began he bought Lympne Castle in

Kent with the assistance of Jimmy White, although the family didn't move there until 1924. After the First World War Henry rented Knebworth from the Lyttons for three years, then moved to Ewanville for the next two years, and by Christmas 1924 was back at Lympne to stay. He was a compulsive gambler on the Stock Exchange and, in spite of his fine business sense, the crash of 1929 was too much for him. He lost his fortune and lived on another eighteen years in quiet retirement.

Thomas's appearances at Hamilton Terrace became less and less frequent until they were restricted to lunchtime, sometimes three or four days in a row, depending upon what else he was doing, and then not again for several months. His sons no longer regarded him as a close member of the family but rather as a kind of uncle figure who was on the edge of the household, yet did not properly belong to it. They enjoyed his comings but were not upset by his goings. Utica, however, was convinced that he would return and be her husband again in every sense of the word. He left her in 1912 but she maintained her devotional dream until his death.

Thomas made over the house in Upper Hamilton Terrace to Utica, and her parents often stayed there. Josephine Beecham was present, too, on these occasions. Mrs Elsie Olive Betts, Thomas's next but youngest sister, recalls that she once went to the address to try and see her mother, but Mrs Welles barred the way in a most aggressive fashion and absolutely refused her admission. In 1911 Dr and Mrs Welles and Josephine took up residence at Mursley Hall, which stood in 120 acres in the village of Mursley between Winslow and Bletchley in Buckinghamshire and was henceforth to become Josephine's home. Utica and the boys went there for short visits up to the outbreak of the First World War, when they all lived there, away from London.

In about 1910 Beecham first met the soprano Maggie Teyte, whom he engaged to sing Cherubino in his Mozart season that summer. They had a passionate friendship which continued into the years of the First World War and which, for Beecham, ran in parallel with another, far longer-lasting, liaison with Maud (or, as she preferred to be called, Emerald) Cunard.

Lady Cunard was American, the wife of Sir Bache Cunard, third baronet and grandson of the founder of the steamship line. He was immensely rich and far fonder of hunting and racing than of music. She had moved to London in 1906, though their separation by mutual consent did not take place till 1911. Her kingdom was the capital city and not the hunting field or the grouse moor. Soon she had captured all London society, and her Cavendish Square – later her Grosvenor Square

– salon became the most important Mecca for musicians, painters, sculptors, poets and writers as well as for politicians, soldiers, aristocrats – indeed anybody so long as they were *interesting*. Ages did not matter, and Lady Cunard was adept at mixing people together so as to get the best results. She was one of the most extraordinary catalyst-hostesses there has ever been. She knew everybody who was anybody and knew their social precedence as if it were her own. She was also extremely well-read in English and French literature, which was generally absorbed at night in the small hours and which, like Beecham's reading, was backed up by an excellent memory.

In late 1906 Emerald Cunard took over 20 Cavendish Square from the Asquiths. This house became her first great centre for entertaining. Such salons were intellectual breeding-grounds in an age when art meant much to a chosen few and science meant little to anybody. Today there are few with the combined wealth and ability to take the place of the great Georgian hostesses; the State instead has become principal patron of the arts.

Lady Cunard then moved to 7 Grosvenor Square, whose large drawing-room was decorated with white and gold panels and whose walls were hung with Marie Laurencin portraits in wide frames, set with looking glasses. The curtains were of pale blue satin, while crystal chandeliers and brackets set off the delicate French furniture. When the room was lit with candles an amazing impression of lightness and gaiety was created – the ideal setting for Lady Cunard herself.

She was a small, birdlike woman with a brilliant personality. She could dominate any assembly at will, not least with her voice. She was always dressed in the latest fashion, with emeralds – her favourite jewel – abounding. She first became interested in Beecham when she read about the Foster divorce case, and she was determined to meet him.

In 1909 she was the mistress of the Irish writer, George Moore, who remained infatuated with her until he died in 1933. He wove her in and out of his novels, always as the loved one, with true and imagined events jostling together in partly accurate settings. He was thus able to crystallise in print some very intimate details of his love for Emerald that a reader who knew them both might succeed in disentangling from fiction. He wrote her a great number of very touching letters, about 250 of which have been published; but none of hers to him – and these were far fewer – have survived.

Lady Cunard was the love of George Moore's life, while Thomas Beecham was undoubtedly the love of hers. Consequently Moore felt that

Beecham had usurped him. They were often thrown together socially, but Moore did not allow any hint of jealousy to show, as he very well might have done were he a lesser man, for he had an Irish temper. He never sought Beecham out, nor did he patronise any of his musical ventures.

Moore and Beecham were both men of the world and each took from Lady Cunard what she was only too glad to lavish on them. Moore received literary inspiration, encouragement and affection, as well as a continual, well-found flow of advice in other branches of art. Beecham received comfort, much moral support (sometimes too much), and a great deal of money. Had he wished it, he could have received her hand too, willingly. She knew perfectly well that a marriage with George Moore would founder after a few months: he put it at six. So their idealistic love-affair lasted long after Emerald's passion for it was spent.

But Beecham was another *affaire* altogether. He possessed, in her mind, all the warmth and passion of an enduring association, which he was not prepared to grant. At first they enjoyed each other's company enormously. When it appeared to Emerald that there was every chance of Beecham obtaining a divorce, she clung to him desperately and in exactly the same way that Utica was doing. He eluded them both. Shortly before she died, Lady Cunard obliquely described what was missing in his relationship with her to the poet John Lehmann: 'No man has ever spoken the words to me "I love you!" But,' she added, 'I have had letters – I have had *letters!*'

The person who had effected the introduction between Lady Cunard and Beecham was Mary Hunter, in her own way as exceptional a hostess as Emerald. She too played an important part in Beecham's social life, but this time there was no emotional side to their friendship. Mary Hunter was the elder sister of Ethel Smyth and the wife of Charles Hunter, a rich coalfield owner from Darlington, a respected citizen, JP and Deputy Lieutenant. She was also the mistress of the celebrated artist, John Sargent.

The Smyth family came from generations of soldiers. In the sixteenth century Sir Thomas Smyth, Secretary of State to Queen Elizabeth I and one of their forbears, had built Hill Hall, near Epping in Essex. The house was altered and added to in the eighteenth century when it assumed a classical style and was completed in the form of a hollow square. In 1910 Mary Hunter persuaded, or more likely led, her husband to move south from Darlington to her family seat, which she completely refurnished with Italian and Spanish pieces. She sought the help of Sargent in the redecorations and turned Hill Hall into a house which was 'almost too luxurious for comfort', in Sir Osbert Sitwell's words.

Mary Hunter was considered by many people the Edwardian hostess *par excellence,* for nothing was ever too much trouble for her. She had a staff of twenty-eight, including a notable French chef, and her weekend house parties were events of the greatest pleasure for those fortunate enough to be invited. Beecham went there often.

Charles Hunter did not enjoy them at all. He saw little of his wife during the Season, when she left Hill in the afternoons to attend the opera, not to return until about three in the morning. He never accompanied her, but used to walk up and down one of the terraces with his hands behind his back, lamenting the fact that his wife's tastes were so far removed from his own. However, the local hunt used to meet at Hill, where breakfast was prepared out of doors. This was his great delight, but summer and its attractions for Mary seemed to come round far too quickly.

According to the Hill visitors' book Lady Cunard did not stay there until July 1913, but that cannot be right. She may have deliberately omitted to sign it, for Hill saw the blossoming of the *affaire* Beecham-Cunard from 1912. This kind of atmosphere well suited the conductor at a time when he was achieving recognition in society as well as in the musical world at home and abroad, and when he had left his wife.

Beecham now had the full measure of southern England. He was perfectly well able to hold his own – and his audience – in conversation of an amusing and elevated kind. He was also highly proficient at chess, carried a small board about with him wherever he went and knew most of the master-games by heart. He greatly surprised John Sargent, another chess-player, by beating him soundly.

On the west side of Hill was a bedroom which had special significance for those who stayed there. Its walls were covered with reproduction Louis XV wallpaper, in the centre of whose wide, recurring design was a troubadour-like figure that looked remarkably like Beecham. So close was the resemblance that this bedroom came to be known as the 'Beecham Room'. Ethel Smyth exaggerates the scene in her book *Beecham and Pharaoh* – interestingly enough dedicated to Lady Cunard – as the photograph in this book shows.

Beecham used to play Mozart and Richard Strauss in the music room at Hill, sitting at the Bechstein concert grand piano beneath portraits of Henry VIII, Charles I, Charles II and Elizabeth I. In 1912 Beecham was probably the only Englishman who could play long excerpts from *Der Rosenkavalier* from memory: this was shortly before he brought out Strauss's romantic opera at Covent Garden in January 1913.

House parties were Mary Hunter's greatest contribution to the artistic and social world of the time. Mrs 'Leo' Hunter, as she was called, always said that she would spend every penny of her husband's fortune, and so she did. He died, poor, unhappy, generous man, in 1916 during the war, when part of the house was given over to wounded soldiers. But its splendour could never be recaptured in the new world of 1919. George Moore was one of its last visitors in March 1921.

In 1910 and 1911 Joseph Beecham had again served as Mayor of St Helens, and in 1911 he was knighted. In 1914 he was made a baronet, and adopted the motto *Nil sine labore*. His deeds of philanthropy (many of them in confidence) and his services to the theatre – especially to opera – seemed to deserve this elevation. He had backed three opera seasons in 1910 and had presented the Russian Ballet and Opera at Drury Lane in 1913 and 1914 – enterprises which had all involved him in great personal expense, which he was well able and very happy to bear. The Tsar of Russia awarded Joseph the highest honour that a civilian in Russia could be given: the Order of St Stanislaus.

When the First World War began, Beecham gathered together all the operatic resources which London had to offer in the way of singers, technicians and a chorus; he disbanded the Beecham Orchestra apart from a few men unfit for service, augmented these to make another orchestra of sufficient size, and put on performances of opera at the Shaftesbury Theatre. This was such a success, a boon to soldiers home on leave, that the Beecham Opera Company continued its productions throughout the war. It was transferred from the Shaftesbury to the Aldwych Theatre, and then, when the Company began to do the larger works, to Drury Lane. It had the makings of a British National Opera Company.

In 1914 Sir Joseph had bought nineteen acres in Covent Garden on mortgage from the Duke of Bedford. This made him landlord of Covent Garden, Drury Lane, the Aldwych and other theatres, besides the fruit and vegetable market and other interesting properties. Sir Joseph loved to establish records of one sort or another, and this was 'the largest property deal ever negotiated in London'. He had the finest collection of English watercolours in London at his house in Arkwright Road, where he liked to sit alone and focus his attention upon a single picture, absorbing every detail with intense pleasure. He had also crossed the Atlantic more times than any other passenger. Despite his grimness, Sir Joseph was an artistic and sensitive man at heart, taking an enormous pride in Thomas's achievements. The Covent Garden Estate was the last record Sir Joseph achieved, for its acquisition probably killed him.

One day in October 1916 he and Thomas were to attend a highly important meeting at which their need to find funds to pay off the balance of the loan for the estate (total cost $£2\frac{1}{4}$ million) would be postponed by general agreement until the war was over and normal loan-raising was resumed. The whole business had greatly troubled Joseph, and although he was unaccustomed to taking tablets or pills of any kind (all his life he had been too close to them), he took some barbiturates on the evening before. Neither he nor anybody else knew that he was suffering from a diseased heart, and at 5.30 in the morning of 23 October he died in his bed at Hampstead. Neither Thomas nor the family ever recovered financially from the disastrous misfortune of Sir Joseph's death five hours before his signature and a number of others' would have put them all in the clear.

Thomas had been knighted in the New Year's Honours List of 1916. The citation in *The Times* read: 'His Majesty has been pleased to confer the honour of Knighthood upon THOMAS BEECHAM Esq., the well-known musical conductor and promoter of Opera. Born in 1879; son of Sir Joseph Beecham.' From this it appears that the knighthood was conferred for musical services alone, but this may not have been so. Several incidents in Beecham's life up to the end of the First World War point to a close connection with the Foreign Office. He was a persuasive man and frequently in a position to obtain information abroad within the social and military circles in which he was a welcome guest.

At the end of 1915 he was actually seconded to the Foreign Office and sent to Rome. His task was to persuade the Roman aristocracy that Britain was a peace-loving and musical nation, far more like themselves than the members of the German bloc. He demonstrated this not only by his handling of the Santa Cecilia Orchestra but also by entertaining his hosts and their guests with his brilliant conversation and equally brilliant wit. Although this can have had no effect, in itself, in detaching Italy from the Triple Alliance, Beecham was there, in Rome, when she declared war on Germany. He was lodging at the College of Cardinals; impressed by their powerful intellects and their excellent wines, he declared on returning to the family at Ewanville: 'I think I might have a crack at becoming Pope!'

Beecham was fully aware, at the outbreak of war in 1914, how little was known in Britain about the true state of affairs in Germany. He had been there often; he had seen the build-up of arms, of a navy, of an obnoxious jingoism. So when cotton, the main concern of all Lancastrians, was left out of national goods prohibited for export, Beecham threatened to call a public meeting at Queen's Hall. He laid everything on and organised important personalities to appear with himself on the platform, but only a few days before the meeting was due to take place the Government announced that cotton was henceforth to be included on the list of contraband exports to Germany and her allies.

There can be no proof that Beecham's threatened meeting had any influence on the Government's action, or that Beecham's presence in Rome tipped the Italian scales one iota. Yet it is interesting to note that he was so highly regarded in spheres which normally did not concern him.

It would seem, in any case, that his honour in the cause of music had been delayed because of his implication in the Foster divorce and his known association with Lady Cunard. Although his knighthood and his baronetcy did not appeal to him quite as much as they had to his father, Beecham agreed with a friend who said that a title goes down well with the public, and that one gets so much better service everywhere, especially on trains and liners.

Ida Haendel, the violinist, recalls that she was crossing the Atlantic soon after the Second World War and the passengers were all lined up waiting to be allocated to tables in the dining-room. She heard an angry and unmistakable voice raised in protest: 'I won't queue, I positively refuse!' Sir Thomas was led quietly to the Captain's table by an apologetic chief steward.

Beecham enjoyed being a baronet, not least because it tickled his sense of the ridiculous to observe how foreigners responded to his style of address. He liked to tell the tale of a doorman at an hotel in the United States who, on hearing that Beecham was a baronet, began by addressing him reverently as 'Your Grace'. But exposure bred contempt. He descended, by way of 'Your Honour' to the ultimate familiarity at the end of the week, of 'Hiya, Old Cock!'

Beecham was tireless in his different spheres of activity; with the untidy condition of his father's estate now causing him considerable concern, it is all the more surprising that he was able to maintain a finger, sometimes two, in every musical pie. When a philistine question was raised in the House of Commons in 1916 as to why Sir Thomas Beecham (then thirty-seven years old) had not been called up, the relevant Minister murmured that he would look into the matter, while both sides of the house joined in laughter.

Beecham had attracted a great deal of what might be called invisible support, not only from the cultivated and intellectual people with whom he associated, but also from those to whom his ideals and tremendous integrity appealed. He had very obvious support from Lady Cunard, who never lost an opportunity to speak up for him, to write letters on his behalf and to make herself his ambassadress wherever she went, sometimes without his knowledge or wish. In 1926 she acquired a portrait of Beecham that had been painted in 1913 by Bernard Munns, showing him in front of the lit house curtains of Drury Lane Theatre, baton in hand, about to commence an overture. Lady Cunard approached another Wadham man, Lord Birkenhead, and asked him to suggest to the Warden of his old college that she should present it to them. It would cost her five hundred guineas. Birkenhead's secretary approached the Vice-Chancellor but there was no response. Lord Birkenhead refused to visit Lady Cunard in London and to inspect the portrait. Six months later he wrote to the Warden of Wadham in a manner which made it clear that he was only being 'a conduit pipe' and, since he was unmusical, had little interest in the matter. 'I have never witnessed his' (Beecham's) 'efforts and I am sure that if I did they would cause me great inconvenience' is scarcely the kind of expression which helps a cause.

The Warden of Wadham was loath to meet Lady Cunard or to accept the picture from her, because of her association with Sir Thomas. Even if the picture had been offered to the college through other channels it would hardly have been appropriate at that time for Beecham's portrait to be hung beside those of Wardens past and present; despite his later fame, he only rated then as an undergraduate who had gone down under somewhat unfavourable circumstances after three terms.

In 1929 Beecham rescued the Oxford Subscription Concerts from foundering by giving a concert in the Sheldonian at his own expense, which he repeated every May. In 1930 he received his Honorary D.Mus. Now all was forgotten and he became 'Wadham's most distinguished musician'. Even so, the contentious portrait offered to Wadham by Lady Cunard remains unhung.

Beecham abandoned music altogether in 1920 to attend to his father's estate, and worked an orderly nine to six every weekday. He proved himself to be a thorough-going businessman, with a flair for getting quickly to the nub of a problem, as well as an adroit and persuasive committee man.

By early 1924 he had managed to liquidate all his father's debts, but he did not return to the Opera House until 1932, partly because of his own bankruptcy in 1931, partly because of the general slump. After 1934 he took over Covent Garden and ran the international seasons until 1939. These years were the busiest for the middle-aged Sir Thomas, who supported the Opera House and his new orchestra, the London Philharmonic, almost single-handed.

In 1936 he employed Furtwängler's Jewish ex-secretary, Dr

Geissmar, at Covent Garden, where she easily settled in, and was a tremendous asset. At home, he employed a Mrs Samuelson ('Mrs Sams'), who was the cook-housekeeper, and his valet Smith. Dr Geissmar was sometimes there too, and they had several code-signs between them so that they could all quickly recognise their master's mood. If Sir Thomas was out of sorts when he entered the house, Smith crossed his arms as a signal to Dr. Geissmar and Mrs Sams.

The 1930s were a time of false hopes and artificial pleasures for many people, determined, it seems in retrospect, to have a good time before the blow fell on them all. If Beecham did not exactly sense this, he was more than usually out of patience with the bad behaviour of his opera audiences. Always a courteous man, he could act snappily when he felt obliged to tell them to 'shut up'. His curtain speeches became, for some people, far too arrogant; his broadsides in the press, and less publicly to a wide variety of bureaucrats, sounded like intolerance.

Beecham was still absolutely determined to present opera and music in London and the provinces at the cheapest possible rates. If 'going to the opera' was a painful duty to some of the stall- and box-holders of Lady Cunard's brigade, nevertheless it did become an annual habit with them. However it needed a greater upheaval, which the Second World War initiated, for a much larger number of young people to experience the joy of music for themselves and to support it with their last shilling.

The only regular artistic attraction during the war years in London (and to a lesser degree outside it) was not opera at all but the magnificent Sadler's Wells Ballet, in which Beecham played no part. (He was in the USA in any case.) Had Covent Garden still been operating then as an opera house and not as a dance hall, it might have been a very different story. If only Beecham had been able to continue his operatic activities in the Second World War as he had in the first...

Lady Cunard followed Beecham to America, ostensibly to visit some silver mines in Ecuador (which had long since been closed and had ceased to yield her a penny), but really to be with him. She stayed at the Ritz Hotel, Beecham's residence while he was in New York, where she held court, if in a less influential or ostentatious manner than she had done in London during the previous quarter of a century. She was still trying to 'run' Beecham until, in 1941, somebody else arrived in his life.

This was Betty Thomas, professionally known as Betty Humby, a former child prodigy who at the age of twelve had won a piano scholarship to the Royal Academy of Music. She had been a pupil of Tobias Matthay and Artur Schnabel, and had first played for Beecham at her mother's house in Finchley, North London, in 1928. He was impressed, and in the early 1930s he engaged her for two of his concerts, at which she played Mozart concertos. He admired her ability and interpretative powers and suggested that she looked at Delius's Concerto.

At the age of eighteen Betty Humby had married the Rev. H. C. Thomas, who was a good deal older than she was. A gentle person, 'Tommy' became more and more Church-inclined, while Betty and her music went in a different direction. By 1939 they were living apart, and early in 1940 she finally left him to go to New York. There she occupied a small flat on 34th Street, almost under the old elevated railway in what was then the Italian quarter of the city.

Betty Humby had a nine-year-old son called Jeremy who was taken across the Atlantic by his grandmother, Muriel Humby, in the summer of 1940; but instead of joining his mother, which would not have been convenient to a concert pianist trying to re-establish her career in another country, he was sent to Connecticut where, for eighteen months, he was cared for by Roy Larsen, the publisher of *Time, Life* and *Fortune* magazines, and his wife.

In May 1941 Beecham was in the USA, where he had arrived via Australia, and was asked by a concert agency whether he could use a pianist called Betty Humby for a broadcast in the following month. Beecham was delighted. And so on 22 June she played the Delius Concerto while Beecham conducted the Columbia Symphony Orchestra, and thereafter they were seen together a good deal – except by Lady Cunard.

Rumours began to circulate about them. By 1945 Betty Humby Thomas was playing concertos at Beecham's concerts in North America and living with him, to all intents and purposes, as his wife. Divorce proceedings between her and her husband were in progress. Beecham, Betty and her son Jeremy based themselves at Sun Valley, Idaho (whose courts eased the judicial processes), in Seattle, and in Vancouver, where they spent the summer of 1942 in an apartment which Beecham rented because of its fine billiard table. That autumn they moved back to New York and for the next two years lived in a penthouse apartment on 79th Street and Madison Avenue.

Jeremy recalls this time in America with Beecham and his mother. Beecham captivated the little boy. They first met one evening in 1941 in the apartment on 34th Street. Jeremy was in bed, supposed to be asleep, when he heard someone talking in a loud voice in the next room: it was Beecham reciting Christopher Marlowe (probably *Tamburlaine*) to Betty.

Jeremy got up and went in to see the owner of the voice and Beecham at once took him on his knee. He told him that from now on he was *his* little boy, and for Jeremy this was the beginning of a happy relationship with the man who always treated him as an ally (often as a fellow conspirator) against the surrounding world of 'knaves and fools'. They played chess and billiards; Beecham instilled in him an abiding love of the English language.

One day, at a luncheon party given by the Princess Bismarck, Lady Cunard met the English actress Leonora Corbett. Sir Thomas happened to be away at the time on an extended tour of Canada; in a sense, he had an alibi. Of course he came up in the conversation. It was then that Miss Corbett dropped her bombshell: 'I had a letter today from my old friend, Betty Humby, in Seattle. She tells me that she is going to marry Thomas Beecham.'

Lady Cunard was careful to hide her feelings, but fainted as soon as she was able to leave the table and be on her own. She was quite convinced that Beecham had been past his amorous days since the middle 1930s, so that this news came as a double shock. He had misled and deceived her beyond belief. She was too proud, and too realistic, to have it out with him when he returned to New York; she knew that he would avoid an incident at all costs. She merely packed her bags and returned to London. In 1942 that might have been impossible for most people, but Emerald Cunard managed it in spite of the Germans, in spite of red tape on both sides of the Atlantic (even more imposing than enemy action) and in spite of the agonising ear-ache she suffered from non-pressurised, high-altitude flying.

In February 1942 Betty obtained her divorce, but it was not until October that Beecham filed his suit for divorce from his wife, Mrs (*sic*) Utica Celestina Beecham. As he considered that she had shared neither his knighthood nor his baronetcy, both of which came more than five years after their separation, he still called her 'Mrs'. This she disputed, and always called herself Lady Beecham. She lived near her two sons, maintaining an Edwardian dignity that recalled an age long since departed. In 1942 she was aged sixty-three, and still didn't believe in divorce.

Beecham was at the Metropolitan Opera on 15 January 1943 when an American judge in Boise, Idaho, declared his marriage dissolved. The way now lay open for him to marry Betty, but first he made extensive enquiries and sought the best possible advice on both sides of the Atlantic to ensure that an American marriage ceremony would be legal in the United Kingdom.

On 23 February the marriage took place in New York, and on 7 September there was another ceremony before the Supreme Justices 'to assure compliance with technicalities of the English law'. Three weeks later the Beechams were back in England after an appalling crossing in a Dutch cargo boat which landed them, appropriately enough, in Liverpool.

Beecham was finding great happiness with his new wife, for she perfectly understood her husband's needs, being an artist herself. She was determined to see that he had quiet, peace of mind and all possible comforts while he was at home. Furthermore, she was, in his eyes, a wonderful relief from Lady Cunard. That *affaire* was over at last.

One morning in 1943, however, Lady Cunard telephoned Arthur Bliss in his office at the BBC, where he was Director of Music, commanding him to call on her to discuss a matter of the greatest importance to them both. Bliss was mystified, but obeyed. His wife and daughters had gone to California for safety during the war, to Trudy Bliss's family home. Lady Cunard played on a totally mistaken idea of the situation when she made her strange proposal. Sir Thomas Beecham, she told Bliss, had become 'emotionally involved in America' and had to be got back to England. Bliss was to persuade the Director-General of the BBC to appoint Beecham in his place while, as a *quid pro quo*, Lady Cunard would use her best endeavours to ensure that Bliss was transferred to the USA so that at last he could be with his wife and children whom he was missing so much and would do anything to be with again. At first Bliss was amused; then he became angry at her presumption. He coolly suggested that she put her ideas to the Director-General herself.

This may have been only one of a number of ruses which the desperate lady invented to get her lover back. But he had to be brought to her by some third party; no direct appeal would ever work. In 1945 Virgil Thomson arrived by air in London late one night and called on Lady Cunard, who was giving a dinner party in her flat at the Dorchester Hotel. After a little while Thomson found himself alone with her for a moment. 'Shall you be seeing Thomas?' she asked. That was all. But it was no good. She had been jilted, and with nothing much to live for any more she shut herself away and died, miserably lonely, in June 1948 at the Dorchester, aged seventy-five.

Beecham's reinstatement in London was, domestically speaking, a long-drawn-out affair. During the time of the 'doodle-bugs' (or V-1s) and later the V-2s, he and Betty stayed at 16 Wellington Road in St John's Wood, where Betty's parents, Dr and Mrs Morgan Humby, lived. They then went to Selsey, where Betty had lived up to the war, before buying an eighty-acre estate in Sussex near Lodsworth, called 'Overnoons'. But it was too far from London, so they rented the lovely Delves House from John Christie's Ringmer Estates; they occupied it for only six months, before returning to St John's Wood, to 39 Circus Road. From there they went to a palatial flat in Grosvenor House, and in and out of Brown's Hotel, of which Beecham was especially fond; then to Grove End Road, still in St John's Wood, a part of London favoured by Beechams from 1910 and even at the present time. They also had a suite at the Waldorf Hotel, recalling days during the First World War when Beecham was its ground landlord; and there were frequent sallies to the Berkeley, the Mayfair and the Savoy Hotels. The Connaught was another favourite, and its cuisine greatly pleased him.

Thus they maintained his reputation for never being found where he was thought to be living. As of old, the more houses he bought, the more suites he rented, the more likely he was to be in an hotel for a great part of the time.

The pianist, Ivor Newton, remembers visiting Beecham at Delves. He was ushered in with the greatest ceremony by White, who had succeeded Smith as manservant; he was given the best chair in the room and asked what he would like to drink. Beecham suggested sherry, making the word sound like ambrosia, adding: 'I shall now summon my wine waiter.' He pulled the bell with a flourish. Presently the door opened and diminutive Jeremy stood on the threshold. At other times Beecham referred to his stepson as Ganymede or Old Cockleorum.

Beecham would often go into a kind of mental cocoon to read scores or – as a means of recharging batteries – detective stories. More often than not he had solved the plot long before the end. He read avidly through half-closed eyes, usually smoking a cigar and wearing pyjamas untidily buttoned-up. Over the top he wore the inevitable silk dressing-gown. He read on until two or three in the morning and would then be up by about five to read scores and to prepare for the events of the day.

He was not a practical man in the domestic sense. He knew that coffee, perhaps even breakfast, would be brought to him; but how it was cooked, how it arrived did not concern him, although the coffee had always to be piping hot. One morning, forced to fend for himself because he was alone, he decided to boil an egg. He knew that this took three and a half minutes, and since that was the playing time of the first side of his 78 recording of *La Gazza Ladra* Overture, he put on the record and made it his egg-timer.

On one foggy morning in London, when he had to get to a concert rehearsal and driving was out of the question, he and his general manager travelled by Underground. On their arrival at Kilburn Station Beecham walked straight through the barrier without a ticket, receiving abuse from the woman on duty there. It was explained to her who her distinguished passenger was, but nothing would pacify her until Beecham turned round and capped her pungent phrases in such a manner that she laughed and felt honoured.

Beecham loved slapstick. He also enjoyed the clever sort of ribald story. King George V knew this, and once after receiving him into the royal box during the interval of an opera before the First World War, asked: 'Well, Beecham, have you got a new story for me?' The story was begun and the King sat smiling and enjoying himself until suddenly the atmosphere seemed to freeze. Queen Mary had come in behind Beecham, who was not at first aware of her presence. The King made to ease the situation by reminding the Queen who Beecham was, but she cut in: 'We have indeed met Mr Beecham.' There was no smile on her face or pleasure in her voice. For the first and only time in his life, Beecham bowed himself out of the royal presence without having been formally dismissed.

He liked to tell this and other stories against himself for, although he was a very particular man, the comical events in life always came uppermost. Silly remarks made by strangers or outlandish pronouncements tickled him, and he was good at imitating their perpetrators.

He was, as it was easy to forget, very much a Lancastrian in his sense of the ridiculous. When he told a tale, the St Helens lad would pop out. 'Some speed,' declared the Manchester woman on the bus when the brakes failed. 'Ay', said her neighbour; 'Ah has, fer wun!'

Beecham did everything in style (even to the telling of jokes) and, as he advised others to do, with conviction. He would put on a great performance about anything at all, given an audience and the right mood. If he had arrived at a strange hotel he generally went through a great palaver about his rooms, probably refusing them for all sorts of reasons. He was a seasoned traveller and knew all the catches, but he might still go through his procedure so as to test out the staff, to put them in awe of him (promising good service later), or for no reason at all. Nobody was ever quite sure.

He was not one paradox but a mixture of several. This complexity sometimes left even those who were nearest to him in doubt. What appeared to be a genuine, towering rage was entirely disproved to the right person by a solemn wink aside. To say merely that he created a façade is oversimplification. Jeremy used the phrase 'trapped in a façade', but one can argue that Beecham's style and manner were straightforward productions of Ewanville, Rossall, Wadham and considerable travel abroad. He had great nobility of manner and of speech, but the broad vowels of Lancashire were always grazing the surface.

Because he was a man above men, he touched the heights and plumbed the depths to a far more incisive degree than ordinary artistic people ever do. His own standards were high and he used his time profitably, so that meaningless, tiresome people only bored him. Although he was attentive when meeting a person for the first time, if they did not match his expectation he delivered a withering silence that was more notable even than one of his epigrams. The habit of twitching his nose, first noticed at the beginning of the century, became a distinct Beecham trademark.

Beecham's English friends were few, considering the number of his acquaintances. The most staunch were Sir Maurice Bowra, Vice-Chancellor of Oxford and Warden of Wadham; Lord Boothby; Neville Cardus; Beverley Baxter; Sir Ronald Storrs and Sir Hugh Allen. He was fond of Virgil Thomson, Leopold Stokowski and Lauritz Melchior in the USA. Towards the end of his life he buried many old hatchets, especially those with John Christie and David Webster.

In the early 1950s Betty was playing less frequently, for she was suffering from a complaint that, in the short term, was alleviated by a habit-forming drug. After a major operation in 1948 her health had deteriorated, but she was convinced that she was not doing enough for her husband. Her participation in the Orchestra's affairs, her voice behind his during telephone conversations, and the letters she wrote on his behalf – or so it appeared – frequently gave the wrong impression.

Then uncomfortable disagreements between them became known outside their house. He was mild and kind to a fault, for he understood her and loved her well. When she was feeling at her worst it would have been far better had she left him to himself, but at these times she tended to intervene even more. He knew that she was desperately ill, and as a dutiful husband he remained calm and loving to her.

Once or twice, when he had a concert outside London, he slipped out of the house and took a taxi to the station, leaving her well looked after. But as the train pulled out of the station the door slid open and there she was, with a look of triumph on her face. She had come, after all, to look after him.

The most careful and devoted of her chaperones was a young woman, only a girl when she joined the Royal Philharmonic as a shorthand typist-cum-Girl Friday in 1950. Her name was Shirley Hudson and she was of the greatest help to Beecham in reasoning with Betty, woman to woman, and calming her in a household that was otherwise dominated by men.

There was Beecham himself, his servant, a secretary-assistant, and frequent visitors from the Orchestra: the manager, the leader and librarian – all men.

In 1956, before the end of the financial year, Beecham and Betty were obliged to live abroad for tax reasons. They relinquished their English domicile, but not of course their nationality, and took up residence at the Villa Grevillea in Cap Ferrat. This delightful spot was leased from the Earl of Warwick, and Jeremy, now in the Foreign Service, spent his honeymoon there in the autumn of 1957. A long letter from Beecham to him contains all kinds of plans for the four of them to be together in Italy afterwards, and its tone and affection are those of a father to his beloved son.

Beecham had two singular honours bestowed upon him late in life. He was made a Companion of Honour; and – which he felt more deeply – he was invited to deliver the Romanes Lecture at Oxford. That he spoke on John Fletcher, the Jacobean playwright, and not upon a musical subject showed the depth of his literary understanding and his penetrating insight into a period with which he seemed closely connected.

In the summer of 1958 the Beechams were in South America. Betty suddenly suffered a severe heart attack and died on 2 September in Buenos Aires during the opera season.

Beecham was shattered. He knew it was inevitable, but when the time came he was suddenly unprepared. He rejected any sympathy with bitterness and anger. Nobody had ever seen him so demoralised. But he did not pause to dwell upon his loss. He threw himself into his work at the Colón Opera House with a demoniac gusto that astonished everybody who worked there.

His devotion and loyalty to Betty during her long illness had brought him very close to her. After all, he was getting on for eighty, no longer the self-sufficient young man who had gone his own way from another wife in 1909. There had been other occasions in his life when – for quite different reasons – he had abandoned those who had grown close to him. Yet now everything was different. Betty's loss in no way made up for the hollow peace which existed around him. He was lonely.

In London that year he paid three quiet tributes to Betty. The Berlioz *Grande Messe des Morts* (although planned some time beforehand) was a blazing performance and united the Royal Philharmonic Society, the London Philharmonic Choir and the Royal Philharmonic Orchestra.

His biography of Frederick Delius was published, as a promise to Jelka Delius and after nearly thirty years of labour. Its dedication, anonymous but obvious, reads: 'To the memory of a beloved companion, brave and beautiful, gracious and gay, to whom the music of Delius was ever a joy and a mystery.'

At the party to launch the book Beecham was borne down upon by a lady who called out: 'Lovely to see you – how's Betty?' By some mischance she had not heard the news, although she did know of the recent demise of the composer of *The Wasps* and the *Antartica* Symphony. Beecham replied, 'She's on tour', and pausing long enough to shuffle away, added, 'with Dr Vaughan Williams.'

Chapter Two

THE ORCHESTRAS

THE GREATEST of all Thomas Beecham's many achievements were in the orchestra field. He raised the New Symphony Orchestra from chamber size to symphonic proportions and by 1907 had made it into the best London orchestra. He recruited, trained and conducted – as well as maintained – three entirely new orchestras between 1909 and 1961 without any form of subsidy from the British taxpayer: the Beecham Symphony, the London Philharmonic and the Royal Philharmonic Orchestras. He almost certainly saved both the Hallé and the London Symphony from being disbanded during the First World War; he prevented the Royal Philharmonic Society from failing from a similar lack of funds, and thereby assured the continuance of its own orchestra. That totals seven symphony orchestras over which Beecham had a powerful influence. Although he never found the Liverpool Philharmonic in dire straits, he frequently conducted them without a fee and was always willing to be called on by them. And there was another, the Beecham Wind Orchestra, which existed for a short time before the First World War. All these enterprises involved him in great personal expense, effort and skill. There were many foreign orchestras, too, with which he was concerned as a guest, from Budapest in the East to the western shores of America. They also form part of his extensive orchestral story.

Beecham's first contact with professional musicians goes back to 1894, when he was a schoolboy. In that summer Rossall School celebrated its fiftieth jubilee with a concert given by their own choir and 'a large contingent of the Hallé Orchestra'. Beecham was at the end of his second year there and still a fairly junior boy.

E. T. Sweeting, the school's choirmaster and organist, conducted. From his photograph he appears to have been a sensitive man, and certainly he was a good musician, for he later became master of music at Winchester. Sweeting has left 'A true and faithful Historie of the Singing Boys of RUSHALE' in which he records certain events at this Rossall concert. 'I got very nervous and all done up beforehand,' he writes, 'but all went well. Lloyd was openly delighted by the singing of his *Ode* and was most complimentary. We also did Bridge's effective *In Inchcape Rock* and in this and the *Ode*, Beecham and Gairdner were useful in the orchestra.'

Beecham had been incorporated into the Hallé as an extra per-cussionist because the orchestral player booked for the concert had lost his way between Manchester and Fleetwood. Beecham confessed little in later life about his abilities as a percussion player, although in a press interview in 1898, when he was up at Oxford, he admitted to having had 'a little to do with an orchestra' apart from writing short pieces for them. (The second part of this statement is a mystery.) He does not seem to have been intimately concerned with any orchestral – or even choral – activities in Oxford, but after going down in 1899 he formed and conducted an amateur society in St Helens. A choral society already existed and had a conductor in J. T. Elliott. Now it became the St Helens Choral and Orchestral Societies, under the joint honorary conductor-ships of Elliott and Thomas Beecham Jnr. There were a number of skilled amateur players in the district and when they were augmented by professional principals Beecham felt them to be ready for a public performance. He found from the start that he could establish, from his point of view, a personal and effective rapport with them all.

The first of the three concerts that Beecham conducted at St Helens in 1899 was on Wednesday evening, 8 November. The Overture was Mendelssohn's *Ruy Blas*, and it was followed by the *Pagliacci* Prologue sung by a Mr Haigh Jackson, the vocal soloist of the evening. Then Beecham conducted the Introduction to Act III of *Die Meistersinger*; the Chorus joined the Orchestra in Elgar's *Spanish Serenade*, and the first part ended with Mendelssohn's D minor Piano Concerto with Mr Osborne Edmundson as soloist.

The second part began with Grieg's *First Peer Gynt Suite*; 'Even bravest Heart' from *Faust* (Haigh Jackson); and then a gradual de-terioration in programme-building to ballads and piano solos by the two protagonists of the evening. Among them, Beecham and the Orchestra played Coleridge-Taylor's *Four Characteristic Waltzes*, and ended the concert with the Overture to *William Tell*. Such was the programme of the very first concert Beecham is known to have undertaken.

When Joseph Beecham became Mayor of St Helens for the first time in 1899 he decided that he would have a concert in the town hall as part of his inaugural proceedings. The local orchestra was not nearly good enough for such an event, and so he booked the Hallé. It was to be a splendid affair, and Hans Richter, formerly assistant to Richard Wagner and the greatest living exponent of *Die Meistersinger*, was to conduct. In an era without radio or television the arrival of one of Europe's prominent conductors was an event of overwhelming interest and importance in St Helens.

But two days before the concert, Joseph Beecham was informed by the Hallé's business manager, J. A. Forsyth, that Richter 'could not appear'. Joseph was furious. On hearing what had happened, Thomas immediately proposed himself. He knew the programme by heart and had no qualms at all.

Joseph was dumbfounded at his son's impudence, and pooh-poohed the idea. Thomas became more excited and argued with his father, who began to get angry – and then paused. He smiled because another idea had struck him: the value in advertising to Beechams. 'All right, lad,' he said, 'have a try.'

Joseph accordingly informed the Hallé that his son Thomas would be conducting them, and they were appalled. Not only did they dislike the presumptuous idea that any amateur might direct them when he decided to, but especially the idea of one not yet twenty years old *and* in place of their great Richter. No, it wouldn't do at all. The Hallé's leader, Carlo Risegari, who had assumed that he would automatically step up to the rostrum and receive the conductor's fee, refused point blank to go to St Helens at all.

If Joseph still had any reservations about letting his son, who had a single concert experience to his name, conduct a seasoned, professional orchestra, Risegari's attitude disposed of them. He got on the telephone, spoke to Risegari direct and told him straight that he might go to the devil; that his son was going to conduct and that if the Hallé were rejecting the date he would engage another orchestra – from London. Then he put down the telephone.

Joseph was now enjoying the situation, for he was by nature a bully and was only calling the Hallé's bluff. He immediately sent Thomas to Manchester to negotiate with J. A. Forsyth, and they came to a gentlemanly agreement: the orchestra would appear at St Helens, but with a deputy leader.

The players came over during the afternoon of the day of the concert, 6 December, and were entertained lavishly by Joseph. Afterwards they rehearsed, but only for ninety minutes. They all responded well to Thomas, except for a bassoonist who had overdone the liquid part of Joseph's refreshments. In the short time at his disposal Thomas was able to get through only a few of the items, and the soloist, a young American soprano called Lillian Blauvelt, did not even present herself. Joseph had to persuade her not to cancel altogether as she was threatening to do.

After the National Anthem the concert began with the Overture to *Die Meistersinger*, thereafter a favourite opener for Beecham. He conducted this work and Beethoven's Fifth Symphony without a score. Although he had observed this practice in Germany and Austria it was uncommon in England, thus confirming many people's views that Thomas Beecham was a most eccentric young man.

Then came Miss Blauvelt's song and aria, followed by the Introduction to Act III of *Lohengrin* and the *Hungarian March* from Berlioz's *Damnation of Faust*. These were not only familiar orchestral works for Thomas but routine for the Hallé and needed little actual work done on them; but the instrumentalists had to become accustomed to their conductor's manner on the rostrum and especially to his baton-less direction.

It was a triumph for one of his youth and lack of practical experience to have come through without mishap, as many of the players grudgingly admitted afterwards. On the following Saturday the *St Helens Newspaper* published a leading article to emphasise the novelty and success of the Mayor's concert, and also, most likely, to show him solidarity. The article read:

> A general chorus of congratulation has greeted the Mayor's Concert. It was a somewhat daring departure from ordinary custom but the experiment has been amply justified. . . . The Hallé Orchestra is one of the most famous bands in the world. It may justly be said too that the people of St Helens feel an added satisfaction that the Mayor's son was so prominent a figure. That a St Helens man should conduct it in such a way as to give added force and fire and soul and artistic expression to the performance of even the Hallé band, is a matter that in a way reflects also some credit on the town, and is a contribution to local patriotism. People have suddenly learned that one of their townsfolk has musical genius.

And that was the first time that Thomas Beecham was recognised for what he was.

On the same day as this leader appeared in the local paper there was an interview with Mr T. Beecham Jnr that occupied a whole column on the back page. 'I play the clarionette and tympanii' (*sic*) 'in orchestras,' he said, 'but the organ and piano chiefly. The piano is most convenient for a person who takes up orchestral study. I like the French horn very much and also the cello.' Asked whether there was a field for clever amateur conductors, he replied: 'Not much unless a very good man has a lot of money and can afford to get a tip-top orchestra of his own.' When asked whether he intended to continue with conducting, Beecham replied: 'I think I may. I hardly know yet.' Already he had formed the idea of employing the best players. As for the money, that was not always to be had so easily.

Beecham went on to praise 'Mr Wood's Orchestra at Queen's Hall' and the Hallé in Manchester, 'the two best in the world. They can compare with any Continental orchestra. I have heard all the best.'

After making this bold statement the self-confident Mr Thomas Beecham Jnr then hurried away to take a rehearsal of the St Helens Orchestral Society for their concert twelve days later. When it took place it was poorly attended by comparison with the Hallé concert, although the reserved seats were fairly full. The programme opened with Suppé's *Poet and Peasant* Overture 'under the clever and "enthusing" conductorship of Mr T. Beecham Jnr.', as the local paper later described it. This was followed by the *Jewel Song* from *Faust*, sung by Miss Ethel Hubi-Newcombe. Then came the *Valse Lente* by Delibes and the Overture to *Figaro*. The programme notes for this concert read as though they were written by Beecham, as the short but succinct description of Mozart's Overture reveals: 'Mozart's famous Opera, *The Marriage of Figaro* (founded on Beaumarchais' play), was first produced in 1786, and has been a universal favourite ever since. The overture is a sparkling bit of comedy, full of bright melodies, sudden changes, and ingenious contrivances of humorous effect.'

This light piece was exactly what was needed before the next work, a choral and orchestral setting by C. V. Stanford of Tennyson's epic ballad, *The Revenge*, set word for word. Following the interval, there were two unaccompanied part-songs conducted by the choirmaster Mr J. T. Elliott, in which Beecham sang bass; and he then returned to the rostrum to conduct Beethoven's First Symphony (one of the few occasions in his life that he did so). Liszt's *Die Lorelei*, Brahms's *Schicksalslied* and Mendelssohn's *Cornelius March* completed this long, varied, but far from uninteresting programme.

There is no indication as to exactly how many members of the orchestra were professional, except for seven violinists (all ladies) and a Dr Holdsworth who was the second oboe. The band had double woodwind with an extra flute, two horns, three trumpets and three trombones beside harp, timpani and percussion, the latter needed in *The Revenge*.

In 1900, following the terrible family row over Josephine Beecham's disappearance and Thomas Beecham's break with his father, Beecham left St Helens for nearly ten years. He set his face single-mindedly towards the composition of operas and the acquisition of a place upon the London concert platform.

The London musical scene in 1900 was dominated by Dr Hans Richter, the conductor of the Hallé Orchestra in Manchester and occasional conductor of special concerts at Queen's Hall. He and his Teutonic tastes governed London's music to the exclusion of Russian, French and Italian works. French and Italian operas were to be heard, of course, at Covent Garden, where the repertoire would have been impoverished without the staple fare of Gounod, Rossini, Verdi and the young Puccini.

The concert platform was occupied by a heavy suffusion of Beethoven, Brahms, Wagner and Elgar, in all of whose works Richter excelled. It was he who wrote the famous (and often incompletely quoted) epigram in a young Frenchwoman's autograph book: 'Les trois B sont les plus grands: Bach, Beethoven et Brahms. Tous les autres sont crétins.' To which the witty Moszkowski made reply: 'Les trois M sont aussi grands: Meyerbeer, Mendelssohn et Moszkowski. Tous les autres sont chrétiens.'

Beecham found three main concert halls in London when he arrived there. Queen's Hall, where the orchestra which bore its name was presided over by Henry Wood, was the biggest. The orchestra were used to playing for Wood for more than half the concerts they gave there. If it meant getting used to the quirks and fancies of guest conductors for the rest of the time, that was a small price to pay for their solid foundation. The orchestra was managed by Robert Newman, the lessee and manager of Queen's Hall.

The St James's Hall, demolished to make way for the Piccadilly Hotel in 1905, was older than Queen's Hall and possessed sentimental attachments for Londoners owing to the past procession of famous musicians who had played there. But it had no regular orchestra or policy.

The Bechstein Hall in Wigmore Street was given over to recitals and chamber orchestras; its standard was consistently high.

Outside Central London there was another orchestra at the Crystal Palace, Sydenham. There the fiery Augustus Manns wielded his huge orchestral and vocal forces, introducing new works to his appreciative audiences, notably the first orchestral music by Schubert ever to be heard in England.

Beecham listened carefully at all these places and probably attended every London concert over a space of three years. This was easy enough for him to do because there were not nearly as many concerts then as now. Beecham was listening from the point of view of a conductor who already knew many of the scores by heart and who knew the players and some of the conductors too.

By 1904 there was another fully-established London orchestra. Henry Wood had been incensed by the number of his players who sent deputies – often of a low standard – to rehearsals and even to the actual concerts, at little or no notice. In many cases he would have paid these people to stay away, so one day Robert Newman, the manager, made a short announcement before the morning rehearsal: 'As from today, there will be no deputies. Good morning, gentlemen!' Nearly half the Queen's Hall Orchestra revolted, and most of them left to form themselves into the first British co-operative orchestra. They called themselves the London Symphony Orchestra and gave their first concert at Queen's Hall on 9 June 1904 with Richter conducting. It says much for Wood's big-heartedness that he attended this concert and applauded vigorously. But perhaps he had already guessed that before very long the LSO were to be plagued with the very same curse as he had been – that of deputies. Nevertheless they were soon firmly established as the first self-administering, self-governing orchestra in London, with each player-member a shareholder in a limited company. Beecham heard the LSO from the start. He also heard Wood frequently, as well as Richter and the great Artur Nikisch, who appealed to him most of all. But before long Beecham felt unable to join in the wholehearted applause which greeted every orchestra after every work they had played. There was something missing, he thought. Nothing he heard was finished: there was no gloss on the performance; in some cases the ensembles were ragged and the intonation suspect. In other words, the standard that seemed to satisfy London's audiences was in need of improvement.

Beecham went abroad with his wife after their marriage in July 1903. At the end of 1904 he came home to London alone, leaving his wife, her parents and the new baby together. His mother promised to finance a concert or two, and so he set about finding players and an opportunity of presenting himself before the public, which for him was going to be the hardest part.

The forty members of Wood's Queen's Hall Orchestra did not take at all to the programme which Beecham put in front of them at their one and only rehearsal. It was, to say the least, *recherché*. A new conductor and a lot of new works were too much for the musicians, and at the concert they blatantly ignored most of Beecham's direction and went their own way. This was noted by the only newspaper critic who reported the event (for *The Times*), and he evidently felt sympathy for Beecham because of the way he was treated.

So far as he was concerned, Beecham was disappointed with himself because the sound which his players produced was not at all as he had imagined it would be. Indeed, for a short time he wondered whether his hearing had not become defective. So most of the treasured French and Italian pieces which his musicians played so badly, as well as Cyril Scott's ballad *Helen of Kirkconnel,* sung by Frederic Austin with the orchestra, seem to have gone for nothing.

Until the name 'Beecham' meant something to audiences, until his presence could command instant attention both from them and from his players alike, until his magic produced willing acceptance of obscure works, such a programme was self-indulgent and largely incomprehensible to his audience. The programme's distinctly Gallic slant was contrary to popular taste.

On Sunday afternoon, 29 October, a talented pianist and musician called Evlyn Howard Jones first conducted a newly-formed chamber orchestra at the Coronet Theatre, Notting Hill Gate, in a cheap popular series of concerts. They were criticised for playing 'unattractive' works – Weber's *Euryanthe* Overture, Mendelssohn's Violin Concerto and Tchaikovsky's Fifth Symphony – instead of English music. They called themselves the Sunday Orchestral Society and included some first-rate musicians, among them John Saunders, the leader; Waldo Warner, viola; Eli Hudson, flute; Charles Draper, clarinet, and Aubrey Brain, horn. The concerts failed to attract more than a handful of people on each occasion and were consequently ended, but the principals decided to keep together and form a committee.

Beecham knew most of these men and had attended one of the rehearsals for the first Coronet concert. When word got round that he was looking for an orchestra willing to play interesting 'new' compositions, the committee sent Charles Draper to call on him in Boreham Wood. Beecham knew that they were exceptionally good and soon came to terms with them. They were renamed the New Symphony Orchestra.

For the past year Beecham had been listening more carefully than ever before to other orchestras and conductors, seeking out any weak points. By the time his private investigation was over he knew that he was going to be able to achieve far better results with the New Symphony Orchestra than had been heard in London for a very long time.

Four concerts were booked at the Bechstein Hall between November 1906 and January 1907. Beecham's business manager advised him not to overload the programmes with totally unknown works, but he ignored the advice and forged ahead with the obscure French and Italian pieces which he had brought back home with him and which the orchestra quickly grew to like. They got on so well together that the orchestra invited Beecham to become their principal conductor, a position which he accepted with alacrity.

The concerts were advertised all over the West End of London with a picture of the conductor fixing passers-by with his magnetic gaze; and from the first concert Beecham seems to have found the key to the kind of orchestral direction and playing which was to be his hallmark for the next fifty years: enormous care lavished upon every bar, with nuances of dynamics, phrasing and rubato which distinguished the performance and presented the composer's intention fully and clearly – and with beauty. For this absolute intention Beecham always produced a melodic line throughout, even though it might not be all too apparent from the score or in the interpretation of other conductors.

The first concert had a long programme and finished far too late on the evening of 2 November. It was devoted, with one exception, to French composers of the eighteenth and nineteenth centuries. The *Morning Post*'s critic stated: 'Mr Beecham proved himself an excellent conductor, sensitive and alert, and he conducted without a baton.' That was all right, as far as it went, but Beecham had to face competition from other concerts and would need to be able to attract audiences away from them. For this he was going to need more than his own competence.

A formidable array of established soloists were to be heard in London in 1907. Richter, of course, had his devoted following with the LSO at Queen's Hall on Mondays; Lionel Tertis was giving viola recitals with York Bowen at the piano; Maria Gay was singing *Carmen* at Covent Garden; Joachim was playing at Queen's Hall, and Harold Bauer was giving piano recitals. For those members of the public who could afford no more than one outing a week, the choice was a difficult one, and Beecham with the NSO came far down the list.

The second concert on 19 November drew the compliment: 'Mr Beecham must be congratulated not only on his idea but upon the manner in which he is carrying this out.' A previously unheard symphony by C. P. E. Bach 'containing some quaint orchestral effects ... was played with great precision and go under Mr Beecham's vigilant guidance.' However, the critics' appreciation was not matched by the public; by the time the third concert took place, on 12 December, it was evident that unless it sold out the fourth could never happen.

The *Morning Post*'s music critic again praised Beecham: 'These concerts possess a very special interest to musicians. Routine plays a great part in the musical life of London and one cannot but feel grateful to those who strike out a path of their own.' But Méhul, Cherubini and

Paisiello were like dead hands on ticket sales and the fourth concert, scheduled for 23 January, was cancelled.

Even so, the three concerts achieved a twofold purpose by putting both Beecham and the orchestra well and truly on the musical map of London. Beecham had been undisturbed by the poor box-office; if anything he was more resolved than ever to show who knew best. He persuaded the committee of the orchestra to augment themselves to symphonic size, in other words from about fifty to eighty players. He and the section leaders between them chose the players they wanted and then rehearsed them in order to gain an approach to ensemble. Normally this takes time, and it is unfortunate that no gramophone record exists of the first, full New Symphony Orchestra from which to judge Beecham's early abilities as an orchestral trainer.

Beecham now made it clear that he intended to become London's first impresario-conductor. Since that implied putting the NSO in his pocket the committee turned themselves into a limited company to prevent him from doing so. This was at the end of 1907, but it only delayed the realisation of his grand plan by eighteen months.

He was still experimenting with and without stick, and in April 1908 invoked the stern disapproval of the *Times* critic for not using one. For the time being he took to the baton again, but there is evidence that during the First World War he put it aside for a while, as he did in several concerts which he gave abroad between the wars. His stick technique tended to be erratic, or at least unconventional. But Beecham was not a conventional person. He achieved his effects by other means and persuaded his players into following him. Even so, eminent musicians would gasp with disbelief to see his right hand entangled with his coat-tails or to observe him extracting splinters of smashed baton from his left hand, which he had impaled in some exaggerated gesture. Many was the time, though, when in soft and delicate passages or when giving one of his inimitable Delius fades, he took the baton with his left hand in order to get it out of the way, while his right caressed the sounds that he was drawing from the orchestra and his fingers magically painted them upon the air. His contemporary in years, Leopold Stokowski, did much the same, but he never used a stick.

The years 1907-8 are the most important in the early part of Beecham's conducting career because they established him as a leading orchestral conductor in London. He had broken the ice with the Queen's Hall players (and got a ducking); he had introduced the New Symphony Orchestra (at a price); and now he was all set to show London, including Wood, Richter and Nikisch as well, that there was a new and

Miss Utica Celestina Welles, aged seventeen, in court dress for her
presentation at Queen Victoria's last Drawing-Room on 11 June 1899. Her
engagement to Beecham was announced a year later.

Richard Strauss (1864–1949), photographed in 1910 – the year in which Beecham championed his *Elektra*; and Frederick Delius (1862–1934), the English composer of German parentage and French domicile whom Beecham first met in 1907. *Below* Ethel Smyth (1853–1944), whose opera *The Wreckers* provided Beecham's entrée to the orchestra pit; and Lady Maud ('Emerald') Cunard.

Thomas Beecham in October 1910, still modelling his appearance on that of the Hungarian conductor, Artur Nikisch – especially in the cut of his beard and the soulful expression.

The Beecham family Christmas card of 1910. Beecham is conspicuous by his absence. *Below left* Part of the wall decoration in the 'Beecham Room' at Hill Hall, Essex, home of Mrs Charles Hunter (Ethel Smyth's sister). The Italianate figure sitting on a step closely resembles Beecham. *Below right* Caricature of Beecham in 1910.

XMAS, 1910.

B

WITH THE SEASON'S GREETINGS.
FROM
MR. & MRS. THOMAS BEECHAM.
32
UPPER HAMILTON TERRACE.
N.W.

powerful contender among them. And he was not yet thirty years of age.

The fully augmented NSO promoted themselves for three concerts at Queen's Hall in the last quarter of 1907, and the first of them took place on 14 October, when 'a talented young violinist, Joska Szigeti', played the E major Concerto by Bach which 'displayed his gifts to advantage'; 'Thomas Beecham deserves all praise for bringing forward... unhackneyed works' in the rest of the programme.

But the main result of this concert sprang from Beecham's meeting with Delius. This composer had come to London with one of his German conductor-champions, Fritz Cassirer, to decide which of the two orchestras known to them, the Queen's Hall or the London Symphony, should be employed for the first London concert of Delius's music. Upon finding that there was a third, the New Symphony Orchestra, Delius and Cassirer attended Beecham's concert and were convinced that this orchestra was the best of the three.

The story of the historic meeting between Delius and his future champion in the conductor's room at Queen's Hall is well-known. They interested each other at once, and so began a partnership which was to be of immeasurable importance to Delius. Although Cassirer and not Beecham gave the first London concert of Delius's music, while Wood and not Beecham gave the second, it was Beecham who then began to make himself the authoritative interpreter of this most elusive and idiosyncratic of composers.

At the second NSO concert, in November, the soloist was a young pianist called Myra Hess. She was known as a recitalist, but this was her first appearance in a concerto. She later recollected that 'still in his twenties but already the martinet, [Beecham] made no effort to hide his disdain for women pianists.' Although she had engaged Beecham and the orchestra for her second début he rehearsed all his orchestral pieces first, and at the very end of the afternoon went quickly through her two concertos, Beethoven's G major and Saint-Saens' Fourth. This rehearsal was still in progress when the doors of Queen's Hall were being opened to the public. Myra Hess's biographer, Denise Lassimone, blames Beecham for causing the pianist enduring stage-fright by leaving her in the artists' room alone before the concert. Tobias Matthay, her professor, expressed doubts about the concert beforehand on a postcard to her: 'Who is this fellow Beecham? If he doesn't accompany you properly, I shall come and do it myself.' Matthay wouldn't have had time to find out, but all was well and the *Morning Post* critic wrote that 'Mr Beecham lent every support to the soloist.'

The third of these concerts took Beecham back six years to the little touring opera company with which he had been associated, for Blanche Marchesi was engaged as the soprano soloist in Mahler's Fourth Symphony and in the Liebestod from *Tristan und Isolde*.

In January 1908 Beecham conducted a complicated and extraordinary work by Josef Holbrooke called *Apollo and the Seaman, A Dramatic Symphony with Choral Epilogue*. Conductor, chorus and orchestra were placed behind a large screen at Queen's Hall, and, as Beecham writes in his autobiography, 'it soon became evident that the most important personage in the whole scheme was the manipulator of the magic lantern.' After a satisfactory final rehearsal, all was set for the first performance on 20 January at 8 p.m., when a carefully planned series of events, from the prompt closing of doors, lowering of lights, soft pedal-note on the organ, darkness, cessation of organ, soft cymbal tap, and the sudden appearance of Apollo on the screen, were all calculated to get the audience in the right mood. But Beecham missed his train and arrived six minutes late. By then the series of events had been started but had stopped at the fifth minute past eight o'clock because Beecham was not there to give the cue to the percussionist. Consequently the audience sat in silent darkness, feeling that something was wrong. At Beecham's appearance behind the screen the cymbal player was so relieved that he dealt his instrument a fierce whack, the huge head of Apollo flashed on the screen, 'everyone in the audience jumped a foot in the air', then roared with laughter, one of the heartiest bursts, Beecham says, that he had ever heard in a public building.

Holbrooke was known at the time as 'the stormy petrel of English music', and he told Henry Wood years later: 'There is one thing I *do* regret – that I did not ask you to conduct the Second Symphony, *Apollo*, but the folk who found the money for that said Beecham – of all the dreadful people in our profession they could not have chosen worse.' This, it must be added, was expressed after Beecham had done his best for Holbrooke by producing his opera *Dylan* during the 1914 Drury Lane season. But Holbrooke, who was without any humour, blamed everybody in sight for not liking his music: 'I with eight symphonies, eight operas, thirty-five chamber works etc... my profession gives me NOTHING.'

Between February and May 1908 Beecham conducted six more concerts with the NSO at Queen's Hall, making a total of eleven there in the 1907–8 season. The series put the orchestra on its mettle, for the programmes were varied, interesting and well-built, although they included works which can seldom, if ever, have been heard again. But, like Holbrooke, the composers may have had backers. There was only a slight smattering of Mozart and Delius to give any indication of the kind of programmes which were to reflect Beecham's future taste and policy and consequently the kind of players that he would be needing.

On 4 December 1908 Beecham gave a performance of Delius's *Sea Drift* at Queen's Hall with the New Symphony Orchestra. The *Morning Post*'s critic wrote the next day: 'Mr Beecham is a fine conductor but his violent and often-times unnecessary gestures detract greatly from the merits of his conducting ... Mr Beecham was thoroughly at home in the *Carnaval Romain* Overture of Berlioz but even in this music we would rather not look at him whilst he conducts, but there is no denying the potency of his methods.'

It was always Beecham's way to have an alternative scheme ready to meet any unexpected contingency; and because he knew that the NSO would never allow themselves to become 'his' orchestra he was already planning to raise another that would respond more exactly to his requirements and standards. He did this with the help of a remarkable man called Verdi Fawcett (one of a number of brothers whose first names were the surnames of prominent composers). Beecham met Fawcett as a violinist in the NSO and employed him as his orchestral 'fixer' with an untold number of other tasks. Fawcett was familiar with many good players who did not belong to the other orchestras, as well as with the best products of the music schools. He snapped them all up, together with a number of others who were already working for the LSO, Wood or Manns and who decided that the change would do them good. The new orchestra consisted of about eighty men, with an average age of only twenty-five years, all very keen and willing to be moulded to their conductor's requirements. To avoid any confusion they were henceforth known as the Beecham Symphony Orchestra (BSO for short).

But there was still no leader. Fawcett told Beecham of a highly promising young violinist in the salon orchestra at the Waldorf Hotel. Beecham went along and over dinner requested he play the last movement of Mendelssohn's Violin Concerto, which the soloist took, as Beecham recalls, 'at a speed which made me hold my breath'. After dinner, when he had suggested to the young man that he play it again rather more slowly, the two men met. Albert Sammons was at once recruited into the BSO, as sub-leader to Philip Cathie for the first few months and then as leader. He stayed for five years. According to Beecham, 'he united a technical faculty equal to any demand made upon it, a full warm tone, a faultless rhythmic sense, and a brain that remained cool in the face of any untoward happening.' Such was 'the best all-round concert-master' that Beecham had ever worked with, and Lionel Tertis' agreement to join Beecham as well meant the addition of a superlative principal in the viola section.

The Beecham Symphony Orchestra gave its opening concert at Queen's Hall on 22 February 1909. Three items already stamped it as a Beecham concert: Berlioz's Overture *Carnaval Romain* and his *Te Deum*, and Delius's *Sea Drift*. There was also Vaughan Williams's *In the Fen Country* and a part song, *The Storm* by Roland Rogers. The North Staffs District Choral Society also contributed to this concert; when asked why, Beecham replied that since there was no decent chorus to be had in London he was obliged to go north for one.

The general public did not show much interest in the new orchestra, but the press realised its potential. *The Times* reported à propos the small audience: 'The public were wrong, for both orchestra and chorus are excellent.' The same critic went on to say: 'The orchestra, which last night numbered ninety-six, is a body of players for which much may be expected in the future. Mr Thomas Beecham is a conductor of ability and determination . . . the enterprise is directed by much earnest intention and musical knowledge.'

The BSO gave one concert a month from February to June, the last of which included the first complete performance of Delius's *Mass of Life*. The second part of it had been heard the previous year in Munich, but now Delius was able to hear his full work for the first time. The *Morning Post* declared that 'the orchestra was excellent and Mr Thomas Beecham conducted with both knowledge and sympathy. The composer was called.' Again Beecham employed the celebrated chorus from North Staffs who sang 'in a manner that fully sustained their reputation'. The great difficulties inherent in this large-scale work seem to have been overcome at this initial performance, but the new sounds that were heard and the unusual direction taken in Nietzsche's pagan text provoked much argument.

Tradition has it that the Beecham Orchestra was by far the best of the three orchestras which he raised and owned. A few records of it exist, but even when the early recording process and techniques are taken into account and one accepts (or overlooks) the string portamenti which were fashionable until the late 1930s, the playing sounds ragged compared to that of the LPO at a later date. Not one member of the original BSO is still alive, and even if he were it is doubtful whether he would disagree with tradition. For whatever the playing was like, the orchestra had a remarkable *esprit de corps*, which Beecham took great pains to foster.

From his office in His Majesty's Theatre Beecham surveyed his prospects and was pleased. He had just made up the quarrel with his father, which meant that relatively limitless funds were at his disposal; and now he had gained for his orchestra its first pit job, accompanying Ethel Smyth's opera *The Wreckers* for five performances. He had already booked Covent Garden for a short opera season in February 1910, when his orchestra would again be in the pit. Everything was moving in the right direction.

Meanwhile he was promoting the idea of using an orchestra at vocal concerts as relief from the inevitable pianist; and he was also suggesting to his society friends that private parties would be considerably enhanced by the presence of a small orchestra. He was criticised in some circles for vulgarly publicising himself and his players: people did not tout their wares as he was doing.

But it was not generally realised that the running of an orchestra is fraught with great responsibilities to its owner. The spectre, ever present, of under-employment – even non-employment – of some eighty men is hard to live with unless the orchestra can be 'sold' for many months ahead. There is also the strain of finding their pay packets every Friday, though in Beecham's case the financial aspect was greatly improved thanks to the solid gold figure of Joseph standing not far behind them all. Moreover, should bookings fall behind, Beecham's best men would undoubtedly leave him and the ensemble which he was building up so carefully would be threatened.

In July 1910 Beecham and the Orchestra made their first records for the Gramophone Company, London – four single-sided vocals from *The Tales of Hoffmann* and an abridged version of the Overture to *Die Fledermaus*. Both these works were in that summer's opéra-comique season at His Majesty's Theatre. In addition they made two records (both single-sided) of selections from *Tiefland* by Eugene d'Albert, an opera which Beecham was preparing to give for the first time in Britain during his forthcoming Covent Garden season. Thus began Beecham's long and busy association with the gramophone.

It was during the two Covent Garden seasons that Beecham showed his predilection for Richard Strauss's orchestral music by commencing the last night of the opera season on New Year's Eve with a performance of *Ein Heldenleben*. The opera which followed was *Salome*. By playing the most taxing of all the Strauss tone poems from the pit Beecham had his tongue in his cheek. Over forty minutes of music, with nothing to look at, was not a tempting thought to the majority of the Covent Garden audience, who stayed in the bar until it was over. But the orchestra had the next day off after so exceptionally tiring an evening, and received a bonus as well. They deserved it, for Beecham was working them hard.

Although, in the opera house, he would sometimes capriciously hand over the baton to other conductors at the last moment or decide at short notice that he would conduct when it was not announced he would do so, Beecham seldom behaved like this in the concert hall. Yet on 1 April 1911, when he was due to conduct a concert of Ethel Smyth's music, he uncharacteristically 'forgot' – according to the composer. A little of Ethel in the opera house was one thing, but an all-Ethel concert was another. Beecham dodged the concert: after all, the date *was* All Fools' Day.

Beecham was adept at avoiding persons and things he did not wish to encounter, and he was equally good at disappearing. One moment he was to be seen leaving the platform at Queen's Hall after a concert; the next, he had vanished by the time his pursuer arrived in the conductor's room. Beecham put so much energy into his work on the concert platform that he was never in the mood to talk to anybody afterwards unless the person was of great importance to him, like the unexpected appearance of Delius. Later in life he became too exhausted even to do his vanishing-trick.

Even so, this running away was indicative of an aspect of Beecham's character. He always avoided a frontal attack of any kind unless he himself initiated it, since he hated to be found in the wrong and refused to concede that he ever was. He organised his life with as great precision as the railway timetables which he knew almost by heart as thought they were scores; he purposely led a very complicated existence in several spheres; and he often indulged in more than one love affair at a time, and rarely with serious intent. Thus he used an enormous amount of energy in his normal day-to-day life. His performances on the platform or in the pit, night after night, show what gigantic strength he possessed.

Beecham returned to conduct in St Helens in January 1911 at another Mayor's concert; the same Mayor – his father – was in office again. This time there was no doubt about it being Thomas Beecham's night; he maintained a firm grip on the programme, on the orchestra (his own) and on the audience. The coloratura soprano, Mignon Nevada, who had sung five principal roles during the previous Covent Garden season, sang four arias in a hotch-potch of a programme which Beecham had tailored to suit the audience. The only unexpected work was the minuet from Mozart's Divertimento in D (K.131). The programme announcement – 'A fanfare of trumpets will be sounded five minutes before the commencement of the second part' – had echoes of Bayreuth, and to round it off the second part began with the Overture to *Tannhäuser*.

1911 was a relatively quiet musical year for Beecham. His orchestra was comfortably ensconced in the Covent Garden pit for the Russian

Ballet and Opera so that Beecham, who had given them over to other conductors, had more time to devote to travel and the ladies. As far as they were concerned, it was a busy year. He had left Utica and begun his liaison with Lady Cunard; and in October the Foster divorce scandal became front-page news. In and out of this pattern, woven by the distaff, went Maggie Teyte, Desirée Ellinger, Clytie Hine, Elsa Stralia and others, all sopranos. It was a moment of relaxation in Beecham's life such as he was not to experience again until the early 1920s.

On 5 November 1911 Beecham gave his début concert with the Liverpool Philharmonic Orchestra, a body with which he was to be happily associated for over forty years.

Beecham's only other concerts at the end of 1911 and in February 1912 were a series of Sunday nights at the London Palladium with the Beecham Symphony Orchestra. There were no concerts scheduled for January but the next month's were sold out and so were extended into March. The programmes were all 'popular' stuff, but they attracted more subtle audiences than those attending the daily Palladium ballets.

On 7 March Beecham conducted the Hallé Orchestra at the Free Trade Hall by invitation. Never since the day when he forced himself upon the orchestra in St Helens in 1899 had the experience been repeated – until now when his reputation was made. The Committee agreed unanimously to bury old grievances against a fellow Lancastrian. Considering the *Manchester Guardian*'s usual attachment to the orchestra, it is interesting to find that the paper reported how Beecham 'would have been more successful still had the orchestra responded with greater alacrity and lightness to his requirements'. The critic granted Beecham 'a most intimate knowledge of the music with which he is dealing'. The programme, which ranged from Mozart, Grétry, Tchaikovsky, and Liszt to Richard Strauss and Delius, was undoubtedly a Beecham mixture. His reading of *Till Eulenspiegel* came in for especial praise. So now he was accepted and in demand from the Hallé, and for the next eight years he was frequently to be heard with the orchestra both at the Free Trade Hall and in surrounding cities, Bradford, Leeds and Sheffield in particular. Before long the Hallé had good reason to be glad of this association.

The nation's most devastating loss prior to the war was the sinking of the *Titanic* in the North Atlantic, and a memorial concert was arranged with the four London orchestras participating. This turned out to be the first of several similar mass-concerts for fund-raising purposes that were held later on during the war. At the Albert Hall they proved very profitable. The *Titanic* concert took place at Queen's Hall on 24 May and caused a sensation by its size and originality.

By way of complimenting his wind players Beecham arranged a concert in the Alhambra Theatre in October with 'The Beecham Wind Orchestra'. The arrangements were by Beecham himself, by his associate conductor, Emile Gilmer, and in the case of the *Meistersinger* Overture by H. F. Willemson ('who worked and scored for Brahms'). At the Alhambra the two most admired works were a selection from *Die Walküre* and Järnefelt's *Praeludium*. When the Wind Orchestra travelled to St Helens to give the Mayor's Concert there on 7 November, the programme was less ambitious – one reminiscent of the early Promenade Concerts – with Rosina Buckman singing, a saxophone solo, and variations on *In Cellar Cool* for solo trombone, composed and played by Mr H. Herring. It is interesting to read of the names in this orchestra: Hinchcliffe and Whittaker, oboes; A. Macdonagh, cor anglais; Waterhouse, heckelphone; Tschaikov, corno di bassetto. The orchestra continued to be brought together from time to time, although many of its players were from other symphony orchestras, notably the first flute, A. Gordon-Walker, who was later a director of the LSO.

After Beecham's busy opera season at Covent Garden at the beginning of 1913, he gave Delius's *A Mass of Life* at Queen's Hall on 10 March, and after more opera at His Majesty's there followed the Saint-Saëns 75 Years Concert in June, where the old man played his Third Piano Concerto. During 1914 the Russian Ballet again occupied the time of the Beecham Orchestra, as well as that of its conductor on occasions, but even so he was able to take it into another gigantic concert at Queen's Hall, this time for the fund for the survivors from the sinking of the *Empress of Ireland* in June. One afternoon in July he again prised his increasingly tired players out of Drury Lane (where they had to be that night) and gave an all-Delius concert at the Royal Academy of Music. It was very poorly attended, but Beecham enjoyed himself thoroughly.

Then war broke out. At once Beecham appreciated the orchestral situation. All Germans and Austrians and Hungarians were repatriated or interned and gaps appeared in the London orchestras. As soon as the most patriotic among the players joined up the position worsened further until, in a short time, there were men playing in prime orchestras who would never have been allowed within hailing distance in normal circumstances. Then there was the question of finance. No orchestra in Britain was secure or independent so far as its upkeep and running were concerned, and before the war was in its sixth month the Hallé and the LSO were in financial straits. Soon afterwards the Royal Philharmonic

Society also looked like shutting up. Beecham came to their aid, and put himself at the very hub of British wartime music; but accompanying this outward benevolence was the fear in many people's minds that his real interest lay in controlling these enterprises and making himself the first British musical mogul. He somehow failed to give an impression of genuine, altruistic patronage.

Whether he was dealing with representatives or with directors of the Hallé, the Royal Philharmonic Society or the LSO – or even of his own orchestra and opera company – Beecham maintained a tone and expression of lightheartedness, often of banter. This enabled him to conceal his hand completely and made him, throughout his life, an exceedingly difficult and infuriating person to deal with. His easy ability to dominate meetings often took the sting out of attacks upon him, while his quicksilver brain generally put him a step ahead of the sharpest antagonist. In argument he was devastating: his logic and power of expression were unbeatable, and when they were tempered with wit there was no gainsaying him.

These complex negotiations with the Hallé, the Royal Philharmonic and the LSO, as well as with the City of Birmingham, where Beecham intended to promote a City orchestra, were carried on simultaneously, with Beecham moving from one place to another, keeping well ahead of events and leaving committees in his wake racking their brains over the next move he might make. One factor, however, was common to all of them: money.

From the middle of 1909 onwards, Beecham had the full support of his father and did not want for cash. Thus he was able to plan and execute a gradual takeover of English orchestras with the best musicians and also of the best singers in the land, and then to manipulate the growing accumulation of talent to its best advantage. In this he was outward-looking and sincere. He knew himself to be the most dynamic conductor-impresario in the world, Diaghilev included, for Diaghilev was not an executive musician, and he knew what was best for the country's music. The coming of the war helped his plan enormously. It upset the former musical structure on which Britain had rested for so long, by incurring a loss of manpower and a loss of ready cash from the usual backers; but these were balanced by one golden realisation – that there existed a new and important desire on the part of the masses to hear music and to spend their own money on it.

Soon after the outbreak of war the Beecham Symphony Orchestra was disbanded. Beecham knew quite well that he could get it together again, but from July 1914 until October 1915 it disappeared from his concert and operatic engagements. Then it re-emerged as a pit orchestra with the newly formed Beecham Opera Company at the Shaftesbury Theatre, and was thereafter in London for most of the war. To call the accommodation at the Shaftesbury a 'pit' is an exaggeration, for there was none. The somewhat reduced orchestra occupied the area normally taken up by the first three rows of stalls together with a minute pit for a tiny orchestra. These forty or so men, the cream of the former full-strength Beecham Orchestra, carried on, sometimes augmented for a concert, until they became a larger orchestra in 1916, when the Opera Company became a Grand Opera Company indeed.

The Committee of the Hallé Concerts Society meanwhile had had to fill Richter's place as principal conductor for the 1911-12 season owing to his retirement. They ignored Beecham, whom they regarded as an amateur, and chose Michael Balling, a German, who merely copied Richter's ways. Now, as soon as war broke out, Balling was sent back home and the Hallé were in trouble on two accounts, the more pressing one being financial. Beecham at once offered the Hallé his services, especially as the players had reluctantly come to the conclusion that in order to survive as an orchestra they would have to accept half salaries for at least twenty weeks. Beecham told them: 'If you want a conductor, you have only to say the word and I'll conduct one concert or any more you please, with one reservation: that I take no fee.' So when the Hallé began their 1914-15 season Elgar conducted the first concert, Beecham the second, Landon Ronald the third, and Beecham two more after Christmas.

It was more than gratitude which prompted the Hallé to appoint Beecham to be their musical adviser in 1915; and on top of this appointment he became chief conductor of the London Symphony Orchestra and sole conductor of the Royal Philharmonic Society concerts. In addition he dallied with the Scottish Orchestra at Edinburgh in November.

The City of Birmingham was also the target for Beecham's interest and patronage, and their present orchestra may well be said to have arisen from his efforts at the end of the First World War. In 1916 he was invited to attend a council meeting, and his speech exhorting them to found an orchestra of their own stirred them considerably. He offered to audition and select rank-and-file players from within Birmingham and principals from outside it; to train and set up the municipal orchestra so as to give concerts for six or seven months of the year; and to help finance the venture for the first three years. Neville Chamberlain, then Lord Mayor of Birmingham, had no interest in the scheme and it was not until the following year, after a further diatribe from Beecham, that the orchestra got going. In 1918 it was disbanded when the town hall, Birmingham's only possible concert hall, was requisitioned by the food controller. However, Beecham had sown the seeds and had spent £2,000 out of his own pocket. In 1920 the orchestra re-emerged with Chamberlain's support and a grant from the rates amounting to £1,250 a year. But by this time Beecham was unable to finance anything.

Apart from the 'untouchable' Queen's Hall Orchestra there was one other in London which still seemed to be outside Beecham's control, and this was the New Symphony Orchestra, whose present importance and following could be said to have been, *ab initio*, his own doing. So he arranged with Landon Ronald, the NSO's conductor, a short summer series of promenade concerts at this orchestra's home in the Royal Albert Hall. Of the sixteen concerts in which he participated he conducted seven alone and shared nine with Ronald. The programmes were adventurous and wide-ranging. But the NSO knew Beecham of old; they were doing all right without his help, and they did not wish now to become part of his empire. He took the hint and left them alone.

Beecham's adventurous plan for an opera house in Manchester, proposed before the war, greeted with delight but never implemented, nevertheless made Beecham a popular figure there, especially after the enormous success of his Opera Company's visits in 1916 and 1917. He reorganised the Hallé Saturday Proms in 1915, under the aegis of the Hallé Society, and ensured the orchestra thirty-two weeks' continual employment against their former twenty weeks. In 1917 he had suggested a series of Promenade Concerts in addition to the Hallé Concerts Society and Opera, all at the New Queen's Theatre. It should be emphasised that Beecham used the Hallé Orchestra, not his own orchestra, for his two great seasons of opera in Manchester.

It is notable that Beecham never took a penny for all the concerts he organised, arranged, conducted. And if, due to special circumstances, he was unable to conduct an advertised concert himself he sent Goossens or another thoroughly experienced musician such as Hamilton Harty or Albert Coates in his place, and he paid them for their services out of his own pocket. This pattern continued for four years.

Then in 1919, because of the accumulation of financial difficulties which Beecham himself was now facing due to his father's untimely death in October 1916, he retired from his position with the Hallé when the orchestra was more depressed and mutinous than ever before. In July 1919 there were only two players on the strength. Beecham had supported and inspired the Hallé during the war years and had given them works to play that had far expanded their former Teutonic repertoire. He had also endeavoured to instil some musical pride in the city's businessmen, but in vain. His coming had been like a breath of fresh air to the Hallé, but his enforced withdrawal, at a moment of some concern about their future, was seen by too many Mancunians as 'ducking out'.

At an emergency meeting in 1919 Beecham and Albert Coates were asked for their advice about a conductor, and both strongly recommended Hamilton Harty, who had already proved himself with them as a deputy for Beecham. Indeed, Beecham had been considering Harty as one of his opera conductors, but felt that he was better placed in Manchester. Harty's career and the success of the Hallé were assured from then on, but Harty seemed to resent the fact that Beecham had been responsible for his appointment.

The Royal Philharmonic Society had been reluctantly obliged, at the beginning of the war, to put their orchestra on half-pay. Its players usually worked elsewhere, but as soon as they were summoned for an RPS concert they considered it an honour to attend. When Beecham heard of this he sent a cheque to the Society, enabling them to pay the men in full as before. He conducted seven concerts for them in 1915, five in 1916 and four in 1917, all without a fee. Then he and his manager Donald Baylis took over the running of the RPS for the 1916–17 season and thus removed any effective control from the Society's directors.

During the 1915–16 season the London Symphony Orchestra seemed to be in impossible financial difficulties. Beecham came to their help and as well as giving them actual cash and conducting without a fee he pacified their bank manager with further payments of cash whenever their overdraft assumed unacceptable proportions.

Obviously all these enterprises needed a great deal of money to keep afloat in wartime, and as long as the money was available all was well. Beecham never stinted any organisation in which he was interested. There were now only two orchestras in London outside his control, the NSO and Wood's Queen's Hall Orchestra. Had Beecham not been there to inject life into the LSO and the RPS, the other two would have reigned supreme. As it was, the competition helped to keep up their standards.

Beecham's conducting programme in the war years consisted of opera, Hallé, RPS and an occasional LSO and Liverpool Philharmonic concert. He was continuously on the move from London to Manchester, fulfilling his promises at the Free Trade Hall.

By 1919, following the death of his father, he was badly in need of cash himself and was already facing one bankruptcy petition. This he fought off, but the signs were ominous and he had to begin to shed his commitments. Some he relinquished gradually; others, like the Hallé, he let go quickly, receiving abuse for his pains. His total financial collapse in the summer of 1920 led to condemnation in voices of mistrust and bitterness from those to whom he had especially shown outstanding generosity and support during wartime.

Perhaps the post-war euphoria had something to do with all this. A reckless, inane public mood now prevailed and there was far less interest in what Beecham was trying to do for British opera and British music than there had been up to 1918. So he removed himself from his musical throne and retired to a small office in the Strand, where he began to put straight his father's estate.

According to *A Mingled Chime*, Beecham was disenchanted with the musical world in 1920 and seriously considered whether he would ever return. But the taste of such success as had been his for nearly five years was not to be lost so recklessly. In March 1923 he made his northern comeback with the Hallé Orchestra at the Free Trade Hall in Manchester. He gave a popular concert consisting of Weber's Overture to *Oberon*, Delius's *Walk to the Paradise Garden*, the *Royal Hunt and Storm* by Berlioz and Mozart's 34th Symphony. After the interval he conducted Hamilton Harty in his first piano concerto and then gave three more short French pieces. One critic emphasised the delightful presence of Beecham's *style* 'that might range throughout everything and do justice to almost everything, yet retain its own features through all and in all.'

On 8 April Beecham reappeared in London where he conducted the joint forces of the London Symphony Orchestra and the Royal Albert Hall Orchestra (once the New Symphony Orchestra). The massed band of 170 players accompanied Dame Clara Butt, with whom Beecham had shared the doubtful honour of *Orfeo* at Covent Garden on the occasion of his last public performance there before his temporary retirement from the musical scene. By engaging the most popular singer of the day Beecham had played safe. 'On a clear day she may quite easily be heard in France', was his description of the formidable contralto. But he need not have worried. The Albert Hall was packed, and Dame Clara, who imagined that the audience had all come to hear her, was disappointed when yet another of her encores was cut off by a voice crying: 'We want to hear the orchestra!' and then another: 'We came to hear Beecham!' The *Times* critic stated that Dame Clara sang poorly but that 'it was a pleasure to hear Sir Thomas Beecham again'.

The programme consisted of the *Oberon* Overture and the same

Berlioz and Delius items as he had given in Manchester on 15 March, together with Dame Clara's contribution in the first half of the programme. The second half comprised *The Ride of the Valkyries* and Richard Strauss's *Ein Heldenleben*. The whole programme proved without doubt that Beecham had lost none of his magic, poise or authority, and the descriptions of his contrasting treatment of the Weber and the Berlioz would have been welcome to any conductor who had remained on the rostrum for the two and half years of Beecham's absence.

But Beecham was not to be heard again in London for another nine months, and this imposing April concert can be seen (together with the one in Manchester) as testing his own responses to a full-scale return to conducting. Was he, he asked himself, to continue with an orchestral life, or was he to devote himself solely to opera? Then, during 1924, he gave a single performance of *The Mastersingers* for the British National Opera Company – another self-searching. But it was as if he had never been away.

His operatic return was prefaced by an LSO tour in January which began at the Albert Hall and continued through the Midlands and to Scotland with one-night stands: twelve concerts in all, the last in Bristol. The public everywhere was enthusiastic; the orchestra were delighted and played well. The programmes were characteristic.

In the following year, 1926, he again took the LSO for more than a fortnight-long tour of the same cities, and in March he gave the Pension Fund concert for the Hallé.

The signs were now to be read by anybody who knew anything of Beecham's ways. If he associated himself with a single orchestra for any length of time it could mean only one thing. Here he was, conducting the LSO up and down the country. If the runes were being cast, the augurers were in for a shock. In November 1926 he called a press conference, promising to make 'a sensational announcement'. Another Beecham orchestra? That must be it. The press turned out in full strength, pencils well licked and poised. What they heard was this: 'England is finished, not only musically, but in every other way. The only thing for anybody to do is to give up and go to America. I am going as a guest and will conduct the Philadelphia Orchestra. After a few months' experience as a guest I will stay permanently.'

He then became more specific and turned his rage on the Labour Party, which was then in power: 'They preach a gospel of thieving and stealing and are quite our worst enemies – worse by far than the Germans ever were.' The BBC was not let off either, especially for their broadcasts of opera (which, to be fair, had only limited equipment for their transmission in 1926): 'It sounds like most horrible chattering, gibbering, chortling, shrieking devils and goblins and they call it Beethoven or Wagner. The sound has as much relation to their music as the singing of Galli-Curci to a roaring bull. It's insanity.'

Beecham's 'farewell' concert on 15 December was a stupendous performance of the *Messiah* at Queen's Hall with 110 players of the LSO. The soprano was a beautiful young singer called Dora Labbette. The public was astounded, for the musty old Handel work sounded fresh and gloriously up-to-date.

However, Beecham's threats and verbal barrages were as a smoke-screen that vanished when the wind blew. He never conducted the Philadelphia Orchestra that year and returned to Europe quietly. He gave one concert with the Czech Philharmonic in Prague on 23 January 1927 that included *The Walk to the Paradise Garden* and then one performance of *Tristan und Isolde* with the Hungarian Royal Opera in Budapest at the end of February. He was back on the rostrum at Queen's Hall on 14 March as though he had never been away. All that was wrong was the lack of that very necessary toy, of which he had been deprived for far too long: his own orchestra. If he thought he could simply walk into the New World and take up any orchestra there he had been greatly mistaken.

The Hallé would no longer have anything to do with Beecham and continued in their way of thinking until 1933. But the LSO wanted him to conduct them. Many there saw him as their permanent conductor, though others argued extreme caution.

Beecham had not conducted an RPS concert from 1918 until 22 March 1928, when he was reunited with them in the happiest way possible. The performance was a re-orchestrated and revivified *Solomon* by Handel and during the interval Beecham received the Society's Gold Medal, the highest award in British music. Coming as it did at this time of uncertainty in his career, the award signified continued hope and expectation on the part of Beecham as well as gratitude for what he had done in the past. King George V and Queen Mary were present at the performance and Dora Labbette was the principal soprano.

Beecham can be seen as Handel's supreme champion in the twentieth century. He not only rescued many of the master's works from neglect, even from oblivion, but he cleaned them up and removed the false patina of Victorianism which had obscured their real beauty. His own arrangement of *Solomon* might have sounded new but he had gone back to the eighteenth-century score and the text as it was before prudishness made nonsense of it. The audience in Queen's Hall that night heard Solomon's Queen declare:

> Bless'd the day when I was led
> To ascend the nuptial bed.
> But completely bless'd the day
> On my bosom as he lay.

Those who might have been trying to follow the bowdlerised Novello score could only see:

> Bless'd the day when first my eyes
> Saw the wisest of the wise.
> Bless'd the day when I was brought
> To behold this favoured spot.

It was in March 1928 that Beecham first began protracted negotiations with the BBC, whose new headquarters in Langham Place were being built now that it had ceased to be a Company and had achieved Corporation status. John Reith was the Director-General and Percy Pitt the musical adviser. Landon Ronald introduced Beecham to Reith and discussions were at once opened about an orchestra to be run partly by the Corporation. It was clear from the first meeting that Beecham had 'a very business-like grip of values in the concert world and it was interesting to find that his figures were not on the whole very much different from ours.' This statement came from Roger Eckersley, who conducted many of the meetings with Beecham and was really in charge of the orchestral negotiations. The BBC acted as part-guarantors in case of a deficit, with the ultimate intention of taking the orchestra over if possible.

The scheme boiled down to the formation of a new orchestra. Beecham suggested the title 'Royal Philharmonic Orchestra', but the BBC disliked the omission of their three initial letters. It was agreed that the Corporation should take care of all administrative arrangements, and since these would be partly bound by the Musicians' Union the BBC's policy from the outset was 'to force a basis whereby the orchestra are absolutely whole-time, and under their contract have to do exactly what they are told without demanding extra money.' Eckersley voiced the pious hope that 'appointment to this orchestra should be ... made so attractive that the players themselves should not allow the Musicians' Union to make difficulties over the contracts.'

So far as Beecham was concerned, he was going to conduct about a quarter of the total concerts and would be at the head of a group of guarantors who would contribute £20,000 (compared to the BBC's £30,000 of public money) against annual loss, which was expected to be up to £70,000. Any actual loss over the joint pool of £50,000 was to be shared equally by the two parties.

Although these negotiations were secret Beecham seems to have leaked the broad outlines to the press, because an article appeared in the *Daily Express* headed 'England's Best Orchestra'.

Beecham now recommended Geoffrey Toye, general manager of the Sadler's Wells Opera (and later Beecham's own partner at Covent Garden), as manager of the new orchestra, since his own experience would enable him to overcome the 'melancholy waste of time and effort' that an ordinary administrator would be unable to do. However, difficulties at once arose over Toye's status and remuneration, since he was not a BBC employee.

Everything so far had pointed to public concerts being held at Queen's Hall, and bookings were made there for a preliminary, pilot series of concerts.

The LSO were disappointed when they discovered about Beecham and the BBC, for most of them had expected him to propose that they should form his new orchestra. Every musical organisation was apprehensive as to the BBC's intentions. Hamilton Harty announced that he wished to co-operate with the LSO, and Sir Landon Ronald argued a complete amalgamation between the LSO, the Royal Albert Hall Orchestra and the Royal Philharmonic Society. The ranks were closing, not only because of financial stresses but because of unknown developments in Portland Place.

The general financial slump of 1929 was especially bad for orchestras. Concert engagements dwindled and the question on musicians' lips everywhere was: 'How long shall we still be together?' The LSO had a particularly bad time. Twice they voted to abandon their constitution and adopt a new one in order to get round difficult corners. There was great dissension among the players, and public opinion as to their solidarity began to change.

But 1929 was not altogether without its musical high-spots, and the most scintillating of these was the Delius Festival which Beecham organised for his friend in the wake of the New Year's Honours List, in which Delius had been made a Companion of Honour.

As he tells us in his biography of Delius, Beecham sought the help of Philip Heseltine (the composer Peter Warlock) in the organisation of the Festival at the end of the year and in the writing of programme notes. Heseltine had at first been a Delius enthusiast, but had subsequently lapsed. Beecham employed him most usefully at a time when he was deeply depressed and in need of the work. Plans were completed between them by early summer for six concerts.

Delius lived in France; he was not generally considered an Englishman and hardly anybody knew what he looked like. Now that he was officially recognised, Beecham felt that he must be brought to London and, as it were, put on show while all the available music that he had ever written was played. But Delius was an invalid and Beecham debated whether he should invite him, in view of his extremely fragile condition. It would mean a long journey by car from Grez-sur-Loing, near Fontainebleau, where he lived, to the Channel port; a steamer to England; then another car journey to London. For a man who sometimes screamed in agony at the touch of a sheet upon his body, this was a lot to ask. But Delius was delighted at the idea and instantly accepted.

The six concerts were given over a period of three weeks between 12 October and 1 November, four at Queen's Hall and two, of songs, piano pieces and unaccompanied choruses, at the Aeolian Hall in Bond Street. It is interesting to note that the LSO did not participate, although the BBC did. Beecham used the Wireless Orchestra with augmentation for the larger works, which were naturally broadcast. The Orchestra of the RPS and that of the Columbia Graphophone Company each played for one of the two other orchestral concerts. By using the Columbia Orchestra, Beecham ensured that some, at least, of the works played would be recorded later. By using the RPS Orchestra Beecham kept his hand on the organisation which meant so much to him.

Such a concentration on the music of one composer, still alive and present, and whose music was still largely unfamiliar to the general public, was a singular achievement on Beecham's part. But however often he said things he didn't really mean, one ideal in his life remained constant: the music of Frederick Delius. Every remark and statement he made in this context was always to be taken absolutely seriously, and at the time of the Festival he said: 'I have no hesitation in declaring the life and work of Delius to be the greatest and most far-reaching incident in music during the last fifty years.'

Beecham conducted five of the six concerts, which ended with *A Mass of Life*. By then all Delius's major concert works had been played, beginning with the incomparable *Brigg Fair*: thirty songs with piano, sung on various occasions by Olga Haley, John Goss, John Armstrong and Dora Labbette, with Evlyn Howard Jones as accompanist; five unaccompanied choruses; the first violin sonata, the cello sonata and the string quartet. Only the operas suffered, being represented by concert performances of the finale from *A Village Romeo and Juliet* and the short *Gerda* of *Fennimore and Gerda*.

After the last concert Delius, who was carried over the road to the Langham Hotel where he had been staying throughout the Festival, passed between lines of enthusiastic, cheering people, delighted to pay their loud, personal tributes to the strange, reserved and ghost-like man who had entranced them with his music that was like no other composer's. Delius was so impressed by the response of the London audiences that it was very likely this which made him declare, on his way back to France, that he would like his chair placed on the deck so that his sightless eyes might face England, the country where he wished to be buried.

With the Festival over and negotiations with the BBC still pending Beecham didn't waste a moment. He took the LSO out for an unusual kind of concert at the Sheldonian Theatre in Oxford. Musicians dislike this place because of its cold stone floor and its capricious acoustic. Beecham had heard that the Oxford Subscription Concerts were on the point of being abandoned for lack of financial support, and although he was on the verge of bankruptcy himself he presented the LSO at his own expense in a programme of Elgar, Debussy, Delius and Mozart. At the time he was referred to as 'Wadham's most distinguished musician' and in the following summer he was awarded his Hon.D.Mus.

Beecham had found the Delius Festival a useful way of avoiding meetings at the BBC. His scheme for a concert hall in Chesham Place, which would enable the BBC to by-pass Queen's Hall, where they feared stranglehold rents from the lessees, Boosey and Hawkes, appealed to them. The new hall, Beecham said, would be of the most up-to-date kind; it would hold an audience of 3,800 and would cost only £8,000 to £10,000 a year to rent.

The BBC set up two committees. One, called the Business Committee, excluded Beecham but included Sir Landon Ronald as his nominee, as well as a representative from among the Beecham guarantors. This was a cunning move because Ronald was already on the BBC's Musical Advisory Committee. The second, the Artistic Committee for the new orchestra, was chaired by Beecham; Henry Wood had agreed to support him, and the other members were BBC staff apart from 'one other person suitable to both sides, ? from RPS'.

Reith's comment on this set-up was characteristic: 'It appears that the BBC can be well satisfied with its control on both committees.'

By January 1930 the BBC had auditioned over one thousand applicants for jobs in the new orchestra and had, with Beecham's co-operation, organised some pilot concerts, for any loss on which he was to be partly responsible. No sooner had the first few players been tentatively offered positions than the usual question was asked: 'May I take on outside work?'

No amount of questioning evoked from Beecham any further information about the suggested hall, except that it was not in Chesham Place after all but in Russell Square. To expedite matters after many legal delays, a draft contract was sent to Beecham for the agreement of his guarantors, who completely disagreed with the BBC's line and refused to approve, let alone sign it. They appended six reasons, of which the fifth is probably the most revealing: 'The Guarantors are of the opinion that the scheme has been modified and moulded by the Broadcasting Corporation less with an eye to the visible than to the invisible audiences.'

So now there appeared to be an impasse. Booking dates for the best months at Queen's Hall had gone by; Beecham seemed to have no concert hall in the offing; the guarantors would not sign the contract. At this point an internal memorandum reads: 'The advantages of single control are almost too obvious to put on paper.' The BBC had committed themselves to an orchestra by their auditions and the press comments, which had so far appeared to be favourable. The Musicians' Union was interested and agreeable, and willing to concede most of the BBC's requests after the normal haggling.

The BBC's line seemed to be straightforward: keep out Beecham, and especially his agent Lionel Powell; run the orchestra from inside; use it for more broadcasts than Beecham would consider desirable; and present the general run of public concerts in the big hall at the new Broadcasting House, rather than at Queen's Hall.

Beecham was therefore given an ultimatum. If by 25 January the BBC had not received a reply to several letters they would consider their discussions with him at an end. Shortly before this date, Eckersley wrote to Reith: 'I do not think it at all likely that he [Beecham] will interest himself any further in the scheme, in which case we shall be in a position to go ahead on our own lines.' On 27 January Eckersley wrote again to Reith: 'Nothing heard from Sir Thomas Beecham. We are therefore free to pursue our own course.' And, as everybody knows, they did.

While the thinking of the BBC officials is clear to anybody who reads their files, Beecham's views can only be guessed. He could not help seeing that the two committees were heavily loaded against him; it was clear that the BBC did not want him as an individual with all his idiosyncrasies but only for his experience, flair and money. Above all it was now painfully obvious that the BBC were far more concerned about the broadcasting aspect of the concerts than about live, paying audiences. That was, after all, their job. The BBC thus had only one course to take; while Beecham had his own line to follow. However, before he could put his next scheme into effect he had a few other matters to attend to.

He had let the BBC know all along that he was involved in many other enterprises, and that their business was not his prime concern. Shortly after Christmas 1929, a group of Oxford undergraduates took the Scala Theatre in Charlotte Street, London, for a festival of opera. Various illuminating articles in the press described it as being 'a quite exceptional operatic treat'. Its producer was Robert Stuart whose knowledge of the art seems to have been lacking. The festival opened with Monteverdi's *Orfeo*, followed in rapid succession by Locke's *Cupid and Death*, Purcell's *Dido and Aeneas*, Handel's *Julius Caesar*, and Mozart's *La finta Giardiniera*. *Alcestis*, by Gluck, failed to materialise. The singers, orchestra and stage-hands rebelled because they had not been paid. In the middle of a great deal of confusion, while the auditorium of the Scala Theatre 'yawned nightly before terrifying emptiness', a *deus ex machina* appeared in the welcome guise of Sir Thomas Beecham. He rehearsed *Der Freischütz* for four days and nights and then played it for five consecutive performances to full houses. He saved the reputation of the 'Festival', which lost only £6,000. As usual under such conditions, he conducted without a fee and demonstrated that genius arrives only after a great deal of hard work.

In spite of the fact that Beecham's association with the BBC as conductor of their new orchestra was over, he still had to fulfil his prior arrangements with them by giving three concerts of an experimental nature. These made the expected loss and the BBC were obliged to dun him for his share. He then had three different series of engagements in Germany, and in the autumn he sought a kind of sanctuary with the Liverpool Philharmonic.

1931 was the year in which he devoted his concerts exclusively to the London Symphony Orchestra, making them feel that he had definite plans for them. But in May and June he was conducting a Russian Opera and Ballet Company at the Lyceum Theatre as its artistic director. He also provided the orchestra, called 'The Russian Opera Orchestra' for convenience sake – all the players were from the London area. From among the sixty-nine whom Beecham employed, twenty-three were later to appear with him under another name altogether. Some of them were so good that he seems to have been 'casting' his new orchestra by trying out a number of key players at the Lyceum to see how they all got on together. An ordinary *ad hoc* orchestra would not normally have contained a third of the best players in London, despite the attraction of a six weeks' engagement during the summer. Some of the names are still famous – Bernard Reillie, George Stratton and Bernard Andrews (violin); John Moore (cello); Gerald Jackson and John Francis (flute); Léon Goossens (oboe); T. Wood and F. Hamilton (horn); James Bradshaw (percussion) and Marie Goossens (harp).

Beecham now had a Board for his yet unborn orchestra, and it consisted of Samuel Courtauld, Robert Mayer, Baron Frédéric d'Erlanger and Lord Esher. Also very much in evidence was a young conductor, Malcolm Sargent; not so much Lady Cunard. Courtauld and his wife had previously offered Sargent the task of raising a new orchestra which they would support, but he declined the opportunity. He was young and it seemed too much for him to take on. But he approached Beecham with a 'package deal' of the Courtauld-Sargent series of concerts, Robert Mayer's Children's Concerts and the Royal Choral Society Concerts. To this Beecham was able to add two months in the pit every summer at Covent Garden and some substantial recordings with Columbia. They thus reduced the financial risk to below fifty per cent.

Lionel Powell, who had been with Beecham during the BBC affair, was their joint agent and one of the most important concert promoters and artists' managers in London from the beginning of the century until his sudden death in 1930. According to his own publicity material and his stationery (which left little room for correspondence) his 'name has been intimately associated with the highest achievements in musical enterprise and he has presented every Artist of note'. He stated publicly that he alone was responsible for 'the re-organisation of the London Symphony Orchestra under Sir Thomas Beecham', which was something of an exaggeration and caused a good deal of anger within the orchestra.

Since Beecham was openly flirting with the LSO, it was understood that if they were to be his chosen new band, to be automatically awarded all the work he now had in his gift, the LSO must replace a number of players who were not up to his standard of performance or, as he put it, up to the high standards of the rest of the orchestra. While the LSO directors knew this well, it remained a touchy subject. Since every member of the LSO was a shareholder it would need a great deal of tact to achieve this object without grave trouble. The directors agreed to hand Beecham their list of players who they felt should not be offered the new contract, and Beecham gave them his list. These lists did not agree in every respect, and one of Beecham's names referred to a director of the orchestra.

In the middle of these difficulties Lionel Powell died, leaving his company more or less insolvent and with a great number of contracted tours and visits unsupported by funds. The most important of these was a rare visit to London by the Berlin Philharmonic Orchestra under

Furtwängler. Mayer and Beecham underwrote them, made £17, and saved British reputation. As Powell had additionally served as the LSO's agent and seemed to be a useful link with the Beecham board, his loss to the orchestra was a serious one.

When a meeting was called at Beecham's office the LSO's directors failed to turn up, knowing that Beecham was in Munich. This was especially tactless of them (and typical of Beecham to have been away) considering that the orchestra had just received a letter signed by Harold Holt breaking off negotiations with the orchestra as a whole and expressing a wish to speak to its board members individually.

Sargent telephoned Beecham and told him that the meeting had not taken place. 'Very well,' came the voice from Munich, 'we'll form an orchestra of our own.' On Beecham's return two of the LSO's directors accosted him about his sudden change of heart. He replied that he liked the LSO very much, as he had always said, but its constitution was an impediment to further progress, and in any case he had been overruled by his Board who now lacked confidence in the London Symphony Orchestra.

So the LSO was 'out'. Their anger when Beecham's board tried to buy their name from them (implying their dissolution) and the stubborn energy which they put into rebuilding their reputation were exactly what was required in the circumstances.

When Beecham left the New Symphony Orchestra in 1909 and told them that he was going to found a new orchestra, they did not believe that he could. Now the same thing happened. When the LSO went to Worcester to fulfil dates at the Three Choirs Festival, their notice-board was covered by telegrams from Beecham inviting some thirty players to join him. Eighteen did, including one of the LSO's directors. That notice-board must have presented a most uncomfortable sight to the loyal members of the LSO.

Beecham's new leader, Paul Beard, came from the Birmingham Orchestra. He served Beecham admirably for four years. George Stratton led the second violins and Anthony Pini the cellos. Gerald Jackson and Léon Goossens were first flute and first oboe respectively, while the talented and eccentric James Bradshaw was the timpanist. The only ladies in the orchestra were the harpists, led by Marie Goossens.

The London Philharmonic Orchestra, as the new band was called, was backed principally by Samuel Courtauld and Robert Mayer. Without them the orchestra could not have been raised and trained. Baron d'Erlanger was a banker more interested in music than in figures, and Lord Esher, who remained a director for only a short time, was an expert committee man. But it was Courtauld and Mayer who promoted the Beecham image.

Beecham trained his orchestra patiently, conducting seven rehearsals by sections and then six as a body. In between section and orchestral rehearsals he briefed his section principals carefully from the piano, impressing upon all of them the vital clues to interpretation. When the full orchestra assembled for the first of their six rehearsals, every player found his part newly marked with subtle dynamic indications. Beecham had given his briefing to the principals and they had transferred his indications to each of their own players' music. This careful, detailed instruction was a Beecham hallmark which henceforward was to become general practice.

Beecham himself had changed his ways from his BSO days. He was never late for rehearsals now. If one was called for 10 a.m. he was present as promptly as if his name was Henry Wood, ready to charge into the first work in front of him. A thrill of excitement and anticipation quickly grasped the orchestra. They realised how well they sounded and responded willingly to Beecham's eyes, those glowing black coals which made them play like demons and sound like angels. After the last rehearsal, held on a Bloomsbury Square dance floor inside an insurance building, they were all at concert pitch, ready for their début.

This took place at Queen's Hall on Friday, 7 October 1932, and was presented by the Royal Philharmonic Society as one of their concerts. At the opening Beecham Symphony Orchestra concert twenty-two years earlier there had been empty seats, but not tonight. As Paul Beard was about to make his entrance, justifiably nervous, Beecham said to him: 'Come along, Mr Beard. Let's show 'em what we can do!'

The first work they played, Berlioz's *Carnaval Romain* Overture, had the audience in a fever of excitement, and at the last crashing chord they were on their feet roaring applause, some reputedly even standing on their seats. This was the finest orchestra ever heard in London; the new BBC Symphony Orchestra couldn't touch them. The rest of the first concert, consisting of pieces by Mozart, Delius and Richard Strauss, was played with equal brilliance and in an atmosphere of heady success. On the next day the newspapers ran out of superlatives.

Beecham was now himself again, with an orchestra that he could take anywhere in the world and dazzle audiences. The Royal Philharmonic Society employed the LPO exclusively for its concerts with Beecham conducting about half of them. The LPO played at Covent Garden every summer up to 1939, and they made more than a hundred records for

HMV and over two hundred for Columbia. Their concert-giving achievements were astonishing.

But soon all was not well behind the scenes. Beecham was used to success and thrived on it. If he felt especially satisfied after a concert or recording session he would say to the musicians: 'Don't go, the night's still young. Let's play some more.' So they went on giving encores or opened up fresh scores and started recording them. In either event it put the players into overtime which had not been budgeted for.

The LPO's board met informally, as a rule. They sometimes invited Beecham along, since he was the orchestra's artistic adviser though not himself a director. Sometimes he would turn up uninvited in an attempt to discover what was going on behind his back. Very soon he was summoned to attend and was questioned as to why he was playing so many unscheduled pieces, and why he was forcing up the costs with so much overtime.

To all these questions he boyishly expressed frank amazement. Was this not the finest orchestra in London? – in England? – in the world? Why was he being asked such questions? He professed a complete lack of understanding of the board and their accountant-like minds.

This state of affairs continued in spite of warnings for four years until, finding that he couldn't change Beecham, Robert Mayer 'pulled out' and was soon afterwards followed by an equally disillusioned Samuel Courtauld. With Mayer went the Children's Concerts.

Some time afterwards Beecham ran into Lady Mayer. 'What's the matter with Robert?' he asked her. 'Why no more Children's Concerts for us?' She replied tactfully that as far as she knew her husband was well, and that they gave their concerts to lesser conductors. 'Robert's an awful ass,' Beecham replied; 'I'll do the next one for you.' Not to be dissuaded, Mayer booked him with the LPO to give a Children's Concert at Queen's Hall.

Sir Robert recollects his astonishment at the performance. Beecham held forth from the rostrum, going into long descriptions of Waltz, Handel's cook, and addressing his audience as if they were adults. The children thought he was marvellous, and the fact that his descriptions, allusions, verbiage and jokes were probably miles above the heads of most of them mattered little, for he brought the music right across and kept them gloriously entertained.

Shortly afterwards Mayer met Beecham and asked him: 'Where's the bill?'

'What bill?' Beecham replied.

'The bill for the Children's Concert,' said Mayer.

'There's no bill, my dear fellow,' Beecham replied. 'It was a pleasure to do it for you.'

This was at a time when Robert Mayer probably knew Beecham as well as anybody did, but even so Beecham never ceased to amaze him. He recalls that Beecham seldom left any written record of his activities since 'he was far more interested in the present and the future than in the past. Indeed his most used filing cabinet was the waste-paper basket.' Yet Sir Robert considers today that Beecham had given himself too much to do. He simply hadn't the time to be patient. Consequently he 'thrived on improvisation and at the same time cast a spell on people. He was a genius – in a class by itself: you either accepted him, or you didn't. He had a brilliance of oratory and personality, and to take the man as a whole he was the most colourful figure in the British scene and must go down in history as the greatest contributor to the music of his time.'

'In his early days, especially to Germanic people, Beecham was regarded as an amateur because he was so debonair and carefree,' Sir Robert says, although 'he was anxious to become popular in Berlin' because he admired precision and good organisation. The Prussians were aghast when they saw him conducting without a score. 'And when he was up to his tricks, and nobody was sure whether he was serious or not, he was merely trying it on to see how they reacted to him. But all through his life the world was divided between Beecham and the philistines.'

Beecham took the LPO on two provincial tours in 1933, to Paris in 1935 and then to Nazi Germany for a week in 1936. Their attendance at Covent Garden during each opera season, at the Festivals and in the recording studio meant that they were being kept occupied in the best possible way. As well as being an excellent orchestra they were a happy one and inordinately proud of Sir Thomas.

Beecham believed in celebrations and conducted at two of the principal Triennial Music Festivals: Leeds and Norwich. But he did not care much for the Three Choirs and ceased to appear there very early on. It all smacked too much of Elgar for him. At the Sheffield Triennial Festival in 1936 Henry Wood was to conduct the LPO. This brought out again what has been well described as his 'anti-Beecham psychosis'. In this instance there was trouble over the leader. Wood expected Paul Beard to be there, but Beard had left Beecham to join the BBC Symphony Orchestra, and there was a new and (to Wood) unknown leader with the LPO called David McCallum. Ultimately Beecham suggested as replacement his sub-leader Bernard Andrews, whom Wood did know, and the matter was ultimately concluded, though with great reluctance on Wood's part. The publicity resulting from the affair was much to Beecham's amusement and Wood's annoyance.

Beecham considered Wood ridiculous when he stood on the dignity of his ten years' seniority, but he himself adopted exactly the same attitude towards such conductors as Barbirolli, who had been a back-desk cellist at the Shaftesbury Theatre in 1915 with the Beecham Opera Company. Beecham also tended to nurse resentment when any of his protégés in an orchestra collected too much acclaim for solos, since he always liked to be the one in the limelight; but because he was such a tease he took every opportunity to poke fun at Wood, who lacked all appreciation of this kind of humour. When Beecham spoke from the platform at the Norwich Festival in 1936 he caused great amusement when he said: 'During my stay in Norwich I found, to my surprise, that I was sometimes addressed as "Sir Henry". It is a fine tribute to my pungent and picturesque colleague in the musical world that his ghost walks so vigorously here.'

In December 1936 Beecham travelled to Manchester for three concerts and then to Liverpool where he gave a conventional programme which included Tchaikovsky's *Romeo and Juliet* and Rimsky-Korsakov's *Schéhérazade*. Beecham found a new first trumpet there, who at the rehearsal seemed to be having a very 'off' day, 'playing under the cushion' for a lot of the time. Beecham indicated to the man (whose name was Harry Mortimer) that he wanted him to play up, but there was no response. He then spoke to the leader, Alfred Barker, who called up to Mortimer and asked him why he didn't answer Sir Thomas. Mortimer shouted back: 'Tell him if he doesn't shut up, I'll not play tonight!' Mortimer was having difficulties because by training he was a virtuoso brass-band musician, not an orchestral player. The Tchaikovsky work requires a trumpet in E and Mortimer couldn't transpose. He had just come to the Liverpool Philharmonic as principal trumpet while also continuing as third trumpet with the Hallé that season. (In the next season he covered principal trumpet for both orchestras.)

In the interval of the concert Mortimer stayed on the platform because he wanted to go over his tricky part in *Schéhérazade*. Beecham, who seldom left his dressing-room, went back on to the platform and spoke to him: 'Now, what is your name? Mr Mortimer? Ah, yes. You play very well, I like your tone. Now what is worrying you?'

Mortimer explained. 'Very well,' said Beecham, and he began to sing the trumpet parts in *Schéhérazade* which Mortimer was shy about. He sounded dreadful, but Mortimer knew exactly what Beecham meant and what he wanted. 'Now keep your eye on me, Mr Mortimer,' he said, 'and I'll keep my eye on you. It will be all right.' And it was.

Thereafter, Mortimer worshipped Beecham. When the BBC Northern Orchestra came to be formed Beecham was on the selection committee. He told the others: 'I want the man who plays first trumpet at Liverpool. He's very awkward, but he's very good.'

Later, on account of Harry Mortimer's great experience with brass bands, Beecham employed him to get the best players for such works as Berlioz's *Grande Messe*. In a huge studio like the BBC's Maida Vale No. 1, full of players and chorus, Beecham would bring Mortimer out in front of them all. 'Now tell me, please, Mr Mortimer, where is Band A? Oh yes, I see. And Band B? Good. Just so long as I know. You wouldn't want me to give an entry to the wrong one, would you?' But Beecham knew perfectly well.

Harry Mortimer played first trumpet in Rimsky-Korsakov's *Coq d'Or* Suite several times under Beecham. The Suite starts with a cruelly exposed and high fanfare for two trumpets in unison. In fact the unison is often impossible to achieve, for one or other of the instruments is almost certain to split a note. Beecham used to sit back and wait for this to happen. Then he would remark: 'You know I've always found this goes better together with one trumpet, so I'll have it with one only, please.' Then when it went perfectly at the concert Beecham gave a little wink: an acknowledgement from one great artist who recognised another in front of the whole orchestra.

When Lionel Tertis, the 'father' of all viola players, at last announced his retirement, due to begin in 1937, Beecham organised a monumental dinner to commemorate the event. It took place on 13 June 1936 and was a great occasion for Tertis and some two hundred fellow-musicians. But Tertis couldn't stand the subsequent inactivity and within three weeks he was back again, playing as nobly and as strongly as before.

It was in March 1938, however, that he incurred Beecham's wrath by speaking out at the Seventy-fifth Dinner of the Musicians' Club in London. He strongly advocated a reduction in all musicians' working hours and described as iniquitous what he thought was the maximum demanded by the London Philharmonic: 'A week's work of the LPO is forty-five hours including three gramophone sessions, five concerts and a return railway journey.' He called for no more than thirty-one hours a week in future.

Beecham replied in the *Daily Telegraph* on All Fools' Day: 'It is a pity that a person of Mr Tertis's usual discretion should have permitted himself to talk wildly on matters concerning which he is completely ignorant.' He then specified the LPO's schedule over the past fifty-two weeks 'which comes to the surprising and amusing result of exactly thirty-one hours. Further analysis of the concert period of seven months or thirty weeks comes to twenty-seven and a half hours a week.' Beecham recalled the French proverb '*Le mieux est l'ennemi du bien.*'

Tertis replied: 'Sir Thomas Beecham is one of the glories of the twentieth-century musical world and the history of orchestral conducting will be no history at all if his unique genius is not given its full due ... I played in the first Beecham Orchestra more than thirty years ago. Young Mr Thomas Beecham was not so experienced as the Sir Thomas Beecham of today, but he was already a brilliant conductor. And good though the first Beecham Orchestra was, the LPO is more brilliant still ... London should subsidise an orchestra.' To which, of course, there could be no reply.

At about this time there had been another disagreement with Beecham, this time concluded with less grace. Beecham had been unable to conduct in Sheffield and the orchestral committee had invited Henry Wood in his place. 'Don't forget that I am the doyen of British conductors,' replied Wood on a postcard as he grudgingly agreed to do it, 'but never ask me again *as a substitute.*' He disliked Beecham's 'ruthless tongue' and did not respond as readily as most to the wit which was one of Beecham's weapons. Their exchanges in the *Daily Telegraph* were rather one-sided.

By 1939 the LPO (or the 'London Pill-harmonic' – to give its obvious nickname) was outwardly a shiningly brilliant orchestra; but below the surface things were not quite so smooth. Beecham owed a great deal of money to his players. Sometimes he was able to settle a fraction of his debts to those who pressed him hard enough, but he was by nature awkward to approach on money matters, and in general the players preferred to go on working for him in the Micawberish hope that something would turn up to their advantage. Sometimes one of Beecham's fixers would telephone a player who was owed money and had not been working for the LPO for several months. After a short silence on the line, the musician would invariably say: 'All right, I'll come. The old bugger owes me £60' (or even more) 'but I'll come.' Beecham not only got the best players, but he got the best spirit out of them.

The LPO's series of Sunday afternoon concerts at Covent Garden had been highly successful artistically, and many a young person found them opening doors of wonder and delight. But – now that Lady Cunard was no longer a rich woman – one of Beecham's prime sources of funds was at an end, though her unsparing efforts and her devotion towards him and his orchestra were obvious by the way in which she attracted rich patrons to him. As for herself, she was sometimes to be seen at one jeweller or another in Bond Street, exchanging a fine piece for something rather less valuable but just as showy – and getting the difference in much-needed cash.

Lady Cunard was approaching a personal financial crisis, and so were the LPO. In addition to the individual balances owing to the players Beecham's own shortage of management funds had prevented rehearsals from being sufficiently numerous, and consequently those which did take place went on far too long. These were the days before inflexible union rules became a bane (often senselessly and inartistically so) to promoters, though it might well be argued that Sir Thomas was one of those responsible for the state of affairs which exists today. Though he paid over the union minimum when he did pay, he took more than his pound of flesh in so doing.

Paul Beard was one of the earliest significant casualties in 1936, when he left to go to the BBC. 'Another Wagner season at Covent Garden from 10 a.m. until midnight would have killed me.' Even so, the LPO was considered fortunate by other musicians to have so much work at the Royal Opera House (where they tended to live like moles), as well as at RPS concerts, recordings and Beecham's own promotions. They appeared to be a highly privileged orchestra.

With the coming of the Second World War, concert-giving suffered a huge setback before a new formula was worked out to suit the changed conditions. Nobody knew better than Beecham the need for music in wartime, but after the 1939 summer season he had been ordered to take a complete rest for up to a year. This he could not do, but he did decide to give up conducting for that length of time. His gout was troubling him considerably and so was his left foot. Surgery was recommended on one toe. So in August he disappeared, to reappear suddenly in the middle of September. When asked where he had been he replied: 'I heard there was a national emergency. So I emerged.' He threw himself into concert work with the LPO until his once-prized appearance on the rostrum was threatening to become a commonplace event. Walter Legge advised him to relax or else his reputation, let alone his health, was likely to be seriously impaired.

In 1940 Beecham went first to Australia, then to Canada and the United States, and he remained in North America for four years. Britain, so reliant on help from her two dominions, Australia and Canada, and on financial as well as moral assistance from the United States, lost Beecham for most of the war. Those who criticise him for leaving London and going to the 'safety' of the USA may care to reflect on his age (over 60); the fact that of the three orchestras working in London the BBC and the LSO were both closed to him; and the final possibility that he was sent there by the British Government.

The LPO without Beecham was at first a headless corpse. By September 1939, according to Thomas Russell, there was 'a doleful meeting of the creditors of the governing company at which Sir Thomas distinguished himself by silencing and dumbfounding the most critical guests with his rhetorical eloquence.' A committee of players was formed and decided immediately and unanimously that they must follow the example of the LSO and turn themselves into a limited company. Beecham was present when the committee was elected, and approved this move. What he afterwards regretted, according to Thomas Russell, was the gift he had made to the players 'of all that the words "London Philharmonic Orchestra" signified. In an historic document of four pages, typewritten copies of which were circulated to each member of the orchestra, Sir Thomas expounded his opinion of the democratic principle as typified by the said committee.'

Although Beecham was at first annoyed to find power over the orchestra, *his* orchestra, snatched from his hands in a perfectly legal and friendly manner, he soon felt relieved to be rid of the responsibility he had shouldered for so long. His suggestions in the 'historic document' were ignored, but after a moment of rage he sent encouraging advice to the new directors. Now that they no longer had to go on fighting Beecham's old battles against the philistines, the new committee were able to show a fresh and unaggressive face to the public.

Financial support, however, had almost shrivelled up, and the emphasis was on survival rather than entertainment in a Britain that was a dull, blacked-out land of utility and self-denial. The LPO was soon in danger of disbandment, and the military call-up created many gaps in the ranks. The violist, Thomas Russell, became the orchestra's first managing director, and it was he who completely rejuvenated them, thanks also to the loyalty of certain members who refused to be tempted elsewhere, and to their pride in the glorious reputation of the LPO.

Help also came from an unexpected source. Jack Hylton, the dance-band leader and impresario, offered to back the LPO under Malcolm Sargent on a tour of cinemas, theatres and variety clubs for a fourteen-week stint in ten cities. Russell instantly agreed, and the LPO began their tour in Glasgow where they played to a total of 30,000 people. On their return to London they played at Queen's Hall on the evening of 10 May 1941. That night the Hall was destroyed by German bombs, as were most of the LPO's instruments. In the days of the Blitz nobody was going to be beaten by the Germans, least of all members of this orchestra, who borrowed or begged unfamiliar instruments from friends and from strangers who heard of their dilemma. The spirit of Britain and the spirit of Beecham carried them through.

At the end of the war the LPO emerged far stronger than it had been in 1939. In 1944 Sir Thomas returned in anticipation of carrying on where he had left off. Dr Berta Geissmar, his former general secretary, had been waiting for this moment all through the war, but she was now pushed aside by the new Lady Beecham who returned from America with Sir Thomas. She wanted none of the old affiliations to be resumed. Beecham had kept a finger on the pulse of British music while he was away, but first he had one important letter to answer.

This was from the Hallé Society in Manchester and had been delivered to him in New York in July 1944, advising him that his office of honorary president of the Society would probably be transferred to the Lord Mayor of Manchester, and thanking him for his past interest. Although Beecham was in an amiable frame of mind when sounded out by an old Mancunian friend called Forbes, he was not in the least congenial when approached in a semi-official manner by the Secretary of the Hallé Society, Ernest Bean. Bean was a shrewd and likeable person but got nowhere at all with his task. He has wittily described his interview as 'a conversation with Puck, Ariel, Beau Brummel, Count Almaviva, the Spanish Inquisitor, Louis XIV, Judge Jeffreys, Till Eulenspiegel and Captain Hook all rolled into one.' Since Ernest Bean was possessed of a great fund of knowledge and humour he decided to enjoy his mock trial and said afterwards: 'I had the exhilarated feeling of one watching a gusty Restoration comedy not only being acted but improvised on the spot. No one would ever believe me if I tried to repeat the extravaganza.'

Beecham did not reply to the Hallé's original letter until October, when he wrote a long article which was published in the *Daily Telegraph*. This began a comic and public exchange of views and of correspondence in the Manchester and national newspapers. After many committee meetings the dénouement might have been written by W. S. Gilbert.

The Lord Mayor of Manchester, who had not yet been approached by the Hallé Society, first became aware of the contretemps when he read about it in the papers, and was understandably perplexed and put out. Supporters of Beecham in Manchester were able to delay the committee motion regarding the presidency, although in so doing they brought the matter into the public gaze via the press.

In January 1945 the Hallé Society discovered that there was no provision for an honorary president in their articles of association, so that none of Richter, A. J. Balfour, Sir Edward Elgar or Sir Thomas Beecham had ever constitutionally 'existed' in the Hallé's orbit. Nor could the Society now approach the Lord Mayor of Manchester with their invitation.

Three days before the advertised extraordinary general meeting of the Hallé Concerts Society, Beecham wrote a long and brilliantly constructed letter to the editor of the *Manchester Guardian*. He set out cogently and logically the events as he saw them from his appointment as President in succession to Sir Edward Elgar in 1934: his departure to America, where he maintained contact with a large number of people in Britain by post and by telephone throughout the four years he was away, and his disappointment at what he regarded as the inept methods adopted by the Society. 'I had not the slightest warning or fore-knowledge of the Society's intentions; I was not even asked if I would like to resign, nor had I been favoured even with a summary notice to quit. What I received was a species of post-mortem announcement that I had already quitted without personal cognisance of the fact.'

He went on to say: 'I desire to affirm, and with all the emphasis in my power, that not only am I still the president of the Hallé Society but that I have not the smallest intention of resigning or permitting myself to be removed from that position. I have also taken the step of causing to be printed on my visiting cards and business notepaper the premonitory inscription "President of the Hallé Concerts Society".'

After this typically Beechamesque stroke of extravagant humour he became more serious, even sentimental as if to touch the hearts of his supporters: 'I have been longer before the public than any other man living in this country as an impresario, a manager, a creator and maintainer of orchestras and opera companies, and, last but not least, as an executive artist. My association with the Hallé Orchestra began forty-five years ago, and my affection for and interest in it are un-abated.'

At the general meeting it was decided that the office of president should remain *in statu quo*, and when the Hallé's new articles were published two years later there was still no provision for the office of president, nor was the omission challenged. Yet one thing was certain: of the four ghostly presidents of the Hallé Concerts Society, Sir Thomas Beecham was the last of the line.

The orchestral situation on Beecham's return to London was very different from what it had been when he went to America. The Hallé issued no invitation to him, mainly because of John Barbirolli's personal feelings against him – and he was now their conductor. Many of the players in the LPO wanted Beecham to come back to them, and there was little prejudice against him because of the many unpaid orchestral fees. The LSO were still unfriendly and had not forgotten the events of 1932. They ignored his return. The BBC Symphony Orchestra was in the hands of Sir Adrian Boult, who did not get on with Beecham personally, although an invitation did not entirely depend upon this orchestra's conductor; for above him sat Arthur Bliss, the Director of Music. On the other hand nothing but friendship was expressed by the Liverpool Philharmonic Orchestra.

The pro-Beecham faction in the LPO won for the time being, and so the first concert Beecham gave on his return to England took place on 7 October 1944 when he conducted his old orchestra once again. There were six concerts up to the end of the year, all at the Albert Hall now that Queen's Hall was irrevocably destroyed, and all characteristically Beecham programmes too, with only one new work, Virgil Thomson's *Episode, The Filling Station* to remind people that Beecham had been in the United States.

For the time being, though, this marked the end of his association with his prime orchestra. The conditions they laid down were that he would become their artistic director and conductor, but that other conductors (of the board's choice) would also be employed, although the orchestra would have first call on Beecham. 'I'm not going to be wagged by any orchestra,' was his comment, although he did not sever connections with them or refuse to conduct them when it suited him. There were members of the LPO who tried hard to get him back, but their new constitution was the stumbling-block. Even so, Beecham was becoming a little more mellow. In April 1945 he was sixty-six years of age.

Liverpool welcomed him back in December 1944 and again in the following June and September; and he conducted the BBC Symphony Orchestra and Northern Symphony Orchestra during the summer. His first LPO concert in October had assured every concert promoter and Beecham fan, as well as a new generation of music lovers, that Beecham was still a magician, and that nobody but he could conjure such sweet sounds from an orchestra.

In 1945 the Gramophone Company (as it was then) appointed Walter Legge to recruit an orchestra of the best musicians available with a view to making recordings. Later that year, twenty-four players from the Royal Air Force Symphony Orchestra (still in uniform) made some records of works by Purcell and Sibelius, and the orchestra was augmented to fifty-two, then to seventy-five players. Beecham was (according to Eric Blom) 'sufficiently interested and impressed to offer to conduct a Mozart concert in London'. This was the first public concert by the new orchestra, called the Philharmonia, and it took place at the Kingsway Hall on 27 October 1945. But he never conducted them again; Walter Legge had complete control of the orchestra and merely offered Beecham the artistic directorship under him. Beecham was not going to change places with a man who had been his assistant in the late 1930s at Covent Garden.

As in 1909 and 1932, Beecham announced: 'I always get the best players', and the cry was heard once more: 'Beecham's starting a new orchestra!' He had been to the USA twice since 1944, he had spent some time with the BBC (as he had done before 1932) and now, on 15 September 1946, he took up his baton at the Davis Theatre, Croydon, on a Sunday afternoon and stood for the first time in public before his own Royal Philharmonic Orchestra.

He had spent the spring in planning who was available and whom he wanted to try out. Many of those who had played for him in the LPO before the war and to whom he still owed money were paid up in full and re-booked. Less than a month before the début concert Beecham's fixers were unleashed and then, with only four days to spare before their appearance, the new orchestra was brought together for the first time in St Pancras Town Hall, a capacious though dismal place for such an historic event. Each department had a core of experienced players, experienced both at their jobs and in playing for Beecham, and also included brilliant young men like Dennis Brain and Norman Del Mar (horns) and Dennis's brother Leonard (cor anglais). The orchestral manager was Victor Olof, who was responsible for making approaches to the more important members of the orchestra.

Gerald Jackson (flute) clearly remembered his telephone call and jumped at the chance even though he had been with Beecham for only a year in the LPO. Another veteran, Archie Camden, became first bassoon and Reginald Kell first clarinet; James Bradshaw was again the principal percussionist.

At the packed Davis Theatre (now long since demolished) the programme gave no list of players. Perhaps this was intentional, since there could be no permanence regarding the personnel. Certainly the strings needed reshuffling and some players were discarded. It was somewhat typical of Beecham that he used only four days before the concert to produce a sufficiently good ensemble for critics and public alike.

There were some who said the orchestra couldn't last, but Beecham used the next year to weld a superb instrument that has continued in being long after his own departure. He had obtained substantial backing from both British and American sources – but not, of course, from Lady Cunard. On the day of the first concert at Croydon she was listening to de Sabata and the LPO at the Stoll Theatre as the guest of poor, cast-off Berta Geissmar, in whose box she was sitting. Felix Aprahamian was also with them, the only one of the three still on good terms with Beecham.

The RPO's first appearance in central London was at the Albert Hall, in the first of seven concerts in Beecham's 1946 Delius Festival, an extension and expansion of the works played eighteen years before. There were four concerts at the Albert Hall and two at the Central Hall, Westminster, all with the RPO; the final concert, again *A Mass of Life*, was with the BBC Symphony Orchestra. Beecham dug deep into the Delius Archive, which was under his control, and brought forth such unknown treasures as *Sur les Cimes*. (This was claimed to be its first performance.) He also gave the Prelude to Act III of *Folkeraadet*, Act III of *Koanga*, and Act III of his beloved *Village Romeo*, without some of which pieces no Delius Festival would be complete.

Beecham was in his element. He paraded the RPO round the provinces, gathering richer bouquets as time went on. Sometimes they played at ill-advised venues like the Harringay Arena for the so-called London Music Festival of June 1947, sponsored by Jack Hylton. The enormous, bare building had a corrugated roof. The orchestra was placed in its centre and there were wooden seats all round. The acoustics were terrible, and there was a constant din from outside of hawkers, aeroplanes, trains and spectators at the adjacent dog-racing track. Beecham's attempts to quell the interference by making his orchestra play loudly were self-defeating, since the building was super-resonant and the result was an indistinguishable roar.

In October the same year Beecham put on a reasonably successful Richard Strauss Festival on Sunday evenings at Drury Lane Theatre, the scene of so many former triumphs. Strauss was present. Beecham's old school, Rossall, had meanwhile reached its centenary year in 1944, but because of the war all celebrations had had to be postponed until peacetime. Now, in October 1947, Beecham accepted the headmaster's invitation to give a concert there and to take part in their festivities. He had the Blackpool Symphony Orchestra at his disposal for a three-hour rehearsal beforehand. After his experiences in America, this shortage of time was nothing new or disquieting to him. He shouted, abused, wheedled and drove the orchestra into shape for a fairly typical concert which ended with the same *Jubilee Ode* as he had taken part in as a boy fifty-three years before. After the concert he held forth in the masters' common room where he was photographed in complete control. Then he signed the register of Old Rossallians, in which was already inscribed:

Thomas Beecham, Knight Baronet of the United Kingdom
Commander of the Legion of Honour
Commendatore of the Order of the Crown of Italy
Decorations – Belgium, Denmark, Yugoslavia
Honorary Doctor of Music of   Oxford   London
                             Manchester   Montreal
Batson's House 1892–97.

The total number of orchestras which Beecham founded has some-times been in dispute. The early one at St Helens was not a professional one, while the New Symphony Orchestra was already in existence when Beecham first conducted it, though only as a chamber orchestra. Then came the Beecham Symphony Orchestra and the Beecham Wind Orchestra, followed by the London Philharmonic and Royal Philharmonic Orchestras. Yet another, seldom if ever heard of, was the Metropolitan Symphony Orchestra. Beecham conducted the MSO once at a public concert at the Gaumont State Cinema, Kilburn, on Boxing Day 1948.

The reason for this ephemeral body of players lay in a double booking of the Royal Philharmonic Orchestra. Muir Matheson was due to conduct them at the Regal Cinema, Edmonton, and Beecham was also booked to conduct them at Kilburn at the same time on the same day. Consequently about half the true members of the RPO attended at each cinema, while the balance of the two orchestras was made up of more deputies than had been seen in one place – let alone two – for a very long time. There had been a similar occasion a few years earlier when the LSO announced itself in two places at once and gave simultaneous concerts. This led to a threatened lawsuit. Beecham had had enough of these.

1948 was also the year of his first appearance as a conductor at Glyndebourne. In July he and the RPO gave four Mozart concerts on four consecutive days to highly appreciative audiences in John Christie's little opera house in the Sussex Downs. The experiment was such a success that it was repeated, with five concerts and a lecture by Beecham, in 1949.

This was the year of Beecham's seventieth birthday, an event which he celebrated first with a concert in Liverpool and then with another in London. At Liverpool he said of the Liverpool Philharmonic: 'This is the best-conducted musical society in the world.' He paid great tribute to the players and commended the care of those present in the audience. 'I am not exactly a Liverpudlian,' he said, 'or even a Mancunian, but if there were any spot in the world that I could call my own, it would be somewhere in this neighbourhood.' With Betty playing the Mozart D major Concerto it was a very happy occasion and Beecham promised that he would make many more 'happy returns' to play for them. 'Sir Thomas still has that rare gift of making things seem even better than they are,' was the somewhat curious observation of the *Liverpool Daily Post*'s music critic.

The second birthday concert, in London, was sponsored by the *Daily Telegraph* (whose circulation must have gained from time to time as a result of Beecham's pithy letters). This was a programme which shouted 'Beecham!': Mozart, Delius, Sibelius and Berlioz, with Richard Strauss and Bax in close support. The elaborate programme contained a worthy tribute by Sir Osbert Sitwell, who described Beecham as 'the most eminent of all English conductors, and . . . the most inspiring and creative – just as he remains after nearly fifty years of active artistic life, the most youthful – figure in English musical life. Genius is rare enough: and Sir Thomas *is* a genius.' The concert was given at the Royal Albert Hall, for there was still no other large concert hall in London. However, on the South Bank near Waterloo station a huge and sleazy site had been cleared and drained, and on it a variety of halls and temporary structures was being built in preparation for the Festival of Britain in 1951. The most permanent of all the buildings was a new concert hall. Beecham watched it going up, rotated his nose in disgust, sniffed 'Giant chicken coop!' and swore he'd never set foot inside it. Pique was added to disgust when Toscanini accepted the invitation to open the new Royal Festival Hall in May 1951.

The Royal Philharmonic Orchestra was now playing superbly for Beecham, and instead of joining in the festivities in London he organised his own tour of the provinces, interspersed with appearances at the Royal Albert Hall. In the end Toscanini withdrew and a variety of British conductors took over, but Beecham was not among them.

His co-conductor was his nearest contemporary, Leopold Stokowski, who he had invited to London as a token of gratitude for friendship during the war years in America. His plan to help establish Stokowski in Britain succeeded. This gaunt and poetic conductor was known to British audiences only from his films *Fantasia* and *100 Men and a Girl* and from his many gramophone records.

At the end of July 1951 Beecham and the RPO reopened the new Colston Hall in Bristol with a scintillating concert. Other conductors then took the orchestra over while Beecham returned temporarily to opera with Balfe's *Bohemian Girl* in Liverpool and London, and while he went on a tour with the BBC Symphony Orchestra.

Since the war he had resumed working with the BBC. Some of the larger orchestral and choral works, which he relished, like the Berlioz *Requiem Mass*, had been performed under his baton in the studio, where costs were not the main consideration. Not only did he conduct the BBC's main orchestra but also their Northern Orchestra in Manchester and the Theatre Orchestra at the Camden Theatre, London, whose resident conductor was Stanford Robinson, elder brother of Eric.

Soon relenting over the question of the Royal Festival Hall, Beecham gave his first of a total of ninety-two concerts there on 28 October 1951. In August the following year he conducted four concerts at the Edinburgh Festival, the last of which, on a Sunday evening at the Usher Hall, was a wonderful performance of *L'Enfance du Christ*. The three other concerts were all-Sibelius; Mozart and Strauss; Haydn and Delius.

Beecham had settled down into a fairly predictable routine with orchestras and concerts. Although he preferred to conduct his own RPO he did not shun the occasional Wednesday Festival Hall concert with the BBC; he even gave some Proms at the Albert Hall; and he continued to work with either orchestra in the studio. Because of his painful gout, which he had borne since the early 1930s, he did not go so often into the provinces for single concerts, although he was able to sustain a visit to the United States almost every year. As it turned out, his last two provincial concerts were in 1954, one with the City of Birmingham Symphony Orchestra, the other with his old friends at Liverpool. He said how glad he was to get back to Liverpool again for Eccles cakes and decent potted shrimps, although he scarcely ever now saw 'the grand old Simnel cake'. He was happy, relaxed and being fussed over by Betty.

Her illness caused her to make very infrequent solo performances in the 1950s. She could no longer concentrate on her work, and what had once been a joyful partnership of husband, wife and orchestra was now a hardship. Betty hated the thought of cancelling an appearance for she was a thorough professional, but eventually there was no alternative. Beecham, too, was upset at having to announce the fact, which he did as lightly as he could before playing a cheerful piece of Mozart, such as one of the Divertimenti. Latterly, Betty played only the Mozart concertos, no longer the Delius or the Handel arrangement which Beecham had made with her in mind.

After her death in Buenos Aires he returned to England in a wheelchair, but recovered in time to give his first London concert as a widower, the first of a series of thirteen public concerts and four BBC studio recordings before the end of the year. The first was a Royal Philharmonic concert with his own Royal Philharmonic Orchestra. Sir Thomas Beecham walked in his stately manner through the green curtain and up the steps on the platform. The applause and cheering initiated the tonic which friends, music and continuous work all began to impose beneficially upon him. He was at the start of the last phase in his life..

Chapter Three

IN THE OPERA HOUSE

TOSCANINI CALLED BEECHAM 'Pagliaccio' – a clown, a cheap showman. It is easy to see why, from Toscanini's viewpoint. Beecham's extraordinary talents and his insistence upon controlling whatever came his way, especially if this were an opera house, must have reduced his activities to the level of a circus act in the eyes of a rival conductor, especially one who spent his entire life conducting. Beecham's all-consuming passion was to produce music for others to hear, and in this respect he was an amateur: a lover of the art. But he was a professional amateur.

The very idea of an impresario being his own musical director, stage producer and conductor was unheard-of in London; and although there were impresarios who sang, Beecham can be directly compared only with Emanuel Schikaneder, the Viennese theatre manager who was the librettist of Mozart's *Die Zauberflöte* and who played and sang the clown-like Papageno himself, staging the opera in his own theatre in 1791. Had Toscanini been alive then he would probably have dubbed Schikaneder 'Pagliaccio' as well.

The command which Beecham enjoyed was part of his natural inheritance. Although Joseph Beecham had fully intended his heir to join him in the family business and in due course to inherit it, he unwittingly supplied his son with the equipment – the music lessons and musical instruments – that imbued in him a far greater desire for opera than Joseph himself possessed. The splendid Swiss orchestrion implanted in Thomas Beecham's mind something like the sounds he was one day to reproduce from his orchestras in opera houses all over the world. While he was content to improve and establish his conducting technique with orchestras – preferably his own orchestras – in concert halls, he was always striving towards opera. Until the end of his days he was planning new productions, and it is greatly to be regretted that he never conducted *Die Zauberflöte* at Glyndebourne or *Les Troyens* at Covent Garden in 1960, and that Grétry's *Zémire et Azor* in 1956 was his last theatrical production in England.

Beecham began to compose his first opera while he was living with the Welles family in London after the break with his father in 1900. His subject was *Marmion*, after Sir Walter Scott, and because of his knowledge of Scott and of literature in general he became his own librettist. *Marmion* was completed, and he looked around for an opportunity to have it produced.

In 1902 a new organisation was being set up to tour outer London, optimistically called the Imperial Grand Opera Company. Auditions were being held, preparatory to rehearsals, at the Old Vic Theatre. Beecham went down to the Waterloo Road with *Marmion* under his arm and sat waiting in an ante-room with a number of strangers, listening to the faint but exciting vocal sounds from within. Suddenly the door burst open and a tubby man asked whether anybody could play the piano, *Faust* in particular, and from memory. Beecham alone replied that he could – all of it. He was at once hustled in and for the rest of the day he accompanied the auditions.

After that he was invited to join the company as their accompanist and assistant conductor, but his suggestion that the reason for his being there at all was to interest them in his opera was met with incredulity. *Marmion* was never performed, but Beecham was launched on two weeks of opera rehearsals and five of performances with an opera company.

The tour started on Easter Monday 1902 and included Clapham, Brixton, Fulham, New Cross and Stratford. Beecham describes the orchestra as insubordinate and recruited from more than a fair share of drunks. Such was the standing of the company as a whole that there is hardly a single review in any of the local newspapers, despite the presence of Blanche Marchesi following her Covent Garden début with the Moody-Manners Opera Company. The excited gentleman of the auditions was Kelson Trueman, who not only managed the company but also sang principal tenor roles such as Don José and Manrico. It is not known which of the operas Beecham was supposed to conduct (for it is most unlikely that he ever actually did so), although the whole repertoire was well within his knowledge: *Carmen, Il Trovatore, Cav.* and *Pag.*, and the 'English Ring' – *Lily of Killarney, Maritana* and *The Bohemian Girl*. The last week at Stratford was well advertised and reported. Seat-prices at the Borough Theatre ranged from two-guinea boxes to a threepenny gallery, but while 'the cheaper parts of the house were quite full', the more expensive seats were evidently empty. If this pattern recurred throughout the tour it is no wonder that nothing more was heard of the Imperial Grand Opera Company. The Leonora of *Il Trovatore* was Marie Duma, who received a good notice and about whom Beecham waxes enthusiastic in his autobiography, saying that he never heard the role sung better by anybody else. Madame Duma from the Carl Rosa Opera Company does not figure in British operatic records, whereas the other prima donna, Blanche Marchesi, was a familiar figure on the London concert platform until the 1930s.

Surprising events seem to have taken place on the last night at Stratford, when G. H. Snazelle, who sang Devilshoof in *The Bohemian Girl*, started a fire on the stage 'as a farewell gesture'. Beecham was much sobered by the low standards throughout, made all the more obvious by occasional flashes of quality like the costumes which some of the principals brought with them, and also some of the singing.

Having failed to get *Marmion* produced, Beecham began to work on another opera, *Christopher Marlowe*. This had a ready made libretto by the celebrated Giuseppe Illica, but was never completed.

Beecham did not venture into opera again for seven years. By 1909 he had travelled a good deal in Europe, was familiar with a large operatic repertoire, and had become thoroughly established as the most interesting orchestral conductor in London. He had also met Ethel Smyth.

This extraordinary woman was twenty-one years Beecham's senior. She had studied composition in Leipzig and, thanks to the interest of Artur Nikisch (the von Karajan of the time), three of her operas had already been performed in Germany. One of these was *The Wreckers*. In 1908 Ethel Smyth had, in her own words, given 'a *Wreckers* concert in London; two acts only with maimed rites, conducted by Nikisch with next to no orchestral rehearsal.' Although the singers had been sufficiently excited by the event to perform without a fee, no London promoter would consider staging the whole opera, especially as the composer was unknown – and a *woman*.

The Wreckers is about a Cornish village where the inhabitants carry out maritime piracy. It is set in the eighteenth century and has an original plot by Harry Brewster, a close friend of Ethel's. The work needs careful staging, especially in the last act when the two (illicit) lovers Mark and Thirza are left to drown in a cave by the rising tide as punishment for having broken the wreckers' code (rather than any moral one).

Beecham and Ethel Smyth admired one another in their professional capacities: she liked his enormous knowledge of music, his ability at the piano, especially in Mozart, and his extrovert personality. He in turn described her as the most remarkable woman he had ever met, although in a broadcast many years after *The Wreckers* he stated emphatically that of all the women he had ever known, Ethel was the one he would least like to kiss. He found her energy inspiring – too much so at times – and appreciated her disinclination to be baulked by anybody. He also discovered that she had friends in high places, for she had only to telephone Buckingham Palace to be put through to a senior member of the royal household with whom she was on Christian-name terms.

Even this was not sufficient to persuade the management of Covent Garden to agree to perform her opera. However, a rich American called Mary Dodge, a supporter of women's rights as Ethel was, came to her aid with an offer to underwrite a production of *The Wreckers* up to £1,000. She also suggested Beecham as its conductor.

Nothing suited him better. Already on the way to becoming reconciled with his father after more than nine years' estrangement, Beecham had his eye on the Royal Opera House, where he intended to promote and conduct operas of his choice during special seasons which would not clash with the Grand Opera Syndicate's normal summer offering. But at present he lacked the funds: he would need the kind of backing which only his father could provide. *The Wreckers* would place him neatly on London's opera map and would also effect an introduction for him and his Beecham Symphony Orchestra before they moved to Covent Garden. He offered to conduct without a fee and was immediately booked by Ethel and Miss Dodge.

Beecham knew Herbert Tree, the lessee of His Majesty's Theatre, which seemed an ideal house for the opera, especially as Tree was a musical enthusiast. They came to an arrangement for four afternoon performances, since *The School for Scandal* was running every evening and could not be interrupted. Although this was far from ideal, with the dates spread over ten days, their plans were accepted.

The virile Yorkshire tenor, John Coates, took the leading role of Mark, Mme de Vere Sapio sang Thirza, and the opera was flung on the stage of His Majesty's Theatre in ten days. It would have needed a good month to achieve anything like a professional result. More precious time was wasted because of Beecham's infuriating habit of arriving at least half an hour late for each rehearsal – sometimes more, because of his commitments elsewhere.

He was concurrently rehearsing a chorus in Hanley for the first British performance of Delius's *A Mass of Life*. This was going to be heard in Hanley on 10 June and in Manchester the following evening, while *The Wreckers* was to open in London on 22 June. That left only ten days on which Beecham was available to give his full time to the opera – ten days and nights, as it turned out. Even so, he did not yet possess enough technical knowledge to integrate all the varied elements of an opera in their unformed state. He accordingly let go with the orchestra, expecting the singers to use full voice at final rehearsals. This occasioned a mild reprimand from John Coates, who stopped singing towards the end of the last act, came down to the footlights and addressed Beecham: 'Sir, will you please explain the situation, dramatic, I mean, at this point? I believed that we were drowned by the sea, not by you and your orchestra.'

Beecham was unaccustomed to the composer standing by him and criticising his tempi, dynamics or anything else. Ethel Smyth did so, unlike Delius, who had merely shrugged his shoulders and said: 'Oh, take it just how you think, my dear fellow.' So, dissatisfied with the way one late rehearsal was going, Ethel vaulted over the brass rail to the temporary bridge across the orchestra pit, sat herself down at the front of the stage, cross-legged, and beat her own time while Beecham in the pit was unconcernedly (and triumphantly) beating his own.

The première was moderately successful in spite of all the difficulties which had prefaced it. The press was, on the whole, kind about the production, and praised Ethel's achievement. Beecham was congratulated for his handling of the orchestra, and he, the composer and the soloists had every reason to be proud of their efforts. There were faint murmurs of surprise about the libretto because it occasionally suggested Lewis Carroll, as *The Times* was swift to point out. Such lines as 'O come with me and have pleasant talk (she said) along the shore', comic enough on the page, sounded more comic still when sung.

After the first night Ethel had been concerned about her scoring, especially in the brass section; and about ten minutes before each of the subsequent performances she went down into the pit in advance of the players and pinned corrections to their parts. Henry Wood delighted in observing this and in pointing it out to his friends.

Ethel Smyth knew that if she could persuade King Edward VII to attend her opera they might be able to carry on for a longer run and achieve some refinements in the production. Working her connections with the Palace to the full, she pulled off a Royal Command performance in addition to the four already booked. Tree was sensible of the importance of royalty in his theatre, and swept aside his play for one night to make room for the King and Queen. On 8 July a royal box was built over the theatre pit, decorated with flowers and made ready to welcome the royal party. The performance went smoothly and in the second interval Ethel Smyth and Beecham were sent for by Their Majesties and congratulated. Queen Alexandra, unlike the King, was really fond of opera.

However, there were no further performances of *The Wreckers* at His

Majesty's Theatre. During a stormy meeting between Ethel and Tree's manager, Henry Dana, she called him a most insulting name for refusing to extend the run of her opera because of his own company's commitments. The settlement out of court cost Miss Dodge an extra £100, bringing her bill to between £500 and £600 to cover the deficit: well within the £1,000 guarantee, to be sure, but still a great deal of money to lose in five days in 1909.

Beecham gained the conductor's feather in his cap as a result of the production, so that it was no surprise either to the musical or to the general public when he announced that he was shortly to give a season of opera at Covent Garden. He had become reconciled with his father during rehearsals of *The Wreckers,* and Joseph's interest in opera and admiration for his errant son's rise to fame had imbued him with the desire to supply whatever funds were necessary to put Beecham and opera into London in the most striking manner possible.

Since the demise of the Moody-Manners Company in 1903 (so far as metropolitan appearances were concerned), and apart from a very few excursions into Covent Garden by the peripatetic Carl Rosa Company, only the GOS (Grand Opera Syndicate) gave anything like regular seasons there. These were the summer seasons with visiting star principals from Europe and America, the smaller parts being filled by British singers. The chorus was also British, composed of hardy men and women who sought work in pantomimes and musical plays during the rest of the year. The Syndicate had a fairly static board of directors and owned most of the costumes, scenery and rights to perform copyright operas at Covent Garden. These rights they guarded jealously. For the rest of the year Covent Garden was either 'dark' or hired out for charity balls and matinées and the occasional visit by another opera company.

The Beechams, father and son, undertook to mount their first season there in the winter of 1910, from mid-February to mid-March. The prospectus which Beecham issued makes it clear that he is, for the time being, sampling public taste as well as challenging an intelligent audience to support him. 'Unless there is a real demand for opera,' he wrote, 'any attempt to found a National Opera House... is at least premature.' So here was a bold venture. He was making it plain that this was not to be an isolated season: he was implying that he was there to stay.

In the previous January Richard Strauss's latest opera *Elektra* had been staged in Dresden and its more lurid details proved irresistible to the public. Beecham (not the GOS) obtained the rights to perform it at Covent Garden, and as soon as this was announced and the box office opened the rush of applications was unprecedented. A black market in tickets developed and the press co-operated marvellously with advance editorial publicity.

Beecham had been to Vienna in January 1910 to see the production and returned with the score of *Elektra* photographed on his memory. Rehearsals were exceedingly trying for everyone concerned except for Beecham, who retained a remarkable composure and led his orchestra patiently through the difficulties and hazards of this 'new music'. Today *Elektra* is easy enough to digest, but in 1910 its violent discords, clashing dissonances and the scenes with two singers carrying on in different keys, quite apart from a seeming lack of melody, took some time for the instrumentalists to absorb. But Beecham's orchestra was recruited from the finest sight-readers and players. Sight-reading has been the standard accomplishment of British musicians for several generations and still is; at all events it gave the orchestra a flying start and a swifter grasp of Strauss's meaning than had been evident from the Viennese. There were far fewer orchestral rehearsals in London than there had been in either Dresden or Vienna.

Eric Coates, sub-principal viola in the Beecham Orchestra, gives a good account of the London rehearsals. Richard Strauss was standing in the stalls beside Beecham, 'with that enormous head of his and arms which reached down nearly to his knees, directing, suggesting, interrupting.' Beecham found it all acceptable and fascinating stuff. Certainly the full score was open on his desk during orchestral and stage rehearsals, but on the first night the score remained shut.

Beecham's own recollections of this first production of *Elektra* are about the sort of amusing accidents that might happen with any opera. But Coates found things far less amusing. Lionel Tertis, principal viola, survived all the rehearsals and the first night, but couldn't go on any longer. His place was taken by Coates, who lasted for the next two nights. Then Siegfried Wertheim, Henry Wood's principal viola, carried on and finished the run. But such pressures not only affected the violas, they brought the whole orchestra near to the point of breakdown.

The story of *Elektra* by Sophocles, expressed anew through the vivid mind of the Austrian poet Hugo von Hofmannsthal, tells how Elektra, daughter of Agamemnon and Klytemnestra, is made to live like a slave under the most bestial conditions in the palace of Argos. Her mother leads a debauched but sleepless life with her paramour Aegisthus, both of whom are responsible for Agamemnon's death after his return from the conquest of Troy. Elektra's brother Orestes, banished for years, now suddenly returns. Brother and sister do not at first recognise one another, for Elektra believes Orestes to be dead and he can only envisage her as a princess. Their scene of recognition is one of the most beautiful in an otherwise barbaric score. Orestes, urged on by Elektra, kills first his mother, and then Aegisthus. Elektra dances in triumph; but she has nothing further to live for, and dies as she dances. The opera still has very great impact on an audience; in 1910 it was a monumental opener to a new season.

King George V (then still Prince of Wales) disliked going out in the evenings; he preferred to dine in comfort at home. But he and the future Queen Mary were at the first night, and the house was filled with musicians and music-lovers as well as members of the public in search of sensation. Press reviews were laudatory, especially for Beecham and his orchestra.

Five different permutations of the three principal sopranos made comparison interesting; among them was the creator of the role of *Elektra* in Dresden, Anny Krull. Strauss conducted two of the performances at the enormous fee of £200 a time, and showed how differently he approached his own opera. When he directed the tenderness of the subject seemed to be uppermost; when Beecham was in the pit the orchestra was dominant, and sometimes obscured the voices altogether. His employment of loud percussion was a feature of his interpretation. However, Strauss, always delighted to have his works performed, expressed his total satisfaction with the playing of the Beecham Orchestra, and was already doing his best to interest Thomas in the production of his other operas.

The public seemed almost as interested in opera as in football, and although their patronage was short-lived, it was clear that, given the right publicity and the right opera, anybody could be persuaded to buy tickets for Covent Garden. But the 'right' opera had to be something sensational. Be that as it may, Beecham had achieved a unique result in a matter of weeks. At the end of the last *Elektra* performance he was presented on stage with a laurel wreath 'as big as a lifebuoy', and there were innumerable curtain calls for the singers and especially for himself. The press made him guest of honour at a special dinner: an exceptional event.

Beecham had built his programme of operas skilfully from only eight works. *Carmen*, *Tristan und Isolde* and *Hansel and Gretel* were standard fare, and a stage version of Debussy's cantata *L'Enfant Prodigue* had been made specially by Beecham to form a double bill with the Humperdinck opera. The rest were experimental, although the success of *Elektra* was a foregone conclusion. *Ivanhoe* was a tribute to a past English composer, Sir Arthur Sullivan, and had not been heard for nineteen years. *The*

Wreckers and *A Village Romeo and Juliet* were tributes to two living composers of English birth. The latter opera by Delius was already nine years old and had not yet been heard in Britain.

Beecham's assistant conductors were Percy Pitt and Bruno Walter. Pitt was a thorough, experienced and popular musician who had been on the Covent Garden music staff since 1902. His Pickwickian appearance and jovial nature always got good results. Walter had conducted in six continental opera houses already and for six years had been Mahler's assistant in Vienna. He was only thirty-four, but his experience and ability were enviable. He was given the first performance of *The Wreckers*, for he had championed Ethel Smyth in Germany.

Beecham conducted seven of the nine *Elektras*, the second *Wreckers* and two *Village Romeos*. The advertised third performances of these last two operas were cancelled to make way for extra performances of *Elektra*. To judge from the sparse second houses they had attracted, this seemed only commonsense. Ethel Smyth was furious.

The Delius opera puzzled its first-night audience with its unfamiliar idiom. Beecham had a personal interest in the work. He had recently become converted to the Delian cult and did everything to make a success of the production. One of his extravagances was a full-sized roundabout in the fair scene of the opera, which was certainly never Delius's intention to show on the stage. At its first appearance at a dress rehearsal Beecham left the pit and insisted upon riding round himself on one of the gaily painted horses. It certainly enlivened the rehearsal but made a number of Germans present shake their heads. They failed to understand how the *Herr Direktor* could allow himself to behave in such a manner and still hope to maintain the respect of his orchestra.

A Village Romeo and Juliet is a low-key opera, with a fairy-tale, almost mystic, flavour. Two lovers, brought up by jealously warring fathers, spend one day of happiness together, and after consummating their love in a barge on the river they willingly drown. The celebrated intermezzo *Walk to the Paradise Garden* was itself drowned on the first night by the chattering of the audience on one side of the curtain and by the hammering and banging of the stage staff on the other. Beecham learned one lesson that night: never to lower the house curtains on an English audience with the lights out and music being played. Delius appeared on stage with Beecham at the end, the only time he was ever seen at Covent Garden.

Of thirty-one performances in his first season, Beecham conducted ten, of three different works. It was a sensible balance.

He had already, during early February, announced a second Beecham opera season at Covent Garden, and this was to take place for thirteen weeks at the end of the year. In March, before the end of the first season, he released the news that he was taking over His Majesty's Theatre in between for a seven weeks' summer season of opéra-comique.

The term 'opéra-comique' means different things to different people in different places. It cannot be completely rationalised, but, broadly speaking, it can be described as incorporating a down-to-earth story about real people, quite often in humble surroundings; dialogue between set numbers spoken and not sung as recitative; and a happy ending. To Beecham it meant light works suitable for light voices; melodious and easy to listen to; attractive to the eye and generally romantic all round. He intended his summer season to appeal to as wide a section of the London opera-going public as possible and for this reason he supported his light-hearted choice of works by cheap prices (stalls at 12s 6d), absolution from evening-dress, and all operas sung in English.

The public were mainly under the impression that it was to be a season of comic opera, and when they found that in some cases it was serious they did not give it the full support that Beecham needed. He included one or two operas for the simple reason that he wished to hear them himself – and admitted as much. His reason went deeper, though, than mere self-gratification. He already possessed a far broader and deeper knowledge of operas than any member of the GOS, and was in a strong position to introduce previously unperformed works to London when these were entirely unsuitable for performance at Covent Garden. He was also building up a strong English company, with voices far better suited to certain operas that he knew than to the standard fare at the Royal Opera. Few of Beecham's singers could expect to compete with those expensive, imported foreign voices. Beecham was seeing to it that they were steering an altogether different route towards building up their own repertoire.

The season got off to a bad start because of King Edward VII's death on 6 May. The opening night was postponed in deference to national mourning, and when the curtain did go up at His Majesty's it was on a depressed and sorrowful London. There were five performances of Offenbach's *Tales of Hoffmann* with John Coates, in Beecham's words, making the English language 'sound not only perfectly clear but beautiful as well'.

This was followed by a single performance of Massenet's *Werther*, from a story by Goethe but almost Russian in atmosphere, with its forlorn characters and its tragic end. Even so, Massenet made a very French piece out of it, and Beecham's Anglo-Saxon singers were as yet unable to absorb any Gallic qualities. *Werther* was not heard again on the London stage for forty-two years.

Another French opera which failed to attract public support was *Muguette*, an arrangement from Ouïda's novel *Two Little Wooden Shoes*. Edmond de Missa's score seemed too serious in its simplicity, but Beecham adored the work. He conducted eight performances in defiance of poorly attended houses. What the public wanted was what they thought they were coming to hear and see according to the season's title: comic vulgarity. This was entirely missing from Beecham's bill of fare; it was a commodity which did not at all appeal to him in the context of opera, but he saw a way of introducing something like it towards the end of the season.

In the very middle was a short 'Mozart Season' of nine performances, all conducted by Beecham, which have gone down in operatic annals as by far the most significant aspect of the whole season. The first performance was *Il Seraglio*, in which an unknown soprano called Maggie Teyte distinguished herself as Blonde and the great English bass, Robert Radford, made an excellent Osmin. This was followed by 'a landmark on the road of operatic development', a revival of *The Marriage of Figaro* in which Maggie Teyte's Cherubino was again singled out for high praise. The *Daily Telegraph* critic wrote that her characterisation 'showed how perfect and natural and peculiarly fascinating is her genius for the real opéra comique'. So somebody understood what it meant.

Then there was still *Così*. This glorious and subtle opera, already 120 years old, had been given only a few times in London since its première at the old King's Theatre, on part of the site of which His Majesty's Theatre now stands. That was in 1811. Meanwhile it had been rediscovered and revived in Germany, where Richard Strauss conducted it at Munich and was especially fond of it. He had spoken to Beecham about *Così*, for they shared a great enthusiasm for Mozart, and now Beecham had at last been able to produce the lovely opera in London. It was so unfamiliar that several newspapers delayed printing a review until after the second performance, to allow their critics to hear it twice before committing themselves.

Beecham appeared a cynic to most people, and many of those who knew him well (or thought they did) swear that he never shed a tear in his life. This is not so. The most simple and beautiful things could move him greatly: and what is more simple and more beautiful than the Act I sextet in *Così* as the lovers leave their women? Each time he played this, at the 'Addio! Addio!' tears would involuntarily come into his eyes and roll down his cheeks. He loved this score, compounded of the twin geniuses Da Ponte and Mozart.

These few performances set the seal upon Beecham as a great Mozart conductor. Maggie Teyte recalls, in her autobiography, his 'electric quality that some people call genius', which she describes as his ability to change an ordinary performance into something elevated and beyond description. This, and the power to magnetise his singers and bend them voluntarily to his will, made these Mozart operas take wing and remain as paragons in the memories of those who were fortunate enough to hear them.

Maggie Teyte remembered long afterwards a remarkable man called Tommy Chapman who was the accompanist and also played the celeste and glockenspiel when required. He was never seen without an enormous and dirty overcoat which he wore while playing, in the saddle-bag-sized pockets of which were vocal scores, usually '*Figaro* on the right and *Bohème* on the left'. Nobody knew where Chapman lived or what else he did, but he was often late for rehearsals and then used to snooze off while waiting for cues. When they came he was as alert as if he had been watching, and then his enormous hands came down 'on the correct chord like the wings of a butterfly'. Tommy Chapman had 'a nose like Cyrano de Bergerac's' and was as big in proportion. He was a great asset to Beecham because of his own excellent memory of the scores, and many a time when a principal had been pushed into a part at short notice it was Chapman who coached him and saw him through.

Then there was George King, the stage director, and a young man called Baylis, who joined the *Village Romeo* chorus in the previous season and was now, at His Majesty's, taking small parts and acting as the company's assistant manager. Baylis was to come into his own later on.

Beecham's next production was – if not vulgar – then decidedly risqué. Richard Strauss's second opera *Feuersnot* ('Fire Famine') is a wildly indelicate one-acter, and was sung in English, leaving little to the imagination. It concerns a provocative burgomaster's daughter, Diemut, who allows herself to be approached by Kunrad, an intriguing newcomer to the town. But she is irritated when he kisses her in front of her friends and without permission. So she invites him to her bedroom that night, begins to pull him up in a basket on a rope so that he may avoid the front door, and purposely leaves him stranded in mid-air for the townspeople to mock at him. But Kunrad is a magician and brings total darkness on the town. No light can be rekindled until Diemut has yielded to him. Everybody urges her, for the common good, to give in to Kunrad. This she does, and a sudden return of light to the town reveals a happy

Diemut in Kunrad's arms, together in her room. It is a jolly, tuneful work, and includes a chorus of children led by three precocious little girls whose obscene remarks about Diemut's virginity must have surprised the 1910 audiences.

But even *Feuersnot* did not catch on, partly because of the need to increase prices of admission. Beecham conducted all five performances and won admiration and praise for the way in which he controlled the extremely difficult and complex choruses of adults and children. *Feuersnot* was not heard complete in Britain again until 1978.

Beecham included two British works at His Majesty's, *Shamus O'Brien* by Stanford, 'a colourful, racy piece' first heard in 1896, and *A Summer Night* by G. H. Clutsam, music critic of the *Observer*. Beecham set much store by this one-acter, but it has not been heard since.

Last came *Die Fledermaus*, by the other Strauss, added to the repertoire to satisfy those who had come to see a red-nosed comic. Beecham had specially engaged the D'Oyly Carte baritone, Walter Passmore, for the part of Frosch, the prison governor, and Passmore gave his admirers full value.

When the season was over there was an absence of the acclaim that Beecham had earned in the previous March. Then the delighted press had described him as 'the man for whom we have long been waiting', and they hoped that 'in the future he will meet with the full reward of his labours'. But now, in their eyes, the ambiguously titled opéras-comiques had not much advanced his cause.

But Beecham was already thinking ahead to his next season and went straight over to Covent Garden to prepare for it. His prospectus contains a number of 'ifs' and 'buts', such as seven projected first performances, one of which could be staged only 'if passed by the Lord Chamberlain'. This in itself was news that would whip up interest in the work, and when it was found to be another 'horrifying' opera by Richard Strauss called *Salome* it proved as profitable to the box office as *Elektra* had been. There is even more in *Salome* to titillate the public interest, for in its hour and three-quarters of action it includes lechery, suicide, attempted incest, nakedness, necrophily and murder. But the score makes all this palatable.

The total repertoire was to be selected from thirty-nine named operas, eventually reduced to nineteen, two of which had not been initially advertised: *Rigoletto*, for the sake of the great Italian baritone Giuseppe De Luca; and a single *Pelléas et Mélisande* because of Maggie Teyte, who had studied the role with Debussy.

Beecham conducted thirty-four out of the eighty-five performances that season, and on two Saturdays, when there were matinées, he appeared in the pit for both performances. It was during this season that he conducted his first *Don Giovanni, Fliegende Holländer* and, because the conductor Alfred Hertz disappeared without good reason, *Tristan und Isolde*.

It is interesting to find Beecham optimistically forecasting a production of Berlioz's *Les Troyens* as early as 1910, for he wanted to conduct this great work in the opera house all his life and never managed to do so. It always remained tantalisingly out of his reach.

But there was still one knot to unravel: *Salome*. Beecham found that the Lord Chamberlain's office rejected the English translation which had been prepared, partly because events were taken from the New Testament. Despite Beecham's protestations and arguments he was told that it would need somebody in higher authority to sanction performances of *Salome* at Covent Garden – or anywhere else in England, for that matter.

Through the agency of his many society friends Beecham had already met the Prime Minister, Mr Asquith, and his wife. So he talked to Mrs Asquith about the matter and was invited down to the country one weekend so that he could approach the Prime Minister informally. Asquith was not in the least musical, but he had a fine legal mind and was a brilliant classical scholar. In this respect Beecham admired him, and the two men got on well together. When the conversation turned to music Asquith confessed that he had one favourite piece, the March from *Tannhäuser*. At his request, Beecham played it to him several times on the piano, and then after some discussion about the *Salome* impasse the Prime Minister promised to have a word with the Lord Chamberlain.

The way out was to be by a new translation that would treat the subject remotely and obliquely. Some characters were renamed, the scene was transferred to Greece, and all hints of lasciviousness between Salome and the Prophet (as he was now called) were obliterated. It could now go ahead.

The singers found their new words and sentiments perfectly ridiculous, and the three principals, being Europeans, found it doubly awkward to learn a new set of words when they knew the original German and had then committed to memory the first English version. But they had to do as they were told.

Then came the first night, and all did not go according to plan. The house was packed as it had been for *Elektra*, and Beecham, conducting, suddenly became aware of a growing excitement among the singers on the stage. The beautiful and talented Finnish soprano, Aïno Ackté, who had already executed her dance, accidentally lapsed into the former, forbidden text. Beecham was powerless to correct her and when, one by one, the other singers followed her until they had all left the bowdlerised version far behind Beecham felt as if he were condemned to be executed himself. The performance finished in the full blaze of 'If you had looked on me you would have loved me' instead of 'If you had looked on me you would have blessed me'. Beecham recounts the degree of his discomfort and how, when he took his call with the cast at the end, he was unable to dodge the Lord Chamberlain's party which bore down on him in the wings. After broad smiles of pleasure and handshakes all round their spokesman commended him upon the complete fulfilment of his master's wishes. Beecham never knew whether slipshod diction, an imperfect understanding of the opera or straightforward British diplomacy had saved his neck.

At the end of his third opera season in twelve months Beecham was more puzzled than disheartened. Out of the twenty or so operas which had never before been performed in England, only four had been complete successes: *Elektra* and *Salome*, *Hoffmann* and *Fledermaus*. But one thing he knew only too well: it would be folly to carry on with another season employing the same formula, for the public and he were viewing the whole scheme from opposite directions. Gone was Beecham's earlier optimism of achieving his goal of a firmly established national opera in three strides; a harder, more businesslike approach was replacing it. For the time being, however, a turn of events enabled him to pause and think more deeply upon how he was to proceed, without having to commit himself to another season founded on as yet unknown lines.

London has now and again become a proving ground for generously disposed people who are convinced they can provide more opera than is currently available to the public. The same is true, in a more modest fashion, for concerts. Vanquished concert promoters come and go with little publicity to advertise their downfall, but with an opera impresario the stakes are higher and the fall, when it happens, makes a resounding crash that is impossible to conceal.

In 1899 a concert agent called Norman Concorde had perfectly sincerely attempted to persuade Frederick Delius to found a permanent opera company in London for the performance of his own operas. All Concorde succeeded in doing was to cause Delius a staggering loss on one concert. And now, in 1910, a new contender in the unequal struggle appeared. His name was Oscar Hammerstein, German-born in Hamburg and later an American citizen who had made a fortune out of cigars.

He was an exceptional businessman with a passion for opera. His

Manhattan and Philadelphia Opera Houses had been so successful that the Metropolitan Opera bought up his interests in the USA in self-defence. This cost them a million and a quarter dollars, but they insisted that Hammerstein must not produce opera in New York for the next ten years. He brought his money to London, took a ninety-nine-year lease of a site in Kingsway, and began to build a theatre there on what he considered to be model lines. Kingsway had only just been developed and was in the news. It is on the edge of Covent Garden, close to the Opera House and to Drury Lane Theatre, lying between them and the ancient site of the Lincoln's Inn Fields Playhouse of Restoration days. So the new theatre was perfectly well sited in theatrical terms. It was to be called the London Opera House, and was completed in just over a year at a cost of a quarter of a million pounds.

When Beecham was asked by a newspaper reporter how he felt about the new competition he answered nonchalantly that he was delighted that Mr Hammerstein was coming to London, delighted for the sake of British music. He stressed that *he* did not produce opera for profit – implying that Hammerstein did – but rather for the love of it among British audiences.

At the first hint of Hammerstein's proposals two years previously Beecham had begun to build up his own interests for 1911 so that, if necessary, he would be in a position to overcome any competition alone. He began by negotiating for a visit of the Metropolitan Opera to Drury Lane, to coincide with the Covent Garden summer season, and he booked Serge Diaghilev's Imperial Russian Ballet; this was with his father's full approval, so the enterprise was financially sound.

Beecham had already seen the Russian Ballet several times in Paris, where they had first appeared in 1909. The British general public and the directors of the GOS were as yet unaware of the enormous attraction and artistic importance of the Ballet, which had had a shattering effect upon Paris. There had already been lovely performances by Russian dancers in London, but only as 'turns' in revue bills at the Hippodrome and Alhambra. The Russian Ballet as an independent concern, with its own costumes, scenery and highly trained dancers, was yet to astonish London.

But the idea of a visit from the Met was altogether understood by the public and the GOS, and the latter were most perturbed. This celebrated organisation had never visited London (nor has it to this day) and, since its singers included Caruso, Melba, Geraldine Farrar, Mary Garden, Ernestine Schumann-Heink, Scotti and many others, with a repertoire of twenty operas, the GOS capitulated. The final straw was the announcement that Signor Toscanini might be persuaded to share the conducting with Beecham.

The upshot was that the Grand Opera Syndicate invited Beecham to join them for the 1911 season. He accepted, and cancelled the Met visit and his planned season at Drury Lane. But the Syndicate approved the visit of the Russians and also undertook to employ the Beecham Orchestra in the pit for the Ballet. So now it was to be the GOS and the Russian Ballet against Oscar Hammerstein in a straight fight, with no third party to confuse the issue. It was partly the presence of Hammerstein which induced Beecham to accept the Covent Garden offer, for although he enjoyed competition the Met visit was not yet signed and sealed, and Joseph usually encouraged prudence and the acknowledgement of the bird in hand.

In any case Beecham knew that London could not satisfactorily support three opera companies at the same time. He happily took his seat on the GOS Board among H. V. Higgins (the chairman), the Marquess of Ripon (whose real interest was in preserving his position as England's best shot), Lord Esher, Lord Wittenham and Baron Frédéric d'Erlanger (a very talented man and a composer), with Neil Forsyth as secretary and Frank Rendle as lessee and manager. That several of these officials were either related to one another or to Higgins's predecessor, Augustus Harris, is not particularly surprising at a time when the control of so many organisations in the British Isles was shared by aristocratic families.

Joseph Beecham could not hold his own in such surroundings. He encouraged his son to be his figurehead, while he provided funds for opera and, in 1911, for the Ballet. This was known as the Coronation Season in London, and there has never been a more splendid one. Joseph had already spent far more than he had anticipated on the three ventures in 1910, and was now recognised as an important artistic benefactor. He received a knighthood from King George V in 1911.

In one way Sir Joseph was relieved that for the 1911 season there was to be a tight control of finance and that his son was not scheduled to conduct at all, because he knew that when Thomas went into the pit he often got carried away by what he regarded as necessities, which would involve extra rehearsals and add to the expense. There were eleven Italian operas and nine French, and the conductors were two Italians, Campanini and Panizza. The German Ambassador was extremely put out that there was no offering to represent his nation in this of all seasons.

Very few Londoners had met the inspiration behind the Russian Ballet – Serge Diaghilev. He was a phenomenon: a connoisseur of all the fine arts and a theatre director of outstanding ability and vision, all of whose talents came to realisation in his productions. The one practical skill he handled himself was stage lighting. His company meant everything to him and he worked ceaselessly for them, exercising a harsh discipline over his dancers, tempered by complete understanding of their individual capabilities. He relied entirely on rich patrons to supply him with the necessary finance which such an enterprise demanded, for the box office was totally inadequate; he always lived on credit and more often than not owed several months' back-pay to his principals, who supported themselves meanwhile by paid appearances in private houses, which Diaghilev arranged for them. Although he was a pederast he was welcome in every salon in Europe, and his relationship with women could be affectionate. They found him alarmingly attractive with his badger's stripe in the middle of his black hair, his heavy-lidded eyes, cruel mouth and plump, delicately manicured hands. He could be meltingly charming. Many of his dancers were terrified of him. His violent temper was often in evidence, usually because somebody had not carried out his precise instructions, for his personal, artistic integrity allowed no room for compromise or mediocrity of any sort. But he always got his own way and was invariably right.

Beecham believed Diaghilev to be the greatest impresario the world had ever known. There was mutual admiration between the two men, although they stood no nonsense from each other.

When, two years later, Beecham asked Diaghilev to provide six star dancers and singers for a single programme, the request was met with astonishment and the Russian replied that such a thing was unheard of. Beecham, who was footing the bill (on his father's behalf), told Diaghilev that he could mind his own business and make the arrangements as requested. On another occasion Beecham gave a dinner for the Ballet and found, to his surprise, that Diaghilev had forbidden a certain dancer to sit at the top table, although Beecham had wanted her there. Diaghilev explained that it was bad for morale and that she must remain with her equals in the company. He was not having one of her rank among the directors and he had already instructed her to sit in her proper place.

Although Diaghilev spoke only French or Russian in public, he and Beecham got on perfectly well in a mixture of English and French. Only once was he heard to utter English words at table, and this was when one of his favourite dishes was being served. He urgently ordered the Savoy Hotel waiter in a low voice: 'More chocolate pudding!'

The GOS considered opera to be their only concern and had probably not considered extending their horizons any further, which was why they had not invited Diaghilev to London themselves. He would have come, sooner or later, because such influential persons as the Marchioness of Ripon already knew him (she was half-Russian herself). But it was entirely due to Thomas Beecham's foresight and flair (and his father's purse) that Diaghilev was able to establish at one stroke an entirely new dimension of production in the British theatre.

It is difficult today to recall the state of affairs before his arrival. Everything he did led directly to the formation of the Royal Ballet of today, yet that could scarcely be more different from the Ballets Russes. For the first time there appeared a complete co-ordination of movement, colour, entirely apt and individual scenery, and a score to accompany it all. If this had not been composed to order it had been carefully and expertly orchestrated from the work of a first-rate composer: *Carnaval* from Schumann's piano pieces, *Les Sylphides* from Chopin's. So when the lights went down on the first night of the Russian Ballet in London, 21 June 1911, the expectant audience in the darkened auditorium heard the surprisingly beautiful prelude to Nicholas Tcherepnin's *Le Pavillon d'Armide*. Here was excellent music played by a first-class orchestra, instead of a rag-bag of old ballet tunes turned out by a pit band.

Beecham was frequently in the Opera House watching and listening, observing closely how the experienced ballet conductors worked. Pierre Monteux was extremely skilled and Beecham had learnt sufficient to take over a performance of one ballet. It needed a special knowledge of dancers' demands and a stricter observation of tempo than Beecham usually cared for. Rubato must only occur when it helps the dancers, not for musical effect.

Hammerstein indirectly did Beecham a good turn by allowing him to be relieved of the simultaneous task of organisation and musical direction, thus giving him time to devote to orchestral activities elsewhere. Hammerstein's prospectus appeared towards the end of the Coronation Season so as to catch as many likely patrons as were still in town. He had his committee of titles, but not the experienced nucleus of Floral Street, who might have prevented him from committing a number of solecisms in print and in person.

He boasted that he had come 'to give London an opera house worthy of her'. There were at that time in London some half-dozen theatres which would have proved very adequate to his demands, besides which Covent Garden, Drury Lane and His Majesty's had seemed perfectly worthy to house opera for the past two hundred years. Hammerstein went on to say: 'The present generation in England has still to see grand opera presented in the grand manner, and... it will be my endeavour to supply the deficiency.' And finally: 'I want it to be understood that grand opera is only beginning its career in these islands; that great provincial cities when they reach the level of musical enthusiasm that obtains . . . abroad, will all support their own opera company.'

These were bumptious pronouncements; but they might quite easily have been made by Beecham. Perhaps the statement by Hammerstein which coincided exactly with Beecham's policy was this: 'I seek . . . to present masterpieces by British composers and writers, who will find in the London Opera House the goal of their highest ambition.'

The palatial, though cold, London Opera House opened on 13 November 1911, after a blast of publicity of the kind that most Londoners felt to be vulgar and inappropriate. Hammerstein was an unsophisticated man, self-educated and self-made, but he was generous and completely sincere.

The opening opera *Quo Vadis?* was coolly received by the press, who regarded it as more of a pageant than an opera. Huge, built sets and enormous crowds on the stage did little to invest the production with the right kind of feeling. The composer, Jean Noguès, was as unknown as the principal singers. The slim list of twelve operas in the first season (which went on until early March 1912) did nothing to improve the situation with the press or the public. Hammerstein's plea for support fell upon deaf ears and when he proposed to extend his repertoire Covent Garden threatened to sue him if he dared to mount any of the twenty-four operas of which they held exclusive rights of performance in London. Then he became desperate and announced that he had engaged Caruso for his second season, when he had done nothing of the sort.

In spite of a non-social atmosphere about Hammerstein's opera house, a Royal Command performance was arranged. King George V and Queen Mary arrived and were greeted by the great Oscar, who advanced towards His Majesty with hand outstretched saying 'How are you, King?'

Lady Cunard paid one visit there, sat in a box next to the proscenium arch and, quickly becoming bored, started to talk loudly to members of her party. Hammerstein generally sat in the wings during performances, and on this occasion he could hear the female voice clearly. Becoming irritated he sent somebody to find out whom it belonged to, and when he heard he issued instructions that Lady Cunard be requested to leave his theatre immediately.

Hammerstein used to sit in the wings on a plain chair, back to front, tipping it to and fro, wearing a top hat and smoking a cigar in complete defiance of London fire regulations. At Covent Garden nobody ever wore a hat in the vicinity of the stage (unless it were part of a costume), or smoked on pain of dismissal, or walked across the stage, which is regarded as a sacred area.

During Hammerstein's second season of thirteen operas, from the spring to summer of 1912, he knew he was beaten. Box-office takings on some nights were as little as £50. He lost one million dollars on his London venture and returned to New York where he began again to produce opera until the Met stopped him once and for all.

Beecham had been 'keeping tag' on events in Kingsway and saying nothing. His father was asked whether he intended to take over the now empty London Opera House with its 'For Sale' notices, but he replied that he intended to build his own. Whether he did or not, the statement was enough to silence inquisitive questioning.

In 1912 Diaghilev's company again visited Covent Garden with new ballets and substantially the same principal dancers as before. Beecham conducted Balakirev's *Thamar* on the first night and was warmly received by the audience. Later on in the season he conducted performances of Stravinsky's *L'Oiseau de Feu*. His orchestra had by now absorbed the Russian idiom so well and had become so skilled at assimilating the unfamiliar scores that Diaghilev engaged them, with Beecham, for his Berlin season at the Kroll Theatre for a month in November 1912. This was the first time that a British orchestra had ever played on the mainland of Europe and their performances were highly praised by the Berlin critics.

On their return to Covent Garden to rehearse for the winter opera season which Beecham and his father again sponsored, there was a new Strauss opera to be learned. This was *Der Rosenkavalier*, 'the greatest high comedy in all opera': no more bloodshed and violence but a gentle, passionate comedy that tickled the senses, and a bitter-sweetness at the end of the first and third acts. Beecham had heard the opera when it was first performed in Dresden in the previous winter and already knew the score by heart. He was banking on a Strauss success for the third time running.

Beecham shouldered a great responsibility in this season by conducting seventeen performances out of a total of twenty-one. *Der Rosenkavalier* opened and closed the season and was an enormous success. Margarethe Siems and Elisabeth von der Osten, creators of the Marschallin and Octavian, appeared only on the first night, after which these roles were changed three times. Claire Dux, from Berlin, had been specially engaged by Beecham to sing Sophie, and some thought her even superior to the creator, Minnie Nast. Beecham was highly praised and congratulated on bringing the opera to London and also for his ability to

conduct it from memory, 'if the expression is at all apt in the circumstances' as one astonished music critic stated. Beecham's influence, he
added, was clearly pervading the whole enterprise; also, thanks to the
generosity of Sir Joseph, seats were not overpriced.

Beecham had wisely obtained the services of the baritone Hermann
Gura as producer. Not only did Gura fully appreciate the singers' needs,
but as director of the Berlin Komische Oper he had a distinct flair for
production. He was then at the height of a distinguished double career,
and in this same season he sang Beckmesser under Beecham's baton.
Such a talented man was an ideal member of Beecham's team.

There was also a revival of *Elektra* which this time did not achieve its
former impact and success, and the press accused Beecham of failing to
bring it into clear focus musically and of missing the climaxes. It was
becoming stale to him. He also conducted *Salome*, *Tristan* and *Die
Meistersinger*, while his father looked on, enormously pleased with his
son's ever-growing skill and perfectly content at the manner in which the
Beecham profits were being lavished.

From Covent Garden back to His Majesty's in May and June 1913:
Beecham and Tree decided to co-operate on the original version of
Ariadne auf Naxos. This had received its première in Stuttgart in the
previous October and was unusually difficult to mount. The entertainment began with a new and abridged version of Molière's *Le Bourgeois
Gentilhomme* by Hofmannsthal, now translated again into English (from
Hofmannsthal's text) by W. Somerset Maugham. Afterwards there was a
one-act opera on the subject of Ariadne and Theseus with surprising
intrusions by a Commedia dell'Arte troupe, again by Hofmannsthal and
to a score by Strauss. Strauss had also provided some piquant incidental music to the play.

Tree played Jourdain, and his style in comedy was a good deal broader
than anything which would be acceptable nowadays. Somerset
Maughan's translation was apt and in good taste, but Tree insisted upon
such interpolations as:

> *Servant:* ... the opera of *Ariadne*.
> *Jourdain:* 'Arry who?

Eric Coates was playing the viola in the chamber orchestra of thirty-seven
musicians, and tells how one night he looked up into the box where Tree,
elaborately clad as Jourdain, was sitting and acting the part of a
thoroughly bored ignoramus. Sitting next to him was a man well-known
to Coates, who had been trying to get in to Tree's office in the daytime to

talk business. The only occasion when such a meeting could be arranged was now, during the performance, and of course the man had to get himself suitably dressed up for his 'appearance'. Coates never knew whether he concluded his business or not, but he was never seen there again.

The eight performances of *Ariadne* were cast from European principals who knew their roles already. Beecham conducted every one of them and was considered to have been very shrewd in obtaining the rights for production of the opera so quickly. He conjured sweet sounds from his players – the nucleus of his own orchestra – and reproduced the Strauss score with great skill. He even went to the trouble of obtaining the special kind of harmonium which is called for.

The 'Bourgeois-Ariadne' was a qualified success, as it usually is unless performed under festival conditions. Unless the audience is as interested in the play as they are in the opera the work will probably fall between two separate sets of spectators. Beecham, at any rate, covered himself in glory, but it was only an interlude for him in the year's activities.

He had resigned from the GOS Board because they did not wish to re-engage the Diaghilev Ballet for 1913. Beecham was determined that they should be seen in London again for as long as possible into the future, and so he and his father went into direct opposition to Covent Garden by leasing Drury Lane Theatre for a month in June and July and inviting the Russians to appear there instead.

There was an additional surprise for Londoners. Sir Joseph Beecham's prospectus for the 1913 season stated that a fortunate opportunity had occurred for him to present Russian opera as well as the Russian ballet. Diaghilev was planning a visit of St Petersburg and Moscow artists, with the celebrated St Petersburg Chorus, to Paris in May, and they would then cross the Channel and appear in London. The expense of bringing them over and supporting them was enormous – far too great for the GOS to consider. In addition Sir Joseph advertised the appearance of Feodor Chaliapin, whose fee was £400 a night. (No wonder the GOS had never engaged him.)

All this was of little consequence to Sir Joseph, whose persuasive tone of voice in his prospectus made it sound as though the whole enterprise were a kind of party to which he was inviting the public to be his guests – providing, of course, that they obtained the necessary little pieces of paper from the box office.

In spite of Chaliapin's stunning effect as Boris in Moussorgsky's opera on the first night, it took the public nearly a week to realise that this was a sensation and not to be missed. After that, all seats were at a premium and the artistic success of the season was assured. Lady Cunard attended, taking upon herself the task of 'chief whip' for the Beechams, who all the time insisted that there was no question of rivalry with Covent Garden.

Chaliapin appeared in *Khovanchschina* and *Ivan the Terrible* as well as in *Boris*, and there were some thirty ballets in the programme as well. These included *L'Après-midi d'un Faune*, which many people found scandalous but which Nijinsky's art made perfectly tolerable to others; and Stravinsky's *Sacre du Printemps*, proably the first 'mathematical' score to be heard in London. It was very much misunderstood, in spite of Pierre Monteux's authoritative conducting. The riot which resulted from its première in Paris was not repeated by the polite London audience, but they clearly disliked the work. Instead of romantic ballets Diaghilev was starting to introduce 'modern' scores to works which were even more modern in subject matter. These scores were all by living composers.

Lady Diana Cooper, reputed to be the most beautiful woman in London, was a fanatical attender at all the Russian seasons and became a close friend of Diaghilev's. She was not a member of Lady Cunard's straightforward society crowd although a daughter of the Duke of Rutland; she was first and foremost an artist. Sometimes she put on costume and joined the chorus on stage at Drury Lane, which was a most surprising thing for Diaghilev to have encouraged. But he, who could tell an artist at sight, knew that she would be a temporary acquisition for him.

Otherwise the first of those who were later to become known as the 'lunatic fringe' began to appear among the audience, led by Gertrude Stein always dressed in a thick skirt, white silk shirt and with a little hat perched on top of her huge head. She was accompanied by a sad-looking young woman in oriental dress. Ethel Smyth was there too, of course, dressed in a mannish way, although there was nothing lunatic about her. The eccentricities which these ladies favoured did encourage others to copy them, and the Russians probably turned the heads of ordinary people who wanted to dress up too.

Sir Joseph Beecham's right-hand man at Drury Lane was a former employee at the St Helens factory called Donald Baylis. He had been put to work there as an office-boy in 1895 when he was twelve, and soon attracted attention for his ability as a correspondence clerk and was duly promoted. By 1908 he was secretary to the general manager and well-known to Joseph who had heard him sing in the St Helens Parish Church Choir. Joseph was impressed with his voice and arranged for him to have lessons from a Mr Young in Liverpool and then to study in Italy at his expense. This study included opera stage management, and when Baylis returned to England he was drafted into the chorus at Covent Garden for

Beecham's first season there. After Baylis had become chorus leader it was apparent that his administrative abilities were being wasted, so thenceforward, starting at His Majesty's in the following spring, Baylis was given stage-management jobs to do while he continued to sing small parts. He worked from a table in the recesses of the stage at His Majesty's, dealing with the personal matters of any member of the company who wanted help. He hated formal dress and invariably wore theatrical costume while attending to his daily tasks at the theatre, ready at a moment's notice to go on and sing his role for that performance. His methods were highly personal yet most efficient, and very soon he was made assistant company manager. By 1913 he was Sir Joseph's general manager, and at last the strain of management was lifted from Thomas's shoulders.

Both the Beechams trusted Baylis implicitly, as did everybody else. Thomas could be evasive; Baylis could always be brought to the point. He had a lot to clear up after Thomas had passed by without definitely agreeing to a particular voice, salary or role. Baylis did all that, and he was invariably right. Yet when something had to have Beecham's approval the way was through Baylis, never direct. It is an especial tribute to him that Beecham managed to appoint him over the head of Diaghilev's capable own régisseur, Serge Grigoriev, when it came to decisions on stage at Drury Lane.

Even though Baylis had exceptional talents it seems unusual, on the face of it, that he was encouraged to such a marked degree by Joseph Beecham. The reason seems to lie in the strong possibility that Baylis was Joseph Beecham's illegitimate son, and consequently Thomas Beecham's half-brother. Baylis went about things in the same manner as Joseph, though his ruthlessness was tempered by a kinder hand; he had the Beecham eyes (as the only photograph which has come to light clearly shows); and he combined his 'father's' astuteness with money and his 'brother's' fine artistic sense. Furthermore, the three of them got on admirably together: it was they who planned the Drury Lane seasons so that they worked successfully, and it is unlikely that Baylis would have been able to assert himself as forcibly as he did unless he were one of the family and not merely a servant to them.

Baylis was born in Halifax and subsequently adopted by a kind, motherly lady of that surname. His true mother (a Miss Ann Perrott) may have been a servant in the Beecham household, and Joseph could easily have taken advantage of her as he often did. In those days a pregnant, unmarried girl was generally sent to have her baby as far from home as possible, especially if the master of the house was also the child's father.

Many years later, while Baylis was with the Beecham Opera Company in Manchester, his secretary reported that a lady downstairs had called to see him, saying that she was his mother. He declined to meet her, telling his secretary that she couldn't possibly be his mother – just somebody, the secretary assumed, who was on the cadge from an affluent man. So she was sent away. But was this woman Baylis's natural mother wishing to see her successful son? Whether he was ignorant of the truth about his birth or whether he did know but wished to shut out the real past will very likely remain a mystery. However, there can be no doubt that Donald Baylis played a vitally important part in the success of the two Drury Lane seasons, whose mechanics were entirely constructed, operated and maintained by his genius for organisation.

Beecham recounts a very good story of the day when the St Petersburg Chorus revolted during a performance of *Boris* at Drury Lane. They considered themselves good enough – and they were – to receive the same treatment as a single star performer, and were equally temperamental and tetchy. Because of a complete misunderstanding against Chaliapin they refused to appear in the Coronation Scene in the first act, leaving only the English supers to represent the vast crowd that normally added so much to the spectacle. On this night the scene went for nothing. Chaliapin was furious and knocked down the first chorus man he saw when he came off stage. At once the whole mob attacked him, but he was saved from actual harm by the soprano Dawidowa (who sang the Tsar's son, Feodor). She threw herself on him, thereby making the men hold back. After discussions during the intervals it was agreed that the chorus would take part in the final scene as usual, and after the opera was finished and the audience had gone their arguments went on late into the night.

Suddenly their mood changed. One Russian expression of goodwill followed another until Chaliapin was mobbed again, this time to be hugged and kissed by every member of the chorus in turn. Beecham and Baylis were watching this performance, but when all eyes turned in their direction Beecham – who had comprehended most of the discussions through watching expressions, though knowing nothing of the language – feared that he might be the next object of their affection, and hastened away with the indefatigable Baylis. The Russians stayed in the theatre all night, drinking tea and celebrating their victory over themselves.

Diaghilev was well pleased with the success of the 1913 Drury Lane season and agreed with Sir Joseph that he would return the following summer, bringing Chaliapin, some new ballets, Nijinsky and Karsavina as usual, but a different opera chorus – from Moscow.

Shortly after the end of the season Beecham's attentions were diverted elsewhere. A new opera company had emerged in the provinces in 1911 under the direction of a Swiss musician called Ernst Denhof. He had previously managed a series of opera tours in Germany and now he organised a successful tour to Leeds, Manchester and Glasgow. In 1912 he proposed to extend his activities and obtained from Beecham the rights to perform Strauss's *Elektra* (in English) and later *The Rose Bearer*. Beecham was pleased to help Denhof and suggested a German conductor whose experience would be useful to him. There were fifty rehearsals of *Elektra* in Hull, where the tour opened, and the opera was well received. To its twelve performances were added five of *The Rose Bearer*, with a mainly English cast.

When Denhof planned another, longer tour for the autumn of 1913 Beecham decided to associate himself more closely with the venture. He introduced his own assistant conductor from Covent Garden, Hans Schilling-Ziemssen, and agreed to be principal conductor himself. The company was the largest ever to tour the British Isles. There were twenty-seven principal singers and a chorus of a hundred; a ballet of twenty-four; an eighty-two-piece orchestra and ten management and staff. To cover costs Denhof had to rely on full houses everywhere, which is not common practice when planning a budget.

At the end of the third week the company were in Manchester and Denhof had lost £4,000. In desperation he telephoned Beecham in London, who was attending to other aspects of his expanding business. Beecham told Denhof to stop the company from panicking if he could, and promised to be in Manchester to speak to them all after the evening performance of *The Flying Dutchman*. He addressed the company on stage and led them to hope that he would be able to save the enterprise which was, at that moment, in grave danger of folding. They would have to have a 'week out' but when they reassembled in Sheffield the tour 'will be continued till the end of the fortnight in Edinburgh at least', he told them, adding that henceforth they were to be known as the Denhof-Beecham Grand Opera Company.

His statement was greeted with wild enthusiasm by the whole of Denhof's 240 employees, whose uncomfortable prospect of ten weeks without work had now evaporated thanks to the veritable *deus ex machina* in the person of Thomas Beecham. He hurried off to catch his train. Denhof was nowhere to be seen.

Beecham had brought with him and had left behind in Manchester the resourceful Baylis and two accountants. Those singers and musicians who knew Baylis felt that his presence among them was a guarantee of success. He re-booked opera houses whose managers, hearing of

Denhof's plight, had started to re-let his bookings. Baylis also instituted 'a hurricane campaign of publicity' that incorporated aggressive assaults in print by Beecham upon the duty of the citizen to art and the artist.

As a result, when the company reassembled in Sheffield ten days later having been helped financially by several philanthropists in the intervening period, they found the house was sold out for the first week. The citizens of Sheffield had reacted in fury to Beecham's attack upon them, and when he arrived in the pit for the opening performance it was to stony silence. But at the end of the opera there was a proud shout of 'Well, Tommy Beecham, are we musical?'

By breaking with convention and peppering the local press wherever they went with what Beecham describes as 'a series of philippics', the tour ended in Edinburgh with only two other Scottish dates cancelled but a provocative week's return to Manchester thrust in for good measure. Edinburgh was Denhof's home town and he ended his days there as he was before he founded the opera company which bore his name: a teacher.

The 1914 prospectus of opera and ballet at Drury Lane for the summer of 1914 appeared in February and promised an even more exciting repertoire than the previous summer's. The season would run for almost ten weeks, starting with *Der Rosenkavalier* and *Die Zauberflöte* given alternately for a week before the Russians arrived and presented *Boris* again.

In 1914 *Die Zauberflöte* was considered by most people, and by Sir Joseph in particular, to be the dullest and most impossible opera that Mozart had written. But Thomas wished to revive it and had been working out his method of doing so for some time past. Sir Joseph refused to back such an idea and so Thomas undertook to make any loss his own responsibility. On this basis, and with sympathetic head-shaking from Joseph, it was built in to the programme, being the second of the two German operas which opened the season. In the previous year Thomas had been delighted at Claire Dux's performance in *Der Rosenkavalier* and had engaged her again to sing both Pamina and Sophie. She was an instant success. *Die Zauberflöte* had such notices that at a subsequent performance a whole host of celebrated singers from Covent Garden – Caruso, Melba, Destinn – as well as Chaliapin, were in front to hear her. According to Beecham, Nellie Melba's words to Claire Dux afterwards, 'You are my successor!', were an artistic accolade that nobody else had ever received from this prima donna. Yet when Beecham found Claire Dux singing moderately well in Berlin it was he who had coached her and modelled her performance of the well-known arias, making them something exceptional. It was Beecham's idea to frame her on that huge stage in a small space for her aria 'Ach ich fühls' so that every eye and ear was concentrated upon her; and it was Beecham's idea to set the dialogue between numbers and turn it into recitative. One of the distractions in *Die Zauberflöte* in the past had been the speech. If it was in German it was probably unintelligible; if it was in English it was badly mauled by the singers. Few British singers can speak without their native dialect intruding. For this original treatment of the dialogue (arranged and composed by Emil Kreuz) Beecham was taken to task by three reputable music critics, and Sir Joseph kicked himself for not having trusted a little in Mozart's genius – and in his son's intuition.

Der Rosenkavalier was once more a great public success and as usual had a number of cast changes. A new Octavian called Charlotte Uhr seemed perfection to Beecham, and she sang with the incomparable Siems as Marschallin for the first five performances and with Dux as Sophie. For the last two nights, however, Dux was replaced by a soprano from Hamburg new to London. Her name was accidentally transposed in the programme with that of the Octavian, Joanna Lippe. The real Sophie's name was Lotte Lehmann; she was not noticed and the absence of Dux was regretted. But the fact that she had sung in this opera at all, in London, led to another misunderstanding ten years later which was to have the profoundest influence on her career.

Beecham conducted all *Rosenkavaliers* and *Zauberflötes* – seven performances in nine days, and without a score. An extra *Zauberflöte* was squeezed in on 6 June because of the public clamour to hear Frieda Hempel as Queen of the Night, but Beecham only had one day off before orchestral and final rehearsals for the first night of the ballet, bringing back *Thamar*, though with a slightly changed ending. Its opaque mystery and exciting sensuality were fully achieved by Beecham from memory, and Karsavina was again the cruel seductress who sent all her lovers to their doom on the rocks below her tower.

The first novelty was Borodin's *Prince Igor*, in which Chaliapin took two completely contrasting roles: the careless, sensual profligate, Prince Galitzy, and the small, wiry, sharp and curious Tartar, Khan Kontchak. With the Russian Ballet transformed into Tartars for the Polovtsian camp scene, the effect and the enchantment of the opera produced the most sensational applause that even Beecham could remember having witnessed from an audience.

Nijinsky was no longer a member of Diaghilev's company, having much upset the impresario by marrying a dancer in the previous September. His roles were now taken by Michel Fokine, whom Diaghilev had taken back into his company after an earlier quarrel.

Le Coq d'Or was another notable addition to the repertoire, a fairy-tale in which Karsavina caused a sensation as the Queen of Shemakhan. The work, by Rimsky-Korsakov, integrates singers and dancers, and Karsavina's singing part was taken by a soprano in the wings. But the composer's son, Alexander Rimsky-Korsakov, wrote a stern letter to *The Times*, complaining that this was not the manner in which his father wanted it done. The singers were arrayed on both sides of the stage in brilliant scarlet ('like Chelsea Pensioners') while the action went on between them. Diaghilev ignored this letter, just as he had ignored Ravel who was equally furious with Diaghilev for having jettisoned the chorus altogether from the ballet *Daphnis and Chloë*. Diaghilev used sometimes to ride roughshod over creators of works which he had commissioned from them, but always so as to simplify, if not to purify, the original intentions. However, this was entirely Diaghilev's concern, and Beecham did not enter into it.

In July Beecham conducted three well-spaced-out performances of *Dylan*, second opera in the trilogy by Josef Holbrooke. Hammerstein had produced the first of these in 1911. 'If a foreigner can mount one of my operas,' said Holbrooke to Beecham, 'I expect you to do the same, if not the whole cycle.' It is a very curious cycle called *The Children of Don*, and it was cash from Holbrooke's patron that made Beecham agree, for it does not belong anywhere near the Drury Lane season of 1914. It is not in the same class. But since Beecham's policy was to help British composers, and there seemed to be a bottomless purse, he got round his father to include it. The critics were scathing and the public gave *Dylan* little support. Those who came rejoiced in some of the naïvely unintentional strokes of humour such as the hero's opening line: 'I have sung, I can sing better.' There was a feebly contrived effect of 'changing a man into a wolf' by means of an obvious, revolving platform, which always produced laughter. Beecham apologised for *Dylan* by saying that he included it for the sake of variety, but its clumsy operatic construction and doubtful dramatic strokes failed to achieve the desired effect. On the other hand, the scenery was wonderful, and a 'projected' flight of birds, representing the chorus, was an interesting idea.

At the end of the penultimate week of the season Pierre Monteux, who was to conduct *Petrouchka* on the following Monday, demanded leave of absence to go to Paris until Tuesday. His wife had just had a daughter. Diaghilev told Beecham that he would have to step in and take over the direction of *Petrouchka* with thirty-six hours in which to learn it. Beecham did so. He had already learned *Der Rosenkavalier, Die*

Zauberflöte, and *Thamar* by heart, and now it was *Petrouchka*'s turn. His orchestra was inordinately proud.

Donald Baylis had the heaviest season in his experience. His was the final responsibility for changes from one opera to another (ballet sets are simple by comparison) and it is to his great credit that there were no major changes to Sir Joseph's prospectus which had come out in the previous February. Baylis was in at the planning stage, of course, and here lay the secret of his success. Apart from the cancellation of the ballet *Antar*, with *Papillons* in its place wherever it was billed; the extra *Zauberflöte*, and a reversal in the order of ballets on the last night, there were no changes to the printed prospectus at all. On more than one occasion it was thought that Baylis had erred in his calculations as to what could or could not be done in the short time available. Chaliapin came on to the Drury Lane stage one morning expecting to find everything in order for the evening's opera. There was chaos. The great man went howling to Baylis to say that the date of the opening would have to be postponed. Baylis merely stated that Mr Beecham knew exactly what he was doing. Mr Beecham (and his father) certainly knew what they were doing when they appointed Baylis to be their general manager.

Richard Strauss came in person to conduct his long ballet *The Legend of Joseph* with a book by Count Harry Kessler and Hugo von Hofmannsthal after the biblical account of Potiphar's Wife and her attempted seduction of the beautiful youth. Nijinsky was to have danced Joseph and to have created the choreography, but since he was no longer with Diaghilev another Joseph had to be found. This was a relatively inexperienced boy-dancer called Leonid Massine. He was put under the tuition of Maestro Cecchetti, his steps were modified so as to come within his abilities, and his looks helped greatly to carry him through his début. The score was as bloated and as disappointing as that of *Der Rosenkavalier* had been fresh and delightful; but the sets, costumes and staging were the most sumptuous in living memory, and contributed very largely to the ballet's acceptance. Some music critics were candid about the score; some damned it outright. Strauss conducted the first four performances and Pierre Monteux took over the rest, although Beecham was due to succeed the composer on the rostrum. Even so, in this season alone he had conducted thirteen performances of opera and three ballets.

Diaghilev and Sir Joseph again agreed to meet at Drury Lane for the summer of 1915, but on 4 August 1914, ten days after the end of the season, England, France and Russia were at war with Germany. The immediate artistic result was the closure of Covent Garden Opera House until 1919. Both Diaghilev's tour in Germany and Beecham's orchestral tour of the same country were cancelled. There had also to be a moratorium on plans for 1915 and beyond.

Beecham did not dwell upon the disaster but looked round to see whether there was anybody in need of practical help. At least one musician benefited immediately. Igor Stravinsky remembers his debt of gratitude to Beecham at the beginning of the war: 'He sent 2,500 Swiss francs to me ... in the event I might be cut off from my income in Russia.' Money was everything to Stravinsky, though jealousy was not far behind, and he also recalled: 'Perhaps because we never shared a concert together, we were always on good terms.' Stravinsky and Beecham seem a most unlikely pair to be 'on good terms' for very long, as may be implied in Beecham's own reaction to Stravinsky when he was asked in a broadcast many years later what he thought of the composer of *Petrouchka*. 'Oh, Igor. Igor's a good egg,' was his reply.

By 1915 Beecham had fresh plans of his own. The singers whom he had collected round him for the opéra-comique season of 1910, and those from the now defunct Denhof Opera Company, were all established British artists who could, without much difficulty, be formed into a self-contained opera company with a repertory tailored to suit their voices: no Wagner for the time being, no *Boris Godunov*, but smaller, more intimate operas written for intimate surroundings in the theatre which Beecham had in mind. This was the Shaftesbury. Several rows of stalls would have to be removed to make way for the orchestra; the acoustic was fair; the house was not so small that a season couldn't pay its way if the bill of fare were attractive enough. And the name: the Beecham Opera Company.

At the outbreak of war all German musicians, including singers, had been sent packing. This meant that a number of important seats in the Beecham Orchestra were now filled by slightly less capable musicians than before. Others had joined up and left further gaps, but very soon the Beecham Opera Company, the Beecham Opera Chorus and the Beecham Orchestra appeared together for the first time on 2 October 1915.

In *A Mingled Chime* Beecham makes the remark: 'It seemed to me that the best individual contribution a single person could make to the necessity of the moment was to form an opera company.' The 'necessity of the moment' was not so much the dreadful war as the lack of employment opportunities for singers, musicians and stage craftsmen.

He conducted Gounod's *Romeo and Juliet* on the opening night, and again three nights later. He then left the running of the season to his capable staff, headed by Baylis, King and Chapman. His conductors were at first Percy Pitt and Hamish McCunn, who between them directed for the opening three weeks. Later they were reinforced by Julius Harrison,

Landon Ronald (who only conducted *Carmen*) and Harold Howell. The repertoire included, besides the two operas already mentioned, *La Bohème, Tosca, Faust, Madame Butterfly, Cav.* and *Pag.* and *Tales of Hoffmann.*

There was no other opera to be heard in London at this time, and troops on leave or stationed close by, as well as office- and munition-workers, all came to enjoy these well-sung and ably directed performances. With seats ranging from reserved stalls at half a guinea to one-shilling gallery seats, the house was generally quite full and the season lasted until mid-December.

A fortnight later the Shaftesbury reopened to another season in which the repertoire was increased and the singers given a short but necessary rest in the evenings while they rehearsed in the daytime. The new season, which opened for a Boxing-Day matinée, had a very large audience, and the *Times* critic complimented the company on what they were doing, suggesting that they were being recognised as a permanent institution. Moreover, the audiences were there to enjoy themselves, and that was exactly what Beecham wanted. He was in Italy and did not return to London until a week after New Year's Day. Beecham was satisfied with the way things were going. He could rely implicitly on 'the machine', and yet he needed somebody else, somebody who could understudy him and be his assistant in every sense.

One night he went to Queen's Hall and watched a young man leave his place in the second violins of the orchestra, conduct a composition of his own, and then return to his seat. The young man was called Eugène Goossens, the brother of Léon, Sidonie and Marie. Beecham invited Goossens to call on him in his Cavendish Square house the next morning, and when he asked whether he should bring his violin Beecham replied: 'Good Lord, no!'

Goossens arrived as requested and found Beecham in pink pyjamas and one of his dazzling mauve silk dressing-gowns. He instantly appointed Goossens in a general capacity as assistant conductor to him – for operas and for concerts – to arrange and score works as required, to take rehearsals, to coach singers, to do anything, in fact, which he required. Goossens was with Beecham for five years, and many times found himself thrown into a new work with little warning. Only one other musician ever occupied the same position on Beecham's staff, and that was Norman Del Mar thirty years later.

The management of the Shaftesbury seasons consisted of Beecham and Robert Courtneidge (father of Dame Cecily). But Beecham was already looking towards another theatre, tours, the expansion of the company and a firmer foot on the ground so that when the war was over he would already be established with a national opera company. He knew very well that he would be unable to hold all the good singers in peacetime, and that events had so far moved very much in his favour.

In 1916 Beecham planned a month of opera in Manchester and after that a winter season at the Aldwych Theatre, which his father owned. Both men were titled now, for Thomas had been knighted in the New Year's Honours of 1916.

Up to now, Beecham's opera company had been of opéra-comique dimensions, but he was determined to enlarge it so that he would be able to mount any opera, especially the exciting and colourful Russian works which fascinated him as much as they did the Drury Lane audiences. In addition, the sets and costumes for these productions were still in London as Diaghilev had been unable to get them out before the war began.

Beecham rested his principals for the heavy works ahead, and the two weeks of opera at the Aldwych which prefaced the company's bursting into flower in Manchester included *The Magic Flute*, *Tales of Hoffmann* and *La Bohème*, all of which Beecham conducted.

He had increased his principal singers in all vocal ranges and had enlarged the chorus, but he gave them and his London orchestra a rest while he used northern choristers and the augmented Hallé in Manchester. He was thus ready to do what every impresario of a large-scale musical enterprise (including Ivor Novello) has done since: he opened in Manchester, where the audiences are notoriously critical. 'What we does in Manchester today, they does in London tomorrow,' as the saying goes.

'Sir Thomas Beecham's Great Manchester Season of Grand Opera' opened at the New Queen's Theatre on 10 May. Seats were at the encouraging prices of a half-guinea stall down to a one-shilling gallery, but the theatre *was* in the 'wrong part' of Manchester. The repertoire not only comprised a selection of well-played-in works from the Shaftesbury, but also included some new ones. Among them was *Boris Godunov*. Those members of the regular chorus who travelled up to Manchester by train rehearsed all the way there in a saloon coach, specially booked and with a piano installed in it. There was great astonishment from other passengers on station platforms when the train stopped en route. In Manchester they met the rest of the chorus and now, for the first time, the Beecham Opera Company had reached the size and strength of one suited to Covent Garden or Drury Lane.

The first scene of *Boris Godunov* opens with a duo by the cor anglais and first bassoon. Archie Camden was the Hallé's bassoon and he recalls his astonishment at finding that the cor anglais player had not arrived, and consequently he had to play a solo at the dress rehearsal. 'It's all right,' said Beecham, 'he'll be here for the performances.'

Boris won great public support and acclaim in Manchester. Beecham conducted the first performance with impeccable Russian style (gained from absorbing all the Drury Lane pre-war performances) while the magnificent sets and costumes set new standards in Manchester. Beecham also conducted a single *Lucia di Lammermoor*, all the *Tristans*, all the *Otellos* and half the *Bohèmes*. *Tristan* was sung and played with such feeling and tension that its German (i.e. enemy) origin did not prevent its inclusion in the repertoire from then on, and it became one of the best patronised operas throughout the war.

Frank Mullings, Beecham's principal tenor, sang a marvellous Otello to Mignon Nevada's Desdemona. Those who remember Mullings still say that his nobility and total absorption in the roles he was playing made his all-round performances finer – in the case of Otello – than those of Zenatello and Vinay.

When it looked as if Baylis and Julius Harrison might be conscripted, Beecham did some judicious arranging with the authorities and the two men were commissioned into the Royal Flying Corps HQ at Regent's Park, attending only a minimal number of parades. Beecham presented their work as being far too important to be interrupted, and their experience and ability made them irreplaceable. Any musician who was exempt on grounds of disability or ill-health wore a khaki armband on the platform or in the pit. (By 1916 the public reacted fiercely to conscientious objectors and scrimshankers.)

By the early autumn of 1916 Beecham was forecasting an annual programme for his company: two seasons in London, a season in Manchester, then others in cities which he knew were able to accommodate a grand opera company. The GOS might well be left to continue its normal, international season at Covent Garden every summer while he was at Drury Lane. He would have to wait and see about that. Meanwhile his principals were becoming welded into a wonderful ensemble and deriving great satisfaction and contentment from what they were doing.

Beecham also kept them on their toes. Sometimes he handed over the baton to another of his conductors at short notice, because he had 'an important engagement'. He might be standing drinks to off-duty singers at the Waldorf Hotel across the road and on Beecham land. He might be in front, making notes. He might suddenly appear through the pass door on the stage. But if he got in the way there he was perfectly prepared for George King to tell him to make himself scarce – politely.

On the other hand, Beecham might tell the conductor of the performance about to start in half an hour's time that *he* was going to conduct, and that the good fellow might have the rest of the day off. The sudden appearance of Beecham in the pit was a sign for great rejoicing by the audience but one of woe for the odd understudy who had not properly learned his or her role. Beecham was a master of precision, and he asked for and expected it from all his company. His eye never missed a makeshift action or object, and it took in every mistake. So did his ear.

Of the singers, Mullings was especially valuable because he sang both Otello and Tristan. Robert Radford was principal bass, as reliable as a rock. Agnes Nicholls, Miriam Licette, Caroline Hatchard and Lena Maitland; Frederic Austin, Frederick Ranalow, Percy Heming, Norman Allin and Robert Parker were some of those who supported the theory that a British National Opera Company was in existence.

A tenor called Frederick Blamey sang a notable Samson in the Saint-Saens opera, and one evening, having partaken of 'a glass of dinner' and then another, tottered on for his last scene as the blind man, well and truly led by a boy. He sang splendidly and rose majestically to his top note. The stage manager, King, stood watching him like a lynx. He sensed that something untoward was about to happen, and his sixth sense saved him. Blamey was about to lunge forward to pull down the columns which supported the temple when King pressed the button for a blackout. He was just in time. Blamey missed both columns and fell flat on his face, out for the count.

Beecham conducted twenty-one performances at the Aldwych between 20 October and the end of the year. But three days after his first *Bohème* on 20 October his father died very suddenly. The performance on the evening of the day of the funeral was cancelled and a number of principals went up to St Helens to pay their respects to the man who had provided for them all.

After this Beecham seemed determined to work out of his system all his grief, sense of loss and apprehension for the future. He did this by conducting more frequently than his singers could remember. On two Saturdays he appeared at both matinée and evening performances to conduct, and when one of these days had *Tristan* beginning at 1.30 p.m. and *Bohème* beginning at 7.30 p.m. one can only assume that he was being driven by some power beyond normal human possession.

Once over this, however, he went on as before. The company paid a second visit to Manchester in 1917, after seasons at Birmingham,

Glasgow and Edinburgh. The *Manchester Guardian* in the spring of 1917 presents a chilling spectacle, even today: there were only two notices of the operas in a month, for the newspaper was filled with lists of casualties day after day.

In the summer of 1917 Beecham took Drury Lane Theatre where his most revolutionary production was, without doubt, *The Marriage of Figaro*. Just as he had rethought *Die Zauberflöte* there in 1914, so now he set about presenting Mozart's social masterpiece anew so that not a single detail should go unnoticed. He invited the greatest authority on eighteenth-century theatre, Nigel Playfair, to produce it, which Playfair agreed to do on condition that he could coach the principal singers himself. The designer, who had been with Beecham since 1915, was Hugo Rumbold, son of a British Ambassador, who wore immaculate clothes and was as great a craftsman as he was a humorist. He painted all his own scenery.

Playfair returned to Beaumarchais and substituted dialogue for the recitatives (the *Zauberflöte* scheme in reverse). As this is generally unintelligible because of the speed at which it has to be delivered, much was made clear by firm, strong and incomparable diction. When singing-actors, scenery and orchestra came together for the first time the impact was magical.

Beecham conducted 'in his most fastidious manner', according to Goossens, who marvelled at the production. Maggie Teyte, who heard Agnes Nicholls sing the Countess (from among the audience and not as Cherubino), described her performance as equal in beauty to Claire Dux's Pamina four years earlier. 'What voices they had, and what style!' she says, and 'Sir Thomas Beecham, that great interpreter of Mozart's music... I know of no one who goes so close to the heart of the matter.'

This *Figaro* has been called a landmark in British operatic history, and it should be remembered that Beecham not only conducted it but also had a hand in the selection and translation from Beaumarchais, as well as advising both Nigel Playfair and Hugo Rumbold in their work throughout. The production filled Drury Lane and was one of Beecham's finest operatic achievements.

He contemplated staging Glinka's *A Life for the Tsar* but events in Russia were moving towards a state of affairs where Tsar Nicholas's life was worth nothing at all. But Bizet's *Fair Maid of Perth* achieved enormous popularity; it is a true opéra-comique.

Beecham was becoming extremely worried about his father's estate, the assets, his own money and general prospects which, of course, affected the future of his whole company. His 1918 season at Drury Lane was ruined by the Zeppelin raids on London and lost him a great deal of money; the public were scared away from large buildings in case they were bombed. Lady Cunard fought a losing battle with her friends and supporters, and it was she who stood up in her box one night during a performance of *Figaro* when the music was being drowned by anti-aircraft fire. She shouted at the audience to follow the example of the singers and carry on as if nothing else was happening. Her motor-car and its chauffeur were to be seen outside Drury Lane every night. Lady Diana Cooper recalls that she found Emerald Cunard on the way there one evening, having dined exceptionally well and sheltered from a raid. She declared that she simply must get to the theatre to die with Beecham.

When peace came in 1918 Beecham was almost at the end of his financial resources. Although he was heavily in debt, even to money-lenders, he imagined that there would shortly be a return to the happy financial ease of pre-1914, and all would be well. In fact he was never financially comfortable again, for 1914 was past and gone – except in one respect. Covent Garden opened its doors again. Beecham had rejoined the Grand Opera Syndicate on special terms, for his late father's newly-constituted Estate Company was now the landlord of the Royal Opera House.

The prospectus was issued in early 1919, announcing the possibility of Toscanini conducting Puccini's *Trittico*, heard for the first time in New York in the previous December. Beecham was back in business for sure, snapping up the latest operas as he had done in 1910. But the *Trittico* did not materialise in 1919 because of a personal feud between Puccini and Toscanini ('that pig', as the composer called him).

Beecham opened the season on 12 May with Melba as Mimi and Tom Burke as Rodolfo in *La Bohème*. He also conducted Massenet's *Manon* (with Edvina), *Thaïs* (with the same soprano), *Roméo et Juliette* (with Melba) and, for the first time, *Un Ballo in Maschera* (with Destinnova, as she now liked to be called since the establishment of Czechoslovakia). Beecham also conducted Isidore de Lara's *Naïl* with a cast of Beecham Opera Company principals headed by Rosina Buckman and Frank Mullings. He shared the conducting with Eugène Goossens and four others, and there were twenty operas in the three months' season of eighty-two performances, an astonishing achievement so soon after the end of the war. It would have been quite impossible had not most of the Beecham Opera Company singers already been engaged and some of the operas cast with them in principal roles. In addition, they frequently took over from the visiting 'stars': *La Bohème* had four different Mimis – Melba, Rosina Buckman, Margaret Sheridan and Jeanne Brola.

Beecham could again command most of the international singers as he had done before the war, and they were needed, in his view, to complement his own excellent singers in the summer season. But they brought with them their usual temperaments. After a stormy meeting with Dame Nellie Melba in his office, when Beecham pretended he did not know who she was, she soon calmed down and they were thereafter on good terms. Although he admired her technique, vocal purity and professionalism, Beecham admitted that there was something lacking, something vital which prevented her performance from being in every sense that of a great singer. Nellie Melba was not welcome on the continent of Europe, least of all in Italy. Only Britain and the United States accepted her wholeheartedly.

Another soprano from Australia called Elsa Stralia, actually the daughter of a German baritone called Fischer who had settled there, was a member of the 1919 company at Covent Garden. She had made her London début there in 1913 (though not with Beecham, who was at Drury Lane) and had become associated with him later on a personal basis, having sung Aida with the Beecham Opera Company during the war. Her promising career petered out in 1929.

Among the tenors, Giovanni Martinelli, Fernand Ansseau and Ulysses Lappas were joined by Tom Burke whom both Beecham and Melba preferred for the opening *Bohème*. He and Martinelli, especially, were in glorious voice; and Martinelli was, in any case, about to inherit Caruso's mantle. Caruso never returned to Covent Garden after 1914, and died in Naples in 1921.

The 1919 audiences were very different from those of 1914. Not all Lady Cunard's followers could afford any longer to subscribe for the whole season, and there were too many empty stalls and grand tier seats. Elsewhere dress was informal, and the old feeling of occasion was somehow missing.

Beecham did his best to trump a rival season by the Carl Rosa Company at the Lyceum Theatre, by promoting a run of Lecocq's delicious *Daughter of Madame Angot* at Drury Lane in co-operation with Arthur Collins. Three of Beecham's singers were in the principal roles and Goossens was in the pit. But it failed to attract the kind of audience which relishes wit and sparkle and a French elegance that had so long been absent from the London stage. Beecham took it off after only four weeks.

He followed what had been an astonishing success at Covent Garden with a winter season of his own. This was in two parts, from early November until just before Christmas and then from the end of February until just before Easter, which fell in mid-April. Since this was not a celebrity season in co-operation with the Syndicate Beecham returned to work with his British singers, who sang 104 performances of twenty-six operas unaided. There were magnificent performances of *Otello* and *Tristan* with Mullings again. Beecham conducted twenty-eight performances including *Bohème*, *Le Coq d'Or*, *Fair Maid of Perth*, *Falstaff*, *Naïl*, *Figaro*, *Otello*, *Samson and Delilah*, *Tosca* and *Tristan*. He also revived *A Village Romeo and Juliet* for three performances, all of which he conducted, and closed the season with *The Mastersingers*. Afterwards he told the capacity audience that the season had been a great success, and that opera in English could now be taken as the rule.

For the 1920 summer season Beecham again joined the GOS and the season lasted for nearly twelve weeks. There were sixty-nine performances of seventeen operas, an opera-ballet and thirteen different ballets. These, to general public delight, were performed by the Diaghilev Company, in London again after an enforced absence of six years. Although Diaghilev had been deprived of some of his most treasured dancers and had met untold difficulties during the war, he was still searching for new ideas and finding up-and-coming young men to help him achieve his artistic ambitions by means of their scores, their designs or their choreography.

Diaghilev brought a fair number of the familiar ballets with him in 1920, but a new element was creeping in: a kind of acid flavour, more subtle than the harshness which had been so obvious in 1914. This was nowhere more evident than in Stravinsky's *Pulcinella* (after Pergolesi), which had a Picasso set. The opera-ballet, *Le Astuzie Femminili*, was based on a Cimarosa score arranged by Respighi and a set by José Maria Sert, humorously out of perspective to some people, aggravatingly so to others. Diaghilev was, as usual, moving just ahead of the times. Beecham left the conducting of these new works to others but was glad to have his former Russian colleague with him again. The Grand Opera Syndicate had never, on the face of it, been interested in the Ballet and only welcomed it to the 1911 season because of the Hammerstein opposition. This time their involvement was going to produce unexpected results.

One of the most interesting sopranos to appear in this season was a Spanish coloratura called Graziella Pareto. Beecham greatly admired her: 'this remarkable artist had a voice of exquisite beauty, haunting pathos and flawless purity' and possessed 'a slight and distinguished appearance'. Of her Violetta, he declared that her representation was 'easily the most attractive and satisfying in my recollection'. He conducted her four performances of Leïla in *Les Pêcheurs de Perles* but

Right Sir Thomas Beecham, Bart., businessman. *Below* a picture from one of the sales catalogues of the Beecham Covent Garden Estate auctions in 1920, showing three desirable lots – the Strand Theatre, Waldorf Hotel and Aldwych Theatre – taken from the opposite site during the building of Bush House.

Left Dora Labbette (b. 1 the beautiful soprano wh sang in Beecham's revise *Messiah* in 1926 and ther at many of his concerts. 1935 she adopted the na Lisa Perli to help gain an entrance into opera.

Right Maggie Teyte (1888–1976), one of the foremost Mélisandes of her time and an exquisite Hänsel. She performed for Beecham during his Mozart season at His Majesty's in 1910 and also for two seasons at Covent Garden in 1937.

Beecham delivers his funeral oration over Delius's second grave at Limpsfield on 26 May 1935. The composer had died in the previous June and was buried in Grez-sur-Loing, but his remains were disinterred and removed to England, where he lies next to his wife, Jelka.

Beecham in action at a rehearsal with the LPO, which he formed in 1932; and playing the part of Sir Thomas Cromwell in a family play at Lympne Castle in Kent, the home of Henry Beecham (summer 1936). *Below* With Ludmilla Tchernicheva and Leonid Massine after a performance of the ballet *Thamar* at Covent Garden, August 1935.

neither of her two Violettas nor two sprightly Norinas in an otherwise poor production of *Don Pasquale*. Beecham afterwards lamented the fact that Pareto never returned to London. She sang at Ravinia (Chicago) and at the Met, where she sang Violetta; and she gave a single performance at the Salzburg Festival of 1931, curiously enough a month before Beecham's sole appearance in the same festival. Pareto was still alive in 1978.

Puccini came to London to superintend the delayed production of his *Trittico*. This triple bill has three contrasting operas: *Il Tabarro* – blood and thunder; *Suor Angelica* – an all-female cast in a convent, with a miracle at the end; and *Gianni Schicci*, a comedy about mourners round the bedside of their rich relative who only pretends to be dead. The conducting was left to Beecham's Italian assistant, Gaetano Bavagnoli, but as artistic director Beecham intervened in discussions over the set for *Suor Angelica*. Puccini refused any changes because it was purposely copied from a convent he knew, but the design prevented significant parts of the action from being seen everywhere in the house; some could not be seen at all. Consequently it was by far the least successful of the three operas (and still generally is, irrespective of its set), so Beecham ordered it to be dropped for four performances. The two other parts of the *Trittico* were played with a ballet as makeweight. Puccini was furious, and referred to Beecham as 'the Purge', presumably with the family business in mind.

Beecham conducted only nine performances in this season, three of which caused him a good deal of trouble. He had persuaded Dame Clara Butt to sing *Orfeo*, a role which demands a real contralto voice. There was no denying that she possessed this, but in other requirements for the opera stage she was found wanting. Nor could she seem to keep in time with the orchestra, and the press was most unkind about her.

Towards the end of the season there were rumours that Beecham's company was in real financial difficulties. At lunchtime on Friday 30 July a notice went up on the outside of the Opera House stating that the evening performance of the Diaghilev Ballet was cancelled. On the advice of his solicitors Diaghilev had removed his entire company from Covent Garden and had issued a writ against the Beecham Opera Company for non-payment. The GOS directors were much put out by the incident and refused to support Beecham, not least because the season had made a staggering loss.

The Beecham Opera Company went out on a provincial tour in something like desperation, in an effort to keep together the wonderful organisation that had all but established itself as the National Opera. But after four weeks in Glasgow they closed with *Carmen* on 4 December 1920. The Company went into voluntary liquidation, and an order in bankruptcy was made against their founder, supporter, champion and figurehead, Sir Thomas Beecham.

After he had achieved such spectacular results it seemed unkind of the fates to demolish his empire so completely. Beecham admits that part of the trouble lay in the unexpected deaths of his two lieutenants. One was his brilliant lawyer, the other was Donald Baylis. The strain of serving as an RAF officer in the daytime and the opera company's general manager at night undoubtedly hastened Baylis's early and tragic death in May 1920, at the very time when, as it turned out, Beecham needed him most of all.

It is tempting to reflect on the possible change in Beecham's later circumstances had Baylis lived and had the Beecham Opera Company not folded. Baylis's presence at the July meeting of creditors could have had dramatic results. Had Beecham 'gone it alone' at Covent Garden without the Diaghilev Ballet in 1920, and had he fulfilled his own statement at the end of the previous season that 'Opera in English can now be taken as the general rule', all this would not have happened. Beecham very nearly succeeded and has been blamed ever since because he had all the cards and played them wrongly. But as with everything else he did, success or failure was magnificent. So, too, was the collapse of the Beecham Opera Company.

Chapter Four

THE COVENT GARDEN ESTATE

BEHIND THE ROYAL OPERA HOUSE, in the silent remains of what was until recently a busy fruit and vegetable market, stands a colonnaded building that was once a zoo. On a pediment at the northern end of it, facing the Opera House, is a coat of arms and the motto *Che sara sara*. This is the family crest of the Dukes of Bedford, owners of the Market and many acres round it since the end of the seventeenth century.

The English Dukes were finding themselves in a decreasingly enviable position in politics and the public eye at the beginning of King George V's reign in 1910. In the previous year Lloyd George had spoken during the Liberals' Budget crisis, saying 'A fully equipped duke costs as much to keep up as two Dreadnoughts, and dukes are just as great a terror, and they last longer.' It was evident, as he also pointed out, that 'public opinion was setting strongly against the accumulation of large landed properties in the hands of individuals.' At an election meeting near Woburn in 1911 the Duke of Bedford was accused of possessing 'vast slums' in London where his tenants lived 'in misery and squalor'.

As a result of these slanders the Duke of Bedford realised that it would be prudent if he were to offer less of a target to jealousy, uninformed opinion and the radical element. So in 1913 his advisers began to make discreet enquiries over the sale of part of his inheritance, the largest and most valuable piece of land that had ever reached the property market, called the Covent Garden Estate.

The Most Noble Herbrand, 11th Duke of Bedford, K.G., was the landlord of Covent Garden Market, the only public market in private hands and a thorn in his side for many years past. Such an important centre of Britain's internal trade might easily be snatched from him by statute, and the ever-increasing laws and by-laws which involved him in expenditure on upkeep caused His Grace to consider selling it outright. The chief adviser in the Bedford Estate Office in London considered it to be 'the most dangerous possession of all'.

Although the Market was at the centre of the property for sale, far more attractive plots within the fourteen acres existed: the Royal Opera House; the Theatre Royal, Drury Lane; the Aldwych and Strand Theatres; the Waldorf Hotel; the Bow Street Police Court; the GPO in Bedford Street; St Peter's Hospital; the National Sporting Club; and many public houses and restaurants, including Rules and the Boulestin.

In the first instance a Mr (later Sir) Harry Mallaby-Deeley, a pioneer in cheap clothing, Unionist MP for Harrow and speculator in land on a large scale, offered to buy the Covent Garden Estate from the Duke of Bedford for two million pounds. It was rumoured for some time that he was acting on behalf of Lord Rothschild. His offer was based on sixteen years' net produce of Market tolls and twenty-two years' net rental of the remaining properties. Although the Duke stood to lose £10,000 a year in income from the tolls and rents at this price, his advisers all urged 'Sell!'

The negotiations, which began in November 1913, went on amid enormous public interest, especially when Mallaby-Deeley disagreed with·the Duke over his wish to reclaim the Bedford boxes at Covent Garden and Drury Lane Theatres. These had accidentally been included in the sale to Mallaby-Deeley, who now refused to hand them back. When His Grace brought pressure to bear on the would-be purchaser he threatened to sue the Duke for breach of contract. He demanded all the theatres, not exclusions within them. In any case Mallaby-Deeley jibbed at paying the £20,000 deposit asked for, and the public was most curious to know how he was going to find it.

By now, other speculators were making offers to Mallaby-Deeley for the Estate, among them James White, famous – if not infamous – property and finance broker whose name had been made overnight when a taxi-load of writs arrived on his doorstep. In May 1914 Mallaby-Deeley commenced an action against the Duke of Bedford, but at the end of June he agreed to sell his option to purchase to Sir Joseph Beecham (whom James White was representing) for a quarter of a million pounds.

Sir Joseph had several reasons for wanting to buy the Estate. Regarding the whole transaction as a purely business deal he intended to float a public company, raise the necessary funds, obtain a large rebate from the Duke for prompt payment, resell the Estate, probably piecemeal, and then retire from the company with a handsome personal profit. He had the means of doing all this, and providing the flow of cash were maintained (and there were probably going to be some crucial moments during the deal) it would be well worth the half a million pounds coming to him at the end.

Sir Joseph recognised that the Market was the least desirable, if not the most unmanageable part of the deal, so that he would quickly have to try and rid himself of it. Nevertheless, the philanthropist in him warmed to the opportunity of making improvements there. Everything pointed to the Market's expansion – or removal elsewhere – and the traders reacted sharply and antagonistically to the news that they were to have a new landlord.

On the other hand, Sir Joseph was tempted to keep the two largest, oldest and most romantic theatres in London. Drury Lane and Covent Garden went back to Restoration times, though the original buildings had been burnt down. Covent Garden appealed to him especially because of what his son Thomas might achieve there. He also liked the idea of being ground landlord of the other theatres and thoroughly relished every stage of the grand deal as it went through.

The Estate was bounded (roughly) by Drury Lane, Aldwych, Catherine Street, Wellington Street and Exeter Street (but exclusive of the Lyceum Theatre and the Strand Palace Hotel); then from the corner of Southampton Row, along Maiden Lane, east of Peabody Buildings to King Street, Floral Street, James Street, Long Acre and back to Drury Lane. Several properties en route were excluded, especially in Long Acre.

On 22 June 1914 *The Times* reported Sir Joseph's interest in buying the Estate, and on 7 July the signing of the contract was given a good deal of publicity. Sir Joseph promised that 'there will be no changes in the management of the property and none of the tenants will be disturbed'. He was in association with Alexander Lawson Ormrod of Lawson Ormrod, stockbrokers of Manchester, and they intended to float a public company at once. Negotiations were in the hands of James White and Charles L. Samson, past president of the Law Society and senior partner of Grundy Kershaw Samson & Co., solicitors of London and Manchester. Sir Henry Paget-Cooke of Russell-Cooke & Co., solicitors of Lincoln's Inn Fields, were also involved, so that the appearance of solidarity and integrity was fully maintained. It was considered to be the most important deal in landed property that has taken place in this country. (Perhaps spurred by the Duke of Bedford's action, Lord Howard de Walden, another patron of the arts, was also selling off land as fast as he could.)

Sir Joseph had paid his £200,000 deposit shortly after signing the contract with the Duke (on 6 July 1914) and then a further £50,000 by the end of July. That left a balance of £1,750,000. If this were paid within seven days of 11 November 1914 there would be a 'rebate or discount' of £70,000 and the deal would be concluded at a net cost to Sir Joseph and his associates of £1,930,000 plus the other £250,000 to Mallaby-Deeley, and the usual costs and charges. The contract contained another, specially itemised sum of '£94 6s 0d which the Purchaser has also to pay for furniture in private boxes and retiring rooms of the Strand and Aldwych Theatres'. The two contentious boxes at Covent Garden and Drury Lane remained in the sale, but were let to the Duke of Bedford: a fine piece of compromise.

In peacetime, before 1914, it was possible to raise funds to deal with this kind of takeover, especially when Sir Joseph Beecham was involved and could almost find the initial deposit from his own pocket. He was accustomed to buying and selling 'big' and had a number of bank accounts for the purpose, of which two at least were run on overdrafts. His private accounts were another matter. They had to be well in credit to enable him to buy the kind of pictures he wanted, and at a moment's notice, as well as to provide for his mistresses in cash with a maximum of secrecy.

When the Great War broke out there were instant restrictions upon transfer and manipulation of capital funds, so that Sir Joseph was unable to fulfil his contract and the Duke's staff continued to manage the Estate. So he had to make new arrangements with His Grace, obviously to his own disadvantage.

On 17 September 1915 a Supplemental Agreement was signed and a further quarter of a million pounds paid to the Duke; but in doing this Sir Joseph requested an extension to complete the transaction. This date should have been in November 1914, but June 1917 was now requested and agreed, subject to two devastating conditions. Firstly there could be no rebate or discount allowed (save a mere £8,750 if the new date was met). Secondly, and much worse, 'as from 11 November 1914 until completion, the Purchaser shall pay to the Vendor interest at 5% on £1,750,000.'

The Covent Garden Estate, which had seemed so attractive to Sir Joseph in the spring of 1914, now took on the character of a waking nightmare. Throughout his life he had firmly refused to take any of the pills or medicaments which were the source of his wealth, or any made by other manufacturers. Yet now the fearful weight of his glamorous but deadly acquisition in London made him so unwell and sleepless that it began to show in his appearance and manner. On his doctor's prescription he accepted barbiturate pills to relax and refresh him during sleep.

By the autumn of 1916, after almost twelve months of constant worry, Sir Joseph was able to arrange a meeting of the individuals who had advanced him funds, as well as others who now promised additional backing. After some energetic work on the part of James White Sir Joseph's creditors all agreed to withhold their demands until peacetime and to meet him on Monday 23 October at 11 a.m. to sign the moratorium, reinforced by the introduction of the new backers.

Sir Joseph breathed again. Never in his business life had he been in such a tight corner. He had negotiated and succeeded in many tough deals, but they were all to do with the family business and there was never any question that he could be involved in anything as hazardous as this. The Covent Garden Estate, so dangerous to the Duke of Bedford, still seemed to have a curse on it. But now all was well. Very soon Sir Joseph would no longer have to fight off his creditors, but merely wait until the end of the war and find £87,500 a year for interest payments in the meantime.

On 14 October 1916 the Beecham Opera Company opened its new season at the Aldwych Theatre with *Samson and Delilah* – not, however, conducted by Thomas. He gave a concert five days later in Manchester with the Hallé Orchestra and his father attended it. Sir Joseph was accustomed to travelling fairly regularly by train between St Helens, Manchester and London, and after the concert he had intended to stay the night in Manchester and travel up to London on the following morning. He then proposed to have a quiet weekend there, to visit Utica and his grandsons at Upper Hamilton Terrace on the Sunday and invite them to go with him to *Samson and Delilah* on the Monday evening. He would have an early night on Sunday, though, ready for the meeting on Monday morning at which Thomas was going to be present.

On the spur of the moment, and because the concert ended sooner than expected, Sir Joseph decided to take the late train to London afterwards, and Thomas accompanied him to the railway station and saw him off. That was the last time they were ever together. On the Monday morning Sir Joseph was found dead in bed of a heart condition that had never been diagnosed, and the meeting with the creditors was called off *sine die*. On that day when Thomas Beecham inherited the baronetcy he also inherited the most appalling financial incubus, which he never fully cleared for as long as he lived.

As the heir to Sir Joseph, Thomas Beecham was due to inherit a substantial annual income from the company at St Helens of which he was a director, although he was not concerned with its running. Sir Joseph knew quite well where his elder son's interests lay and valued them greatly. Thomas also inherited the large house in Arkwright Road, London.

This palatial mansion suited Beecham very well, with its concert hall, picture gallery and capacious rooms; but soon he was obliged to sell it, together with the wonderful pictures it contained. These fetched £120,000 at Sotheby's. West Brow, Arkwright Road, had been a prized Beecham family possession since 1903, but in the present crisis Sir Thomas was obliged to agree with his father's Trustees that it must be sold. The house was bought from them in 1918 by Mrs Cecilia Gylsen of Caterham, and she quietly sold it to ASLEF (in 1921). There was a good deal of distress and indignation from the neighbours at this piece of news, but by then it was too late for them to carry out their corporate fund-raising to exclude the unwelcome trade unionists. West Brow, Hampstead, is still the headquarters of ASLEF.

It looked on paper as though the second son, Henry, was more favoured. He was given the American manufacturing company outright and Ewanville with all its contents. Henry was a working director of the St Helens company and as the son whom Sir Joseph had trained as a businessman he became titular heir to the Beecham pharmaceutical empire. Thomas had, nevertheless, received huge sums of money from his father since 1909, in the form of loans which were never repaid and which were now wiped out by the will.

Henry Beecham, two of his brothers-in-law and the general manager at St Helens were all appointed 'Managing Trustees' of the estate, and instructed to form a new company as soon as Sir Joseph's death had occurred, consolidating his pharmaceutical interests therein. Thomas and Henry were each to receive 46% of the shares of this company, and three of their sisters were to have 2% each. Thus Thomas was well looked after by his father and assured, at the time of the will (September 1916), of enough to keep him and his opera company afloat.

However, from Thomas's point of view there was a catch. His father was well aware of the vagaries and pitfalls of the musical and operatic worlds, and in order to protect his son against total loss of his inheritance he ordered that he was to receive only the dividends from the shares but not the shares themselves. They were to be in trust to the Managing Trustees. Thereafter the shares and dividends were to go to Sir Thomas Beecham's elder son, so that the holder of the baronetcy in the third generation was provided for. There were other clauses in the will which regulated the financing of Thomas's wife and children, present and future, but Sir Joseph had taken care to ensure that his elder son would receive sufficient to keep himself properly and that there would always be funds available to his dependants at the discretion of the Managing Trustees.

Because Sir Joseph's financial affairs were so complex at the time of his death, his estate was put into Chancery. While this continued the will could not be put into effect, but all those concerned agreed that a private company should be formed at once for the prime purpose of fulfilling the contract with the Duke of Bedford. This was called the Covent Garden Estate Company, of which Thomas and Henry Beecham were the directors. They brought in their family financial adviser, a brilliant accountant from Liverpool called Louis Nicholas, as company secretary.

At first Sir Thomas was optimistic about the chance of clearing the mortgage to the Duke, and put the new position to His Grace. Though sympathetic he was as tied to the contract as the Beechams were. For a while nothing happened to ease the financial situation because Thomas was much occupied with his opera company, and in anticipation of an early settlement in the Chancery Court he borrowed heavily and at crippling rates from money-lenders.

Henry Beecham went to live at Ewanville, but his was a very different case from that of his brother. As a working director of the St Helens board he received a large salary and lived, as he admitted, 'like a millionaire'. Had Thomas not been running his opera company from his own pocket, or at least making up the continual deficiencies from it, he would undoubtedly have enjoyed far greater financial freedom. But this was not his way. He was determined to make the Beecham Opera Company into the National Opera, which its prestige and quality certainly deserved, but he only succeeded in digging himself deeper and deeper into debt until, in July 1920, his company was forced into bankruptcy by its creditors.

It was Diaghilev, strongly advised by his lawyers, who first brought about Beecham's financial downfall by withdrawing his dancers from Covent Garden in July 1920 and issuing a petition for bankruptcy against the Sir Thomas Beecham Opera Company, who were his employers in London for that season. Beecham called a meeting of creditors, from backers to suppliers of ballet shoes, and explained to them that there was going to be enough money to pay them all in full once the season was over. All the creditors agreed to hold off, with the exception of one, a money-lender. He was not convinced by Beecham, but maintained his demand and took the others with him, more in self-defence than in genuine agreement in case the company (but not Beecham himself) was made bankrupt.

The hearing of the case was postponed several times but eventually came up before the senior official receiver at Bankruptcy Buildings on 15 September 1920. Beecham's 'rough statement of affairs', as presented, was very rough indeed. It showed unsecured debts of £58,567; creditors fully secured of £10,000 (the securities being valued at £100,000); partly secured creditors of £55,545. However, since all that was shown on the assets side amounted to £518 *at present*, it could not be accepted. Beecham's counsel emphasised that his client had very seriously attempted to come to an arrangement with his creditors to avoid the gazetting of a receiving order, and had it not been for his father's unexpected and untimely death in 1916 all the debts in question would have been paid in the ordinary course of events. Although Sir Thomas was controlling the Sir Thomas Beecham Opera Company, he was under no financial liability in connection with it. He received no remuneration but gave his services to this company, which was his hobby. The nominal capital of the opera company was £150,000, the main object of which was to acquire costumes, scenery, furniture and stage properties for new productions.

Under his client's father's will, Counsel went on, Sir Thomas became entitled to a life interest in the manufacturing business which should have produced about £100,000 per annum for him, but as yet there was a delay in the receipt of this income. It was in anticipation of it that Sir Thomas had gone ahead and involved himself in large expenditures. However, if Sir Thomas was made bankrupt, he would lose his patrimony absolutely.

The official receiver baulked at the discovery of £60,000 worth of debentures in the opera company, which made it a Chancery matter; and of course this gentleman was perfectly aware of the other family business that was languishing there. However, Beecham's Counsel firmly declared that the debentures would be paid up in full, and the case was adjourned.

And so it went on. Beecham was in and out of the courts for the next three years. When it suited him to do so he threw in some baffling new line of argument or evidence, which further delayed matters. He had good advisers, especially in Louis Nicholas, who enabled him to talk about intricate subjects as if he were an accountant and a lawyer himself.

The Beecham Opera Company foundered in late 1920 from sheer lack of petty cash, quite apart from what the company might or might not be obliged to pay its creditors. At one point during their last tour that autumn, Beecham telephoned his touring manager and ordered the company back. But he was met with a firm refusal. They couldn't just pack up and leave in the middle of a week's work and with other weeks already assured. But there were not so many weeks, and the curtain finally came down on them in Glasgow in December.

Between the end of 1920 and February 1924, Beecham was out of the music business except for two or three surprise performances, usually for fund-raising purposes and to show that he was keeping his hand in. He says in *A Mingled Chime* that he was so disgusted at the public's response to all his efforts and expenditure on opera that he was in a mood to seek some other permanent occupation. But this cannot be taken seriously. He does also say that he admitted the necessity of clearing up his father's debts, but of course until he had done so there was nothing forthcoming for himself from his father's will.

Beecham's three years in exile were far from idle, and in the end proved a most useful and healthy experience. They were spent in selling off the outlying properties of the Covent Garden Estate and in improving the revenue of the rest. He had quickly sized up the potential of the Estate and was convinced that it could be run at a greater profit; and he was perfectly right.

The Covent Garden Estate comprised 1,664 separate units or plots, varying in value from over one million pounds to below £2,500. No two were alike in value or in rents payable to the new landlords. In January 1920 the first auction took place, at which the prime properties were sold. These were the Theatre Royal, Drury Lane, the Waldorf Hotel, the Strand and Aldwych Theatres, Bow Street police court and two public houses. The rentals for these properties were remarkably small: for Drury Lane Theatre only £6,950 a year, and for the Aldwych Theatre £3,500 a year. At a second sale in May, the chief properties were Garrick House, Rules Restaurant (at a most inadequate rent of £150 a year) and the Catholic church in Maiden Lane. The proceeds from these sales and adjustments in rents produced one million pounds.

Thomas Beecham had adapted easily to his new way of life. Although he is said to have 'attended daily at the offices of the Covent Garden Estate Company and superintended the sales', he went abroad quite often and never lost touch with what was going on among orchestras and opera companies in England and on the continent.

In the summer of 1920 the Covent Garden Market was the target for attacks from both the Ministry of Food and the Ministry of Agriculture and Fisheries. They had each set up independent committees to investigate a takeover, and for two years had slowly dragged their findings round their respective departments. That summer, Beecham offered to sell the Market to the London County Council, which put both Ministries on the defensive. But he had already sold off so many of the smaller properties on the south side of the Market that there was now no possibility of enlarging it; and that, he knew, was vital to any ministerial plan. The two Ministries were thoroughly rude about the Market, 'a confused and unorganised anachronism', 'owned privately by a company which has not set itself to make the necessary alterations.' But they recognised that 'the heavy initial programme of renovation and improvements' (including the installation of electric light, which was done by the Duke of Bedford) 'had for several years prevented the payment of any dividend.' Had the Duke of Bedford taken the advice of his London steward in 1897 he would have demolished the properties on the southern side of the market and enlarged the area, which would have made it ripe for a takeover later on. As it was, the London County Council rejected Beecham's offer on the grounds that the Market could not be enlarged or expanded.

This was only one of Beecham's extremely able achievements. His persuasive manner and rapid brain soon established him as a first-rate businessman, something not generally appreciated by those who saw him merely as a profligate spender of money for artistic purposes – large sums that had to be spent in order to achieve the proper rehearsal and presentation of his operas.

By 1922 the debt to the Duke of Bedford was fully paid and the mortgage was redeemed on 7 September of that year. In May 1923 Beecham's own debts were also settled (in part) and he was released from the clutches of the official receiver.

In May 1924 a new public company was floated called Beecham Estates and Pills Limited. It had a nominal share capital of £1,850,000 and combined all the assets formerly held in Britain by Sir Joseph Beecham. Ownership and purchase of property as well as the original St Helens enterprise gave the new directors greater scope.

Beecham held a substantial shareholding in the new company of which he, Henry, Louis Nicholas and a newcomer called Philip Hill were among the directors at the outset. But he did not remain a director for long. Assured of an income again, he relinquished his newly acquired business interests, for although he still owed a great deal to his money-lenders he was itching to get back to music.

Chapter Five

IN THE OPERA HOUSE AGAIN

SIR THOMAS BEECHAM'S return to the opera house was made in an uncharacteristically tentative fashion during the summer of 1924. His office job had given him time to think and time to travel, so that he was abreast of musical events on the Continent, especially in Germany. Operatic activities at home were, paradoxically, of less interest to him, for since he could do nothing about them (and they were in a poor way) he merely watched out of the corner of his eye as his own splendid Beecham Opera Company was transformed into the British National Opera Company (known as the BNOC).

When Beecham's Company closed down in the winter of 1920, several of its active members called a meeting in London to try and arrive at some way of carrying on Beecham's work. He had employed many of them since 1916 and a total collapse had to be averted.

Norman Allin, Frederic Austin, Walter Hyde and Agnes Nicholls were four of the strongest characters among the singers, and they were joined by the conductor, Aylmer Buesst, to form the board. Percy Pitt was appointed their artistic director. Three businessmen, Sir William McCormick, Sir Charles Sykes and Brand Lane, supported the board with cash and with the right kind of experience. The BNOC was formed in 1922 and opened in Bradford on 6 February with *Aida*, in English.

Orchestral players do not make very satisfactory administrators, but opera singers with their extrovert, self-centred and self-preoccupied personalities make even worse ones. The conception of a self-governing opera company turned out to be a great mistake.

After several refusals, Higgins, Chairman of the Grand Opera Syndicate who were lessees of Covent Garden, was eventually obliged to yield to the demands of the BNOC to be allowed to give a season there. Higgins could not bear the idea of opera in English. On 1 May 1922 they opened with *La Bohème* (Miriam Licette as Mimi, Tudor Davies as Rodolfo), the first English *Ring* since Richter's in 1908, and thirteen other operas.

Beecham's first season at Covent Garden after the war had been made possible only because of the ensemble and the quality which his company possessed having worked together throughout the war. Beecham was no longer with them, but something of the energy and spirit with which he had inspired them seemed to linger, filling them with pride and hope for the future.

Beecham, the businessman at his office in the Strand, was far from deserting his chosen profession. In fact, as he tells us in *A Mingled Chime*, he was carefully planning his return.

The BNOC gave four seasons at Covent Garden to satisfactory box-office receipts and press, and toured successfully in between. But after a six weeks' season in early 1924 their directors were informed by the Syndicate that the Opera House would not be available to them during the summer months because of the resumption of the old summer seasons. The BNOC were shut out, and never appeared at Covent Garden again.

It will be remembered that when Beecham was unable to gain entrance to Covent Garden he went to His Majesty's. The BNOC followed his example and opened there in the summer of 1924 in direct competition with what turned out to be a remarkable season at Covent Garden. Grand opera returned there in earnest with foreign singers such as Lotte Lehmann, Elisabeth Schumann, Frida Leider, Alfred Piccaver (who was born in Lincolnshire and adopted by the Viennese), Friedrich Schorr, Richard Mayr and many others, whose names and reputations drew the public in crowds away from the Haymarket to Bow Street.

At the end of their season the BNOC approached Beecham to return and conduct his old friends in a single performance of *The Mastersingers* on the penultimate evening. This was more than he could resist, and on 17 July, a stifling hot day, he arrived at the stage door of His Majesty's to take a single rehearsal.

At once he noticed changes, and all for the worse. The orchestra was enfeebled, especially in the strings; there were too many new recruits on the stage who had never been put through their paces by his producers and staff, had never felt the disciplinary sting of George King or known the tooth-picking parsimony of Donald Baylis. To these new musicians and singers Beecham was a myth. Many a time the old hands had told them; 'Ah, but you should have been here in Tommy's time, *then* you'd have. . . .' Well, here he was, in the flesh, possibly a little quieter, more careful, and certainly more punctual than they remembered. But he was like a ghost to the new element.

The biting tongue was still there. He lashed out at Walter Widdop merely for walking through the rehearsal instead of giving a performance;

and he drew sounds from the pit which had never been heard from that orchestra before. Everybody gave Beecham 150 per cent of their normal best, which, for him, was the acknowledged percentage. The performance was supreme in the season's work.

Two days later, an editorial on opera appeared in *The Times* which in many ways bears the mark of having been written by Beecham. The *Mastersingers* performance was not mentioned. The article summed up the BNOC's past season as disappointing – no wonder, with the competition – but it stated that their activities have 'an importance beyond the immediate interest of each performance as it occurs . . . Opera in English is the only way to make the art flourish on English soil.'

Opera in English is still a subject for fierce argument. Beecham knew that his audiences in wartime had come in their thousands because they wanted to be sustained mentally and intellectually, and were not just paying for their seats because it was fashionable to do so. Consequently his operas were in English so that the action might be more easily understood and followed. In those days when excellent diction and vocal production were the rule and not the exception, and before mechanical sound-boosting from the stage had come in, the audiences were well able to gather what was being sung. In *A Mingled Chime* Beecham cites as a peak in enunciation the celebrated 1917 *Marriage of Figaro* at Drury Lane: 'One evening I went up to the top gallery and stood right at the back to listen, and from there I could hear not only every syllable of the songs, but of the ensemble pieces as well, all was as clearly enunciated as if it had been spoken instead of sung.'

There were times – and there still are – when gawky and ridiculous translations were better not heard in English; but Beecham knew well enough the artistic damage that translation did to the whole work. Those syllables and sounds which the original librettist had carefully placed, and the composer had equally carefully set, had to be cast aside in favour of English, ill-suited to music though a wonderful language when spoken. But since Beecham's intention had always been to get opera over to the masses he was prepared to sacrifice this purist approach until later when, it was to be hoped, he had captive audiences in a fit state to accept and enjoy opera in its original tongue.

The fortunes of the BNOC declined in direct proportion to the reassumption of the summer seasons of international opera at Covent Garden. It looked as though all the efforts of the Beecham Opera Company had been in vain so far as the establishment of a truly national opera in Britain was concerned. Percy Pitt resigned from the BNOC in 1924 to become a senior musical executive at the BBC, and was replaced by Frederic Austin as artistic director. *The Times* reported, however, that Austin 'took up his artistic direction too late to impose his principles on the company's policy'.

Frederic Austin had begun his musical career as a baritone and made his debut in Richter and Pitt's English *Ring* at Covent Garden in 1908 as Gunther. He was principal baritone in the Beecham Opera Company, and between this and his appointment with the Imperial League he had made a new arrangement of *The Beggar's Opera* in 1920 with Nigel Playfair's designs at the Lyric Theatre, Hammersmith. It was a tremendous success, and Austin sang Peachum.

During the summer of 1926 Beecham returned to the orchestra pit for Diaghilev at the Prince's Theatre on 7 July to conduct Lord Berners's *Triumph of Neptune* at a gala performance in honour of King Farouk of Egypt. This renewal of business association with the Russian Ballet resulted in a commission from Diaghilev for Beecham to arrange the score for a new ballet to be given at His Majesty's Theatre in the following summer.

This ballet was called *The Gods go a-Begging* (otherwise *Les Dieux Mendiants*) and had its première under Beecham on 16 July 1928. He had selected some obscure and delightful pieces by Handel; Danilova and Woizikowski were the principal dancers; and Balanchine arranged the choreography. Later on, the Sadler's Wells Ballet used Beecham's score, but with entirely different choreography.

When the Russian Ballet went on tour in Britain Beecham used their stage as a platform to attract publicity for his latest scheme, the Imperial League of Opera. Indeed, he used every possible opportunity to speak to audiences on the subject. The scheme was launched in 1927 and by 1929 *The Scotsman* newspaper recorded that Edinburgh audiences had been privileged to hear Beecham's 123rd dissertation on the League.

The idea for it had been maturing in his mind for three years while he was out of music. It was a grandiose idea for making opera part of life in London and the provinces. 'The Imperial League of Opera' was a good name when the word 'Imperial' was synonymous with Britain's glory and began the title of every organisation which emulated that glory. It all depended upon private investment of a modest nature: one pound per person to join and ten shillings a year for three years guaranteed. Providing there were between 150,000 and 250,000 subscribers on whom he could rely, Beecham would be off to a good start with the League. Lady Cunard had already promised to be his devoted and tireless supporter, and advanced £5,000 of her own money. In the past Beecham had financed his opera company alone; now he could no longer afford to finance anything. However, the League would need an opera company and the opera company would need an orchestra. These thoughts also occupied him.

It sometimes happens that similar ideas seem to be in the air at the same time, almost as general property for anyone perceptive enough to pluck them and go to work. On 16 July 1924 the wealthy composer, Isidore de Lara, had spoken at a meeting at the Criterion Theatre, London, with the object of raising two million pounds 'for the establishment of a permanent opera house in London'. The funding of this enterprise seemed rather vague, though well-intentioned: 'It would cost one million pounds to build the house to seat 4,000 comfortably at 1*s* to 5*s* each all the year round.' The deficit from these utopian prices would be £50,000 a year, 'and the other million pounds was to come from everybody interested in the country at the rate of £1 per person.' Mr de Lara's assumption that there were a million people sufficiently interested in opera seemed far from reliable. Beecham and de Lara knew each other well; indeed his opera *Naïl* had been given by Beecham in his 1919 Covent Garden season. ('The *Nail* in Beecham's coffin' was what the singers uncharitably called it.) Yet nowhere in *A Mingled Chime* does Beecham mention de Lara in the context of this opera scheme, nor did de Lara invoke Beecham's assistance. In any case his plan never got off the ground – more's the pity, for an amalgamation between them might perhaps have helped them both.

Beecham was now giving orchestral concerts with the London Symphony Orchestra, which seemed to be the most likely candidate for his pit orchestra at Covent Garden when he returned – as it was generally believed he would. But until that day dawned his time was almost entirely given up – when he was not conducting the LSO – to propaganda work for the Imperial League.

One of his broadsheets from 161, New Bond Street in 1928 contains the following exhortation:

It is a waste of time to criticise the general public for [its] attitude of mind. Owing to limited opportunity the bulk of the public has never heard opera. But although of moderate dimensions, there does exist a select public which patronises opera in London and in the provinces, and there is no actual insufficiency of first-rate artists of British origin on the modern operatic stage. Many of these artists, however, are rarely heard in England... The plain reason why they are not here is that there is no home to house them. Such a home has long been overdue and it is the immediate purpose of the Imperial League of Opera to bring it into existence... To found and maintain an organisation of the front rank that shall give seasons of five or six months opera in London and shorter seasons in six provincial cities would involve an annual expenditure of £50,000 per annum. To this figure let there be added a safety margin of a further £10,000 and we have the total annual sum of £60,000 per annum. This is the amount which the organisers of the League are seeking to raise.

Divided among 150,000 persons £60,000 works out at less than 10s per head or about 2d a week. The burden is not exacting. Now a single year of trial would be useless... Nothing less than five years is worth considering in a scheme of this sort. Accordingly everyone who is interested in music generally and in opera particularly is invited to become a member of this League...

Sir Thomas Beecham will be solely responsible for the productions and for the selection of the artists. He will have the assistance of an advisory board of experts including Sir Landon Ronald... and Frederic Austin... The business affairs of the League and the organisation of the opera seasons will be in the hands of a committee of which Lionel Powell Esq. is the Manager and General Secretary.

At first subscriptions came in steadily, many with cranky messages accompanying them, others with cheques far in excess of the minimum thirty shillings. Beecham's catch-phrase 'twopence a week', which was all he asked for, was really so little that it gave his antagonists a ready weapon for mockery: 'the twopenny opera' and suchlike. From Beecham's viewpoint, when he had a bee in his bonnet about something (as he usually had) there were only two camps. In one stood Beecham clad in shining armour. In the other grovelled the philistines. There was nobody in between. So in 1927, when he spoke with burning enthusiasm about the Imperial League on his journeys round the hustings, he made it all sound far more important than any general election could possibly be. When subscriptions lagged or simply failed to come in at all, as happened in places where the inhabitants had never heard any opera, the local denizens were slanged, insulted and treated to the best (or worst) of Beecham's venom.

In 1928 Beecham conducted for the first time at the Leeds Triennial Festival, where his associate conductor was Sir Hugh Allen, Director of the Royal College of Music. Sir Hugh invited Beecham to direct some student performances of *The Magic Flute* in the following summer. Beecham readily agreed. He liked young people, especially when they were working at a subject as dear to him as this opera. The students liked him too and responded gallantly to the most unconventional demands he made on them. He would sometimes take a scene that was meant to go slowly at a very quick tempo, then do the opposite with another which, marked allegro, he would beat lento. He would then suddenly ask the orchestra to transpose an accompaniment to an aria at sight 'to help the singer'. At the two performances which Beecham gave, everything was in place and the student instrumentalists found that they not only understood the score much better than before but it all went so much more easily for them than they had anticipated. Genius at work?

Sir Robert Mayer is not alone in considering Beecham a genius. Although it is a description that must be used with the greatest care, even those few who suffered at Beecham's hands and did not like him for one reason or another still declared that he was far above the ordinary mortal in foresight, ability and energy. In the 1920s and 1930s the time had not yet come for the arts to be subsidised by the state. Beecham was probably aware that eventually they would have to be, but until that time he was prepared to go straight to the taxpaying public and extract what he needed by direct means. The Beecham Opera Company had established opera as never before, but that company had been lost to him and what remained of it had wriggled awhile and then lain still. Had he been able to keep the Beecham Opera Company alive under his own direction, the story would have been very different. It might have formed the core of the League, as well as being a strong, living body that had every right to call itself a national opera.

But so far the League had nothing to offer but promises, plans, hard words and insults from Beecham when there was insufficient response to his brilliant idea. He was keeping it going, but very little had happened in five years. Sir Robert Mayer, who watched it all from the start, believes that Beecham tried to win over his supporters in the wrong way: frustration led to bullying, which was a pity. An early piece of literature about the League contained just the right kind of phrases calculated to put the public right behind him:

'A big push now all round and our labours will be crowned with complete success.'

'We are the only civilised nation in the world that possesses an Institution that will be to the world of music what the Royal Academy, the National Gallery and the great Museums are to the world of Art.'

'Assist us to remove this deficiency in our national life and you will be doing something of which afterwards you will be justly proud.'

'We ask you to act promptly. The future of English music is today in your hands.'

In 1929 Britain was suffering from a world slump, and a Labour Government was in office under Ramsay MacDonald. Subscriptions towards the League slowed down even more, despite Beecham's protestations that members would be Founder Members and that their subscriptions were as to a club. 'My organisation is not a business. No man in his senses imagines that by payment of a guinea or whatever it is annually, he is entitled to go into the club dining-room every day of the year and order anything he likes to eat and drink.' This was to counter allegations that subscription money would disappear and members would still have to buy tickets.

'I have not asked for a subsidy,' Beecham went on, 'and my intention is that Opera shall pay its own way.' He then added, somewhat tetchily: 'The fallacy into which most of my critics have fallen lies in comparison with an industrial concern. I might point out by way of answer that some of our most important industries are hardly paying their way at the moment.'

The British National Opera Company was, alas, also in this category. By 1929 they had come to grief for want of a mere £5,000 in general expenses – or petty cash, one might almost say. The swingeing demand of £17,000 entertainments tax from the Treasury had killed them. Their last performances were at Golders Green in April 1929. Beecham came and conducted a *Mastersingers* on the 15th, with May Blyth, Aylmer Buesst's wife, as Eva. On the following evening they closed with *Cav.* and *Pag.* At a meeting of the whole company during the following week it was announced that they had gone into voluntary liquidation. Many of the chorus were instantly out of work, but most of the principals had concert engagements elsewhere and were less affected. All the BNOC's stock was sold up, including a few of their new productions like *Hugh the Drover* (Vaughan Williams) and *The Perfect Fool* (Holst); but the bulk of it belonged to the Beecham Opera Company.

Covent Garden came to the rescue at once and 'took over' the chorus and made arrangements with some of the principals to become a new touring company under the banner of the Royal Opera House. This company lasted only from 1929 to 1932, when they disappeared altogether as a corporate body and ensemble after some seventeen years of working together.

In January 1930 Beecham announced the opening of the League's first opera season towards the end of May, with *Prince Igor*. No theatre was specified, but it was announced that the other operas were to be *The Bartered Bride* (designs by the celebrated Russian artist Polunin), *The Tales of Hoffmann*, *A Village Romeo and Juliet* (designs by Procter-Gregg), *The Snow Maiden* (sung in Russian and with designs by Edmond Dulac), *The Italian Girl in Algiers*, and *The Damnation of Faust* (designs by Augustus John). The expenses of this first season would be borne 'by a private group' and no League funds would be used until the full complement of members had been enrolled. Funds now stood at £40,000 against the required £60,000. Here at last was something concrete that the League had to show for itself; but despite a good press coverage of these opening details, both at home and abroad, this attractively planned season, which would surely have brought in many new members, sank without trace.

Shortly after this season was announced, a circular letter was sent to all members over the signature of Frederic Austin, the League's general manager, recommending an amalgamation with Covent Garden. This was, of course, Beecham's doing. Although he probably knew by this time that their season could not take place, he refused to admit that the League as a whole was a failure. He frequently sent ideas, suggestions, propositions and occasionally demands to Colonel Blois, the managing director of the Grand Opera Syndicate. Because Beecham had first set foot in the Royal Opera House as a lessee in 1910 and had carried out two successful seasons there in that year alone, he sent Blois his recommendations as though he were a kind of superior artistic adviser in office. He was convinced that he knew far more about how to present opera there than any of its present incumbents did.

As a result of this and of Beecham's general enthusiasm, the Syndicate suddenly announced that it was prepared to put up £30,000 a year towards a general fund in which the League would participate, and that Beecham had accepted a seat on the Syndicate's board. Eustace Blois was a remarkable man: he had been engaged by Mr and Mrs Courtauld in 1925 when they had financed the Syndicate. He was at that time a businessman working at Courtaulds, but he had a strong musical background and education. He was a former pupil of the prominent Italian conductor, Leopold Mugnone, and had worked as an opera stage manager in Italy and Germany. With three or four languages at his command, as well as a proven business sense, he was admirably suited to this job.

It was not at first apparent how the Covent Garden Syndicate was going to be able to afford £30,000 as their contribution towards this new and exciting venture until it was revealed that the BBC were also to be involved. Even then the penny did not drop, and Beecham was delighted at the idea of the amalgamation for it would put the League in the right place from every point of view. It seemed a healthy move.

But not for long. Very soon it was made known that £25,000 of the £30,000 was public money, paid by the Exchequer *through the BBC* to Covent Garden. The Syndicate had only £5,000 to find from public subscription. Beecham wrote one of his most blistering letters to the

Daily Telegraph, demolishing the Government, Covent Garden and the BBC, and calling off the whole deal there and then. He was especially angry with Covent Garden for not having come clean with him at the start, and with the BBC for double dealing. Who, Beecham asked, was now likely to take money from his own pocket for the League when the Government was already extracting it from him in direct taxes? This was the moment when the future of the Imperial League of Opera was well and truly blighted. No more subscriptions came in.

What made the whole situation so bitterly disappointing for Beecham was the aftermath. The Government reduced its subsidy, before the first payment was made, to £17,500 – a uselessly inadequate sum. By 1932 it had ceased altogether, after the National Economy Act of 1931 had imposed a 10 per cent cut in all salaries.

This was the first governmental subsidy to opera, although it fizzled out rather quickly after another payment of £17,500 and then a final one of £5,000 had been made, and it came about partly in connection with direct relays of opera by the BBC from Covent Garden and partly because of John Barbirolli.

Barbirolli was a deeply dedicated musician, first a cellist and then, in 1930, conductor of the Covent Garden Touring Company. On one occasion he had been making music by invitation at 11 Downing Street and had found himself in conversation with the Chancellor of the Exchequer, Sir Philip Snowden. Barbirolli always boasted afterwards that it was as a direct result of their conversation that Snowden persuaded the Cabinet to agree to sponsoring the Opera House. After all, it was a government of the people, for the people, and such a move would stand it well in future campaigns. John Barbirolli was a gentle and lovable man, and his simple, trusting nature led him to believe that he was doing the best any man could do for opera. If he was a contributor to that fatal decision by the Labour Government he can be considered as one of the hanging judges of the Imperial League of Opera.

In the summer of 1931 a Russian Opera and Ballet Company appeared at the Lyceum Theatre, presented by Lionel Powell and with Beecham as its artistic director. Diaghilev had died in 1929 and one of the directors of the company was a W. de Basil, later known as Colonel de Basil. He had revived the Ballets Russes from the bankrupt state in which they had unexpectedly found themselves on the death of their founder, although de Basil lacked a personal fortune and had to go on begging as Diaghilev had done to keep the company alive. The star of this Russian Opera Company was Feodor Chaliapin, who was making his last appearance in London (he died in 1938). His magnificent voice was in reasonable trim and his presence was still gigantic, although he had acquired more eccentricities in the intervening seventeen years.

The Lyceum season lasted from 18 May to 27 June 1931. The repertoire was to have consisted of six Russian operas but this proved to be far too expensive for Powell, who settled for *Sadko* and for Chaliapin in all performances of *Boris Godunov* and *Prince Igor*. In the last performance of *Prince Igor* he sang the two contrasting roles as before. In consequence of the cut-back in operas, the ballet played a greater part in the season than had first been intended and included *Petrouchka*, danced by Nemtchinova and Woizikowski. Beecham conducted one performance of *The Gods go a-Begging* on 26 June and six performances of *Prince Igor*, not always with Chaliapin. He also conducted the third act of this opera together with the last act of Massenet's *Don Quichotte*, featuring Chaliapin in his celebrated role of the dying Don at a gala performance on 23 June.

The season was a moderate success for Powell and for Beecham. It revived his interest in conducting the ballet, and it showed the public how greatly one artist could respond to another. At every performance when Chaliapin was 'off' he sat in the auditorium and led the applause for Beecham in a manner that demanded the same from the whole audience.

On 1 December and twice on 2 December, Beecham again conducted at the Royal College of Music. This time he took the students in a new opera, *The Devil Take Her*, to a score by Arthur Benjamin. The synopsis printed in the programme runs: 'The Poet, grieved that his wife is dumb, longs to hear her voice; a doctor arrives, the operation is more than successful, and the Poet regrets the doctor's skill.' Singing a small role for two of the three performances was Ruth Naylor, soon to become a leading soprano at Sadler's Wells.

During the latter part of 1931 Blois and his Syndicate at Covent Garden came to the conclusion that they could not afford an opera season in 1932, nor could they any longer afford their Touring Opera Company. There was such an outcry from the press and from Covent Garden's usual supporters that once more they approached the League with suggestions for an amalgamation. This time it failed for a different reason, namely that opposing factions had grown up within the League's membership.

Blois was keen to acquire Beecham as one of his conductors. He cabled him in the United States, inviting him to be the principal conductor of a short season of German opera in May–June 1932. Since it had been the German, especially the Wagnerian, opera which had attracted high-capacity audiences in the past three summer seasons, this seemed a sensible line to take.

Beecham accepted, and on 9 May 1932 he was once again to be seen in the orchestra pit at the Royal Opera House conducting *Die Meistersinger* with Friedrich Schorr as Hans Sachs and an unnamed London Symphony Orchestra accompanying. This was prefaced, of course, by Beecham's inimitable performance of the National Anthem, and proved at once, more clearly than the whole season of opera which followed, that Beecham was back and intending to stay at Covent Garden.

He also conducted three *Tristans* with a first-night cast of Leider and Melchior, and two *Tannhäusers*; and he completed each of Robert Heger's two *Ring* cycles with the *Götterdämmerung* – a typically Beechamesque stroke. It gave him the opportunity, after the *Götterdämmerung* which closed the season on 3 June, to cap Colonel Blois's speech on behalf of the board with one on behalf of Beecham, who, he hinted darkly, was likely to be back the following season.

Certainly the country's severe financial circumstances had helped Beecham back to Covent Garden. Once there, he decided that he would remain as artistic director only and would never again attempt to take charge of every aspect of that demanding and complicated house.

Meanwhile he was at once involved in conferences, manipulating, arguing and advising until November, when he attended a full meeting of the Syndicate Board together with Geoffrey Toye, H. B. Phillips of the Carl Rosa Opera Company and representatives of the BBC. A press notice on the following day explained that Beecham and Toye had been made directors and that a new organisation called the National Opera Council was to be set up. This was going to be initiated by the joint efforts of the Covent Garden Company (as distinct from the artistic Syndicate), the Imperial League of Opera, the Old Vic and Sadler's Wells and the BBC. While the Old Vic and Sadler's Wells were going to operate independently, though with the benefit of Beecham's artistic advice, the enlarged Syndicate Board would in future 'receive all sums payable by the Broadcasting Corporation and all funds raised by the League and by the Council and will decide how these funds shall be apportioned.'

These rather loose propositions seem today, even without hindsight, highly impractical, more especially as Beecham's personality – in the very centre of it all – was anathema to most committee members; and his recent negotiations with the BBC, which had ended so unhappily, gave him ample opportunities for sniping at its representatives at succeeding meetings.

However, at the end of 1932 the BBC and Covent Garden severed relations and the subsidy was lost. Shortly afterwards Beecham accepted a much more welcome invitation to be artistic director of the Opera House Syndicate. However, the whole future of the Opera House itself was in jeopardy.

In early 1929 the Syndicate had at last relinquished their lease to Covent Garden Properties (the public company which had arisen out of the Beecham family's joint private companies). After 1930 there were many suspicions to the effect that by 1933, when the final lease expired, a new street was going to be cut right through the middle of the site on which the Opera House stood.

Unfortunately for everyone at Covent Garden, Colonel Blois, who had been unwell and had gone to Italy at Easter to recuperate, died on his return to London in May. This was a blow for Beecham, who admired Blois and got on well with him. Charles Moor, the resident producer, was appointed acting manager in Blois's place, but the job only fitted him where it touched. The chairman of the board was a Hungarian banker called Szarvasy, not the kind of person that Beecham would normally take to his bosom. But they had to confide in one another a good deal, since they were by far the two most active and forceful personalities there.

At precisely this time Beecham was being bombarded by letters from John Christie of Glyndebourne, cajoling him to conduct at the first season's offering of Mozart operas in 1934. Many invitations for Beecham to go down there were politely turned down, once at the very last moment. Christie expressed his reasons for wanting Beecham to meet him there thus (the German spellings are his):

(a) in order that my wife [the soprano, Audrey Mildmay] should have the pleasure of meeting you;
(b) that you should form an opinion as to the suitability of the Opera House for the Mozart Festspiele which has been planned;
(c) so that we can discuss the advisability of the German and the English Mozart Festspiele at the beginning and the end of June;
(d) so that I can have a further personal discussion with you on the Covent Garden plans.

Christie's plans seemed so enterprising as to be beyond all possibility in that minute opera house, as it was then constructed:

(1) Two performances yearly of Parseval about Easter.
(2) A Mozartfest of say two operas for a week.
(3) The Ring.
(4) A July–August Festspiele.
(5) Monthly concerts.

In asking Beecham's advice and help Christie was endeavouring to link the two Houses from the outset, and in an early letter to Beecham's manager Christie wrote:

The opening operas should be next year in the early summer perhaps before the Covent Garden season. This would give us plenty of time here to be ready. The doors will be closed during the performance. We are asking Sir Thomas to undertake the opening performance – if not all of the later ones – because we aim at the highest standard and because there is no one else in England.

But Beecham would not bite. He remained aloof and elusive, to Christie's annoyance, and never attended performances there when they began in 1934.

The 1933 Covent Garden season opened with general appreciation shown to Beecham, for, as *The Times* critic wrote, when he 'took his place he secured more than the conductor's customary applause. The audience felt the season owes its existence in some measure at least to his personal efforts.' Which was only right and proper. And in this season, for the first time, the orchestral list, printed in the programme, showed that the Royal Opera House Orchestra was none other than the London Philharmonic, Beecham's new orchestra which he had formed in the previous autumn. Although this was known to most people it had never appeared in print within the Royal Opera House.

Beecham's second *Tristan*, with Frida Leider and Melchior, elicited praise from the same critic: 'If the singers did much, Sir Thomas Beecham did even more, for the poetry of his reading and the lyrical playing which he draws from the orchestra carries the whole drama forward in a ceaseless flow ... so that the whole ensemble seem to sing together.'

Yet there was an uncertain feeling in Bow Street. Covent Garden Properties Ltd had plans to pull down the Opera House and erect a series of shops and office buildings on the site.

The season ran its scheduled course of six weeks with nine operas and *Der Ring*. The last production was a revival of Verdi's *Don Carlos*, which Beecham conducted. It was poorly cast and the lovely work was totally unfamiliar to Covent Garden audiences; it had not been performed there since 1867. This time it failed. On the last night Beecham was obliged to express his lack of knowledge about the future of the Opera House, but stated emphatically that no matter what happened in Bow Street there would be a season of opera in London in 1934, if necessary at some other theatre.

As soon as the season was over Beecham returned to the Royal College of Music to conduct the students in Vaughan Williams's *Hugh the Drover*.

The college had a close connection with this opera; they had given its première in 1924, ten days before its first professional production by the BNOC. They were now performing a revised version, reinforced by eight ex-students of the RCM who had taken part in the original production there, among them the tenor Trefor Jones, and Dunston Hart, a member of Ivor Novello's company who appeared in all his musical plays. Although Vaughan Williams's music was known to be only on the fringe of Beecham's taste and preference, he threw himself with gusto into this production and had the College orchestra playing on top form.

According to the 'Survey of London' Volume XXXVI, plans had been submitted in December 1932 'for the formation of a new street extending across the centre of the site of the opera house'. The existing sub-lease of the theatre, originally due to expire in February 1933, had been extended for another five months, and the Chairman of the Properties Company, Philip Hill, explained that it was unfair to his shareholders to let the Opera House at a rental which was admittedly only a fraction of its true, normal value. 'This rental had, since the previous February, been £1,000 a month' instead of £715 p.a. under the Duke of Bedford's ownership. But the theatre was rescued yet again. By December 1933 a new company, 'the Royal Opera House Company Ltd ... had obtained an agreement for a new lease ... depending on improvements to the theatre which ultimately cost some £70,000.'

The directors of the new company were Philip Hill, chairman of the company which owned Covent Garden (that is to say, the Beecham Manufacturing Company which had been merged with the Covent Garden Estate Company in 1928); Lady Cunard; Viscount Esher; and the Hon. James Smith. Beecham was artistic director again, and the new managing director was Geoffrey Toye. Toye was an excellent conductor (especially of Delius) and a composer best-known for his ballet score *The Haunted Ballroom*. His brother was Francis Toye, the critic and Verdi expert. Geoffrey Toye had been managing Sadler's Wells Opera Company for three years before joining the Covent Garden Board. He and Beecham both talked the same language and, on the face of it, their partnership appeared ideal.

The inclusion of Philip Hill found Beecham in touch again with St Helens, though at one remove; and this co-ordination was due to a joint effort on the part of Lady Cunard and Beecham to interest Hill in the Opera House and possibly make funds available for its upkeep. Hill turned out to be a wise, sympathetic and useful director.

As well as the extensive modernisation programme of the House which the new Syndicate was obliged to make under the terms of their lease, they also decided to commission a newly designed *Ring* and *Fidelio*. Gabriel Volkoff was to do the Wagner and Rex Whistler the Beethoven. They also engaged a 'German Representative', one Dr Otto Erhardt (soon known backstage as 'Dr Earwig'). He was an opera producer of some distinction, but his knowledge of singers' values, especially the Italians', soon offended and alienated too many. He cast so many Germans in Italian roles that his employment seemed a mistake even before the season had started; by then the damage had been done.

The Spanish coloratura mezzo, Conchita Supervia, had been engaged by Toye to sing both *Carmen* and *La Cenerentola*, but the upsets which this highly-charged lady engineered at Covent Garden were many, and stories about her abound. Originally Beecham had decided that he would conduct *La Cenerentola*, but finding Supervia's dictates over tempi, cuts and production details far too demanding he handed it all over to Vincenzo Bellezza. There were further upheavals when the singer made her own rules about rehearsals and the sequence of performances, so that the Opera House had to make her toe the line by forcing her to agree to sing in only the Rossini opera. She threatened to sue for breach of contract and at one stage walked out altogether. Beecham and Toye charmed her into staying but only after her friend and accompanist Ivor Newton performed a miracle of diplomacy in persuading her to agree to dictate the time and place when she 'could spare five minutes' to see Toye at her hotel. Then it was all resolved.

In many ways Supervia resembled Beecham. They both insisted on dictating their own terms, they both enjoyed rumpuses, and neither of them bore any grudges afterwards. It was all a game.

Mme Supervia then began rehearsing in earnest. One day she demanded a carriage and pair to take her to the ball. There was a carriage in the prop room, but no live horses for early rehearsals. So to celebrate the entente, Beecham and Toye became the horses, high-stepping their way down the stage at Covent Garden, the volatile lady in the carriage, cracking a whip over them with a delighted grin of victory on her pert little face.

In her autobiography, *On Wings of Song*, Lotte Lehmann has a few charming words to say about some of Beecham's sweeping changes at Covent Garden: 'Dusty old stage decorations were the background to artistically incomparable performances ... but we all felt at home there and scarcely noticed the grotesque incongruity between our costumes, frequently of regal magnificence, and our surroundings.... After ... came Sir Thomas Beecham [and] new ideas, modern productions, sparkling life, stage reconstructions. Sir Thomas, witty, elegant with a genius for comedy . . . Now there was something to look at as well as to listen to!'

The 1934 summer season opened with *Fidelio* in Rex Whistler's beautiful and appropriate sets. Beecham was conducting and suddenly, during the overture, his voice was heard raised in an angry shout: 'Shut up, you barbarians!' The performance was being broadcast and thousands of people sitting at home were astonished at the interruption, especially as the noun was taken by some to be another word altogether. There was far greater coverage of this in the next morning's newpapers than of the performance itself, and factual accounts varied considerably. *The Times* explained the 'outrage' fairly: 'The audience may have been a brilliant one socially and it was crowded. But it was not artistically brilliant enough to realise the elementary musical points of behaviour in the Opera House. The exasperated conductor (or it may have been another official) had to shout "Stop talking" while the overture – as far as we could hear, beautifully played – was in progress. The peripatetic stall-holders, unconcerned with the music, sought their seats guided by the electric torches of the attendants, flashed to and fro as in a cinema. The first thing the new management must do is to educate its audience and perhaps it would have been better to wait a little before casting Beethoven before them.'

Beecham conducted eighteen performances that season, including *Die Meistersinger* as well as the *Fidelios* and two cycles of *Der Ring*. The Austrian conductor Clemens Krauss and his wife, the soprano Viorica Ursuleac, made their débuts at Covent Garden during this season. She sang Queen Ice-Heart in *Schwanda* (which Krauss conducted), and also Desdemona. Their coming was connected with the visit of *Arabella* from Dresden. This was Richard Strauss's latest opera, only a year old, in which Ursuleac sang the heroine and Krauss conducted. The visit was such a success that the planned performances were increased in number.

This was the first season in which Beecham conducted the complete *Ring*. The cycles were extremely well cast and Beecham delighted everybody by the clarity of his interpretation. The main change in personnel in the two cycles was the Wotan: Rudolf Bockelmann in the first and Hans Hermann Nissen in the second; the Brünnhilde (Leider), Siegfried (Melchior), Sieglinde (Lehmann), Siegmund (Völker), Hunding (Kipnis), Hagen (List) and Alberich (Habich) were constant.

Although Beecham had no time for dictators, least of all for Adolf Hitler, he had a healthy respect for German musical organisations and was convinced that the way opera was supported by the state in Germany and in Austria was ideal. Various other plans for bringing over German productions during the 1930s came to nothing, and the Bayreuth

Lohengrin was turned down flat when Hitler offered it as his personal gift to the King at his Coronation.

As had been usual in Diaghilev days the ballet followed the opera season. In 1934 it was the turn of Colonel de Basil's Ballets Russes, and Beecham conducted the opening ballet, the second act of *Lac des Cygnes*, after the two National Anthems.

He then went across to the Royal College of Music in South Kensington and conducted three student performances of Delius's *A Village Romeo and Juliet* with the College First Orchestra. Among the student singers were Frederick Sharp as the Dark Fiddler and Peter Pears as the Poor Horn-Player in the second performance. This was Beecham's last appearance with the College students; when Sir Hugh Allen ceased to be the Principal there Beecham's connection lapsed. Even so, four operas and one concert had certainly infected a lot of young people who afterwards proudly declared that they had indeed played (or sung) for Beecham.

Christie's first Mozart season had been a great success at Glyndebourne, so much so that it seemed to have turned his head. Julius Harrison, the very experienced opera conductor, who had been on Beecham's staff throughout the First World War, asked Christie for some seats. He was musical director of the Hastings Council and conducted their municipal orchestra. The correspondence which followed was acrimonious and only displayed Christie's ignorance of the professional opera house. Harrison sent the file to Beecham who wrote a letter to Harrison which was intended to be passed on to Christie – and so it was. The part which stung most, and for which Christie never forgave Beecham, was this: 'I have had an opportunity of hearing the tests of some of the gramophone records made at the first Glyndebourne Festival, and if these be fair samples of the general results obtained there then I more than agree with you that in the important matters of execution, style and accuracy in the interpretation of Mozart we have not only nothing to learn but a great deal to teach!'

Beecham's main objection was to Busch's plain unadorned treatment of Mozart's score of *Figaro*. But because this was the first complete *Figaro* ever to be recorded (albeit drastically out of sequence) several generations of music-lovers were brought up on it, apparently oblivious of the defects which Busch's interpretation imposed upon the opera. The three early Glyndebourne recordings always had an aura about them.

Supervia was now on such good terms with Beecham and Toye that she wanted to return, on her own rehearsal conditions, to sing three operas in 1935: *La Cenerentola* again, the postponed *Carmen*, and *L'Italiana in Algeri*. However, she was not the only female attraction that season. When Toye, with an eye to the general public, suggested the singing film star, Grace Moore, both Lady Cunard and Beecham hotly refused to support him. None the less, Toye carried the plan through and she was approached. Grace Moore, whose film *One Night of Love* had made her famous, did not know *Butterfly*, which Toye wanted her to sing for him, but she offered Mimi instead. The offer was accepted, for three performances.

In his highly entertaining autobiographical book, *At the Piano*, Ivor Newton paints a charming and thoroughly likeable portrait of Grace Moore, whose magnificent ways and complete list of friends to command, including the President of the USA, should have commended themselves to Beecham. It is possible that had he been allowed to approach Miss Moore with an entirely open mind he would have fallen for her, and that may be the reason why Lady Cunard was so insistent that the two of them never meet. Lady Cunard met her, though, and was extremely offensive to her in public.

The three *Bohèmes* sold out almost at once, and that is about all that could be said in favour of them. Compared with Dino Borgioli, John Brownlee and Ezio Pinza, who were supporting her in the cast, Grace Moore was completely lacking in style or operatic experience, though she had a good voice with 'quality and power' as *The Times* graciously put it. In a way it was a pity that Grace Moore had to appear in an opera so close to Beecham's heart. But whether or not it was really desirable to pull in a star from the periphery of the opera and try to pretend that she belonged there is a debatable point. It was a gamble that came off financially, but failed artistically.

Beecham and Toye had been disagreeing on a number of matter partly due to Lady Cunard's interference, and the Grace Moore episode put paid to any further co-operation. As managing director Toye was the stronger man on the board, but he was weaker in character than Beecham, and resigned. This left the artistic director in sole charge, and the vacant post was never advertised, let alone filled. Although Beecham had determined that he would never again control the whole Opera House, he nevertheless assumed command of the building which had been such a trial, delight and doubtful asset to him, on and off, since 1910.

Before the end of the 1935 season there had been another newcomer to the conductor's desk, a tall, very shy and gangling German whose knowledge of Wagner and methods of interpreting him caused certain hardships to the orchestra, especially as he seldom put into practice at performances what he had rehearsed. Most of the time he had his eyes shut, for he had the score memorised, and his head not only swayed in a great arc on account of his height but sometimes looked as though it was about to fall off. His name was Wilhelm Furtwängler. For the first time it was possible to make some assessment of Beecham's conducting compared with one of equal standing. They each conducted two performances of *Tristan und Isolde*, and Furtwängler's was described as 'a wonderful symphonic poem for orchestra with voices: a poem set to music or "poetry fertilized by music" (Richard Wagner) – but not poetry superseded by music.' The result of Furtwängler's performance was 'one of the most sensitive and well-balanced performances that have been heard at Covent Garden for many years'. The result of this statement was that the critic had his tickets withdrawn by Beecham for the remainder of the season. The same critic had disliked the way Beecham had beaten on his score, 'a practice which we hope will not become a habit with him'. Yet he stressed the apparent ease with which the players sensed exactly what Beecham wanted – the old magnetism again.

He always nursed his orchestral players and generally seemed to be far more attuned to them than he was to singers. Some singers he virtually ignored; others he coaxed if they were nervous or in any way troubled. He did not much care for them as a breed and detested vain, foreign tenors. But of course he loved a number of British sopranos dearly. At one *Bohème* rehearsal he wanted to go through the whole of the last act again, and it was already well past midnight. The Mimi was exhausted. 'Sir Thomas,' she objected, 'it is extremely difficult for me to sing when I am lying down, and it is very tiring.' Beecham replied: 'My dear, I have achieved some of my most remarkable successes from that position. Now, ladies and gentlemen, the last act again, please.'

Orchestral rehearsals were something of a disgrace during the inter-war Beecham seasons. The orchestra would rehearse from ten in the morning until about five in the evening – not so late on *Götterdämmerung* nights – and then play for the performance. If there was no performance that night, and certainly during the rehearsal period before the season had started, the orchestra might well be working until four in the morning, with Beecham as sprightly and witty as ever. Sometimes, if it was a particularly arduous session, he sent over to the Nag's Head (opposite the stage door) for sandwiches and liquid refreshment for the whole orchestra. The trouble was that since the seasons were being run on a shoestring there was not nearly enough rehearsal time allowed at reasonable hours. Beecham did his best by telling stories to keep his players as happy and amused as he could.

Beecham with Eva Turner at Covent Garden in 1935, where she sang several roles during the Imperial League of Opera's season; and (*below*) with Wilhelm Furtwängler in the summer of 1936, at work on plans for the 1937 Coronation Opera Season at Covent Garden.

Beecham as guest-conductor of the Berlin Philharmonic Orchestra in Berlin, November 1935. *Below* The fake press photograph of Beecham (right) talking to Hitler in the Führer's box during the interval of the LPO's concert in Berlin, November 1936.

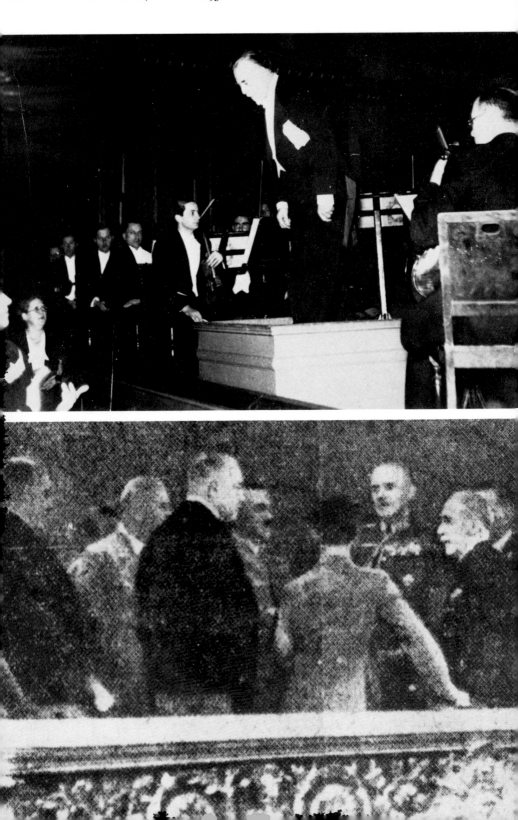

At a complimentary dinner at the Savoy Hotel given by the LPO to the Berlin Philharmonic Orchestra in May 1937, Beecham sits with Furtwängler on his right. Harold Holt is seated three places away on his left, Léon Goossens (1st oboe of the LPO) in front of him and to the right. *Below* Beecham on the set of *Das Rheingold* at Covent Garden during a rehearsal. The producer, Otto Erhardt, is on the left.

Below Betty Thomas a[...]
son Jeremy, c. 1933.

Above Betty-Humby
Beecham and Sir Thomas in
duet, c. 1949.

In Act I of *Götterdämmerung*, soon after Siegfried has arrived at the Gibichung Hall, there is a moment of suspense while Hagen watches him. At this moment there is a solitary D below the bass stave played by the eighth horn. It is awkward to get such a low note out, exactly on the beat, at the right pitch and with a degree of purity. At one dress rehearsal the horn player in question, Raymond Bryant, achieved a perfectly timed, perfectly placed fat sound. Beecham called out to him: 'That'll need a lot of paper!'

Because of a huge bill for entertainment tax and income tax, totalling almost £15,000, after the 1934 season, Beecham had consulted lawyers and found that if the orchestra traded in future as a non-profit-making company they would be exempt from entertainment tax. So this arrangement was set up for 1935 under the name of the London and Provincial Opera Society. The Imperial League was also able to enjoy the advantages which this offered, and between September and October they gave a short season at Covent Garden during which Beecham conducted three performances of *Der Freischütz* and three of Delius's *Koanga*.

Ever since the Delius Festival of 1929 the composer had tried to persuade Beecham to mount his Negro opera. And when Delius died in 1934 Beecham saw this as a fit moment to accede to his wishes. *Koanga* opened the season and gave good singing opportunities to John Brownlee as the captive Negro chieftain and to Oda Slobodskaya as his mulatto love, Palmyra, and other glorious opportunities to Beecham and the London Philharmonic Orchestra, who were to remain in the pit at Covent Garden until 1939.

John Brownlee had to colour all his visible flesh for the part he was taking, whereas Leyland White as the planter, Don José, didn't have to 'colour up'. This gave rise to a number of jokes in the company about brown and white, which didn't make the process any less tiresome to Brownlee. It seemed that Beecham enjoyed the three performances of *Koanga* far more than did the public, who gave him little support for the venture.

In the *Freischütz* performances Eva Turner sang Agathe with great distinction. Dame Eva, as she now is, recalls Beecham on her first night with the utmost affection and gratitude. Her father, Charles Turner, was sitting in the auditorium before the curtain went up when he died of a heart attack. Beecham was told at once but refused to let his leading soprano know until the opera was over. Then he gently broke the news to her himself. He had thus saved her performance.

La Bohème was one of Beecham's favourite operas, and on one occasion when auditioning for a Mimi he was in front with Clarence Raybould, who was going to conduct it. Among those who came on stage and sang was an unknown singer who went merely by a number – 3. After several more had been heard it was already evident that No. 3 was the best singer by far. She possessed a pure, girlish voice, very musical, well produced and absolutely in the middle of every note. So they called her back. The stage manager reported that she had gone – had left the Opera House. 'Well, you'd better find her,' said Beecham.

After some searching about she was run to ground in Harold Holt's office. 'No. 3?' asked the impresario, 'you mean Lisa Perli, yes, she's here.' She was at once engaged for the two performances under Clarence Raybould, with Heddle Nash as Rodolfo. When the first orchestral rehearsal took place one of the musicians looked up to catch a glimpse of the lovely new soprano and gasped in surprise: 'Blimey, it's Dora!'

It was Dora Labbette, the concert singer whom Beecham had cast in his performances and in his complete recording of the *Messiah* in 1927, and who had frequently sung with him afterwards. He knew all about the practical joke, of course, and lunched her after the audition, but she had completely fooled everybody else. Whether it was Beecham or Harold Holt who had put her up to it we can only guess, but it was she who contrived the name, having been born in Purley.

Dora Labbette had been a successful concert singer for twenty years, but wanted to sing in opera. It was not easy to cross from one field to the other, and she had a voice that was on the small side. But she had great purity in her favour, and certain roles were ideal for her: Mimi certainly, Mélisande, Desdemona, Marguerite, Mignon and Antonia in *Hoffmann*. In addition she possessed a fine personality and presence and had a delicious sense of humour.

After the 1935 season Beecham announced that it was his intention to reinstate at least a thirteen-week summer season of opera and to 'make an effort to restore this old theatre to something near the position it once occupied in the world of European music'. Toye's resignation and Beecham's assumption of the control of Covent Garden led to a good deal of interest in the press over the House's future, to which Beecham replied, saying nothing about the business side over which he claimed no responsibility. He revealed that a foreign opera company was going to appear there in 1936, and that the Beecham Sunday concerts would begin in the autumn.

Since he proposed to 'go it alone' at Covent Garden, without the irritation of interference or the obligation to confer, Beecham realised that he needed somebody to run his office. He or she would have to be a thoroughly experienced musical administrator, multilingual and acceptable to the European opera houses and agencies. Such a person was not easy to find, but in early 1936, while he was in New York, Beecham found exactly what he was looking for. At the moment the woman in question was temporarily engaged in other activities, but she declared her wish to work with him at Covent Garden and he replied: 'Why not? You are just the person I want.'

Her name was Berta Geissmar, born of Jewish parents in Mannheim in 1892. She had a Ph.D. from Frankfurt, had lived in England for six months in 1911, and was fluent in four languages. But the most interesting thing about her, from Beecham's point of view, was her past association with Furtwängler, who was a friend of her father's. She had known him since 1915, had been his secretary–cum–personal assistant since 1922 and then his touring manager for the Berlin Philharmonic Orchestra. She knew the European musical business intimately and was well liked by everybody in it, which meant that she was competent at her job. This included the management of singers when Furtwängler was conducting at the Berlin State Opera. But since 1933 she had been 'undesirable' in Nazi Germany and only after the greatest difficulties had she been able to leave to take up a short-term research job in New York.

Beecham had known Dr Geissmar for a number of years through Furtwängler, the Berlin Philharmonic and the Opera, and could scarcely have found a better general secretary. She joined him at Covent Garden during the 1936 season and has recorded some interesting facts about his methods of work in her autobiography. When she arrived at Covent Garden Beecham was running the whole place more or less single-handed, was conducting frequently and was also preparing for the forthcoming Coronation season in 1937. In addition there were occasional concert engagements with the LPO, and there was his very active private life. Throughout each hectic day he maintained a constant urbanity and cheerfulness combined with a paternal attitude to everybody in the Opera House. Quite clearly he adored what he was doing.

Beecham addressed both Melchior and Furtwängler as 'my boy', although each of them was nearly twice as tall as he, and Melchior was certainly twice as broad. Beecham was charming to all the female singers providing they did what he required of them on stage. He had a way of saving his voice at rehearsals by blowing a police whistle which hung round his neck on a black ribbon, to indicate that everybody was to stop and listen to him. This was, of course, when he was sitting in front for a piano rehearsal or when one of his assistants was conducting the orchestra.

At first Dr Geissmar found him awkward to work with. He never gave her any detailed information about people or customs at Covent Garden, expecting her to find out for herself. This was a great change from Germany where everything was strictly laid down. She also had to deal with Lady Cunard, which she did admirably, retaining her friendship; and then there were Beecham's constant disappearances. On one occasion, at her wits' end to find him, she tracked him down at the Euston Hotel, comfortably established with his loyal servant Joseph Smith in attendance. Another foible, akin to disappearing, was a disinclination to answer the telephone when it rang. He would calmly sit beside the instrument until it stopped, but now and again, when he did pick it up, the growling noise he made down the mouthpiece was usually enough to convince the caller that he had a wrong number.

As soon as Dr Geissmar had proven herself in her new and unfamiliar surroundings Beecham reorganised their offices. Previously he had worked from the ground floor at Covent Garden whence, no doubt, it was easy to disappear through one of the many doors leading into the street. But now they moved up to the first floor where he had furnished a suite of three adjoining rooms. Dr Geissmar sat in the first, Sir Thomas's office came next, and leading out of that was his own music library. On the opposite wall was an iron (fire-proof) door that led on to the stage and to which Beecham and the chief fireman alone possessed keys. This meant that he had immediate access to any performance as well as a ready means of exit from unwanted visitors. He frequently put both these advantages to good use.

Beecham sent Dr Geissmar to make arrangements for the next season with her friends in Paris and Berlin, obtaining from the German Ambassador to Britain, Joachim von Ribbentrop (known to some as 'Droppenbrick' or 'Ribbensnob'), a guarantee that she would be unharmed and would be treated with all proper courtesies as Beecham's personal emissary. The astonished woman found herself able once more to pass freely in and out of Nazi Germany whenever the occasion – and Beecham – demanded that she should. Furthermore, she was always given VIP treatment by her racial enemies.

Once, but only once, Dr Geissmar made out a train timetable for Beecham when he was about to travel to the north of England. He looked at it curiously, stared her in the face and put the timetable down. She soon discovered that he was a master at travelling and carried most of the important train timings and connections in his head. He was also an adept at planning, using a variety of charts which dovetailed their information.

The 1936 summer season was a spectacular one, especially as Beecham had attracted the Dresden State Opera for nine performances after his own grand opera season. This lasted from the end of April until the middle of June, and Beecham made himself responsible for the two *Ring* cycles again, for two performances of *Hoffmann* and three of *Die Meistersinger*. It was with the first of these that the season opened on 27 April. Some gramophone records have survived of this *Meistersinger*: the opening *Chorale*, the *Prize Song* (Torsten Ralf) and part of the finale, which gives a tantalisingly brief indication of how beautifully Tiana Lemnitz sang Eva. There are also recordings of Ludwig Weber in *Hagen's Watch* from *Götterdämmerung* and of the whole scene with Hagen and the Vassals. Kirsten Flagstad sang her first Brünnhilde in the second *Ring* cycle, and also four Isoldes under Fritz Reiner's baton.

Beecham remembered his allies throughout his career, and in this instance arranged for Malcolm Sargent to conduct three performances of *Louise*. They were successful, and it is surprising that Sargent never conducted an opera at Covent Garden again until 1954.

The Dresden State Opera season was very well patronised. Dyneley Hussey wrote in the *Spectator:* 'At last it has happened! The permanent company from a famous foreign opera-house, with its singers, orchestra, conductor, producer and technical staff, for all I know down to the call-boy, has come to Covent Garden ... the team-work has been of a kind that is unobtainable in the "grand" seasons when a number of singers from various sources are thrown together under strange conductors for a few performances.' The aspect of this company's work which most attracted critics was the thoroughness with which their production had been conceived and executed so that 'sharper definition of the details [was] achieved by exact timing and the skilful handling of the movements of the singers – in a word, in the acting.'

Nothing made Mr Hussey's point more clearly than a comparison between Beecham's *Marriage of Figaro* at Drury Lane in 1917 and any revival of the opera during subsequent short summer seasons. There had to be a permanent company in order to achieve unity, as Beecham had proved nearly twenty years earlier. Although the Dresden visit was an inspiring event it threw into sharp relief a number of grave deficiencies in London opera.

At the end of 1936 Beecham once more reverted to his 1910 plan of a winter season starting on Boxing Day and lasting four weeks. Again he conducted *Hoffmann*, with John Brownlee singing all the three baritone roles with great distinction. The attraction which produced full houses was a German *Salome* conducted by Hans Knappertsbusch (his only appearances at Covent Garden) and sung by a cast of visiting principals. Beecham wanted a double bill of *Salome* and *Elektra* but Knappertsbusch refused to consider it 'on artistic grounds', so *Gianni Schicchi* preceded *Salome*: an odd conclusion to the arrangement.

Beecham's leading tenor, Dino Borgioli, had been unwell throughout the month, and there were consequently an unusual number of announcements before performances in which indulgence was sought either for his non-appearance or for his poor vocal condition. At the end of the season Beecham capped this in a speech when he suggested that there had been as many pronouncements from the stage as there had been people in the audience, but he hoped that for the forthcoming Coronation season every seat would be filled. He promised to give the audience of his best, and asked that their attendance be likewise.

For all his personal preferences Beecham had never seemed to devote as much care and interest to the French and Italian side of Covent Garden seasons as he had done to the German operas. Owing to Dr Geissmar's experience and help, and as a result of his own meetings with Furtwängler and Heinz Tietjen of the Berlin State Opera, he had been able to secure a very good list of singers with Furtwängler to conduct. All the rest of the repertoire was left in the hands of a distinguished Italian baritone called Cesare Formichi, an arrangement which had been made before Dr Geissmar's arrival

Formichi was on the point of giving up his singing career and becoming an impresario, but as far as Covent Garden was concerned his activities were about as diplomatic as Erhardt's had been a few seasons earlier. Nor did he bother to consult Beecham about promises already made to artists before going ahead and booking himself, his friends and a number of cheap artists whom he put 'on his books' and from whom he extracted personal commissions for the favour. The veteran conductor Vincenzo Bellezza was dropped and so were a number of first-class Italian singers who were already favourites with London audiences. A time came when it looked as though Formichi had booked too many singers altogether and there weren't going to be enough roles to go round.

The proportion of operas turned out to be six Italian, five French, one each of English and Russian, and seven German (counting *Der Ring* as four). This meant far fewer German operas than in the past, and in his prospectus Beecham pointed out that 'our effort has been to redress the balance a little in favour of other countries and other composers'. Conditions in Nazi Germany made this statement all the more pregnant for those who had eyes to read.

The one English opera was *Don Juan de Mañara* by Eugène Goossens, which was receiving its première. Beecham ensured that Goossens was given full artistic support, with new scenery and costumes, and adequate rehearsal-time, but the work received little support from the public, although the critics praised it highly.

Beecham's administrative work kept him away from the conductor's desk for longer than in past seasons. He gave four performances of *Otello* and of *Tristan*, each a peak in its own operatic genre, and Barbirolli was persuaded back to conduct three performances of *Turandot* with Eva Turner and Giovanni Martinelli. Formichi's chosen Italian conductor, Francesco Salfi, achieved a lower standard than the other two.

John Barbirolli had Italian music in his blood, for he was of Italian parentage, though born in London and a British subject. He used to queue for the gallery seats at Drury Lane before the First World War to hear Beecham's performances there, and occasionally played in his orchestra at the Aldwych and Shaftesbury Theatres when a cello deputy was needed. In the summer of 1917, when Beecham and his opera company moved to Drury Lane with a far bigger orchestra, Barbirolli was taken on.

Beecham always treated him in a cavalier manner and the younger man grew up to mistrust him. In 1935 Toye and Beecham invited Barbirolli to talk, and gave him drinks, cigars and and congratulations on his fine operatic conducting. Barbirolli records that Beecham was full of 'my dear John', getting him to agree to conduct *Bohème* on tour: 'T.B. extremely friendly and listened to a lot of my *Bohème* (nearly all), put his arms round me and said "John, it's grand to hear you conduct again, it sounds beautiful," etc. I went to supper with him after the show at which he kept me until 2.30 a.m. Had the most amazing conversation – he cannot any longer carry on alone with all his enterprises and must have a colleague, and "My dear John, there is nobody but you." It's all a little puzzling ... the plan would be that I share his concerts and opera with him and conduct the Phil. [LPO] while he is away. What a mixture he is!'

This plan came to nothing but in the following year Barbirolli's appointment as chief conductor of the New York Philharmonic infuriated Beecham because somebody whom he considered his junior had been invited before he himself had been given the chance to refuse. In 1936, when Beecham was planning the Coronation season, he again invited Barbirolli to come and conduct for him – *Tosca* and *Turandot* at £60 a performance. Barbirolli records: 'Met T.B. who was full of "My dear John", dished out drinks, cigars and congratulations. The bugger.' But this time he did conduct for Beecham.

The offering of French opera in the Coronation season was somewhat mixed. Lisa Perli sang Mélisande in the Debussy opera in an idiomatic production conducted by Albert Wolff of the Paris Opéra. *Alceste* and the rare Dukas piece, *Ariane et Barbe Bleue*, with French principals, were conducted by Philippe Gaubert, while *Orphée* was conducted, rather at the last moment, by Fritz Reiner, since Beecham had been forced to withdraw on account of 'pressure of work'. Maggie Teyte sang Eurydice beautifully, the Orpheus was a tenor (according to the Paris version) and the soprano whom Formichi had cast for Amor because she was so lovely couldn't sing a note and had to be replaced. Two choreographers were in conflict on the ballets and there was a total absence of style due to all the misfortunes which the production had suffered in London. This was unfortunate because Dr Geissmar had heard it in Paris and persuaded both Rouché of the Opéra and Beecham to include it in the Coronation season.

The two magnificent *Ring* cycles were conducted by Furtwängler, with Frida Leider, Margarete Klose and Max Lorenz in the first cycle, and Kirsten Flagstad, Kerstin Thorborg and Lauritz Melchior in the second. Rudolf Bockelmann and Ludwig Weber were the Wotan and Hagen in both. Such casting would inspire any Wagnerian to attend twice.

Beecham's *Carmen*, which was given on the eve of Coronation Day, was vocally not up to scratch at all. The much-admired Georges Thill (that *rara avis*, a lyric *Heldentenor*) failed dramatically due to stagefright, from which he always suffered. At the second performance he had to be replaced as Don José by Martinelli. Renée Gilly (daughter of the celebrated French baritone who was singing Pelléas that season) was a good Carmen, but the first-night Escamillo was so poor that he, too, had to be replaced at once, and the part was sung at future performances by Dennis Noble. So much for Formichi's casting.

Despite the appearance of such artists as Lawrence Tibbett, Ebe Stignani, Germaine Lubin, Herbert Janssen, Vanni Marcoux and others, the total effect of the season was not at all what Beecham had intended. By casting his net wide, as seemed to fit the occasion, Beecham had lost control (not only through Formichi) because of lack of proper rehearsal time and slack production standards. It was a patchwork season in which one or two items stood far above the others.

The press were candid about the failures, and several critics had their tickets withdrawn by an irate Beecham, who expostulated from the stage on the last night: 'Never before in the history of Covent Garden has the press attained so high a state of excellence. We, on our side, have not been able to live up to it.'

Ernest Newman, the profoundest music critic of the time, wrote a thoughtful article about the season in the *Sunday Times*, making suggestions which Beecham must have realised were proper guidelines for the future. In essence Newman proposed better production (the recent Dresden Company's visit had not yet been taken to heart); no more 'off-beat' operas; a concentration on 'safe' works; and avoidance of giving wrong impressions about masterpieces, as had happened particularly in the season under discussion at the hands of Signor Salfi.

During his talks in Berlin Beecham had been invited not only to conduct at the Berlin Opera but to take charge of a complete recording of *Die Zauberflöte* there for HMV. This enabled him to work with members of the Berlin Opera, whom he had not yet invited to London but was thinking of doing for the 1938 summer season.

In 1938 John Christie was still planning a scheme for co-operation between Covent Garden and Glyndebourne – or rather (to his way of thinking) between Glyndebourne and Covent Garden. He appeared to be oblivious of the international situation. His unawareness of anything except his own ideas and milieu was at best charming, at worst the bewildering attitude of a crank and an egoist. In a letter dated April 1938 (quoted by Spike Hughes in his *Glyndebourne*) Christie wrote: 'I hope there may be a reasonable chance of managing Covent Garden as well as Glyndebourne, but I suppose it depends on whether Beecham makes a muddle and a loss again this year.... I want Covent Garden to be combined with us. It would mean, I suppose, thirty performances at Covent Garden followed by thirty performances at Glyndebourne – about twelve weeks.'

As the year went on, Christie was blithely planning for Toscanini to conduct at Glyndebourne and for his company to appear at the Lucerne Festival the following summer and at the New York World Fair in 1939. The only possible link that ever existed between the two houses had never been properly forged; when Beecham offered Rudolf Bing, Christie's general manager, a similar job in Bow Street, Bing refused.

On one occasion Fritz Busch, Glyndebourne's musical director and principal conductor, was in direst difficulty when the Glyndebourne organisation failed to book a singer he desperately needed and the season was almost upon them. He described Christie as 'an innocent and an amateur'. Once Glyndebourne had seen two or three seasons Christie's attitude to Covent Garden and to Beecham became one of superiority and disdain; and Christie would not visit Covent Garden even incognito. Beecham for his part referred to the Glyndebourne Opera as 'Christie's Minstrels'.

Beecham's bill of fare for 1938 seemed to have been made with Ernest Newman's suggestions partly in mind. It included only two operas which might possibly be called 'off-beat'. One was *Elektra*, which had been dropped from the Covent Garden stage after 1925; the other was *Die Entführung*, which had not been heard there since 1927. Both were strong Beecham favourites and he conducted them with characteristic devotion. On the whole it was back to the German repertoire, with twelve operas sung in that language and only *Rigoletto, Tosca* and *La Bohème* in Italian. The season was especially strong in tenors – Gigli, Tauber, Nash, Ralf, Melchior, Kullmann and Patzak – but it was also characterised by Nazi intrigue and pressures against non-sympathisers in the company.

The chief casualty of this political ill-feeling was Lotte Lehmann, who had a temporary mental collapse after the levée scene in Act I of *Der Rosenkavalier* when she announced: 'Ich kann nicht mehr'. The act was being broadcast, and those who heard it will always remember the feeling which this moment aroused. For that great trouper, Lotte Lehmann, to give up meant that something was seriously wrong. After the great house curtains were closed Walter Legge, Beecham's assistant artistic director, announced that Mme Lehmann could not continue but that Hilde Konetzni, who was in the audience, would take over after a short and unscheduled interval. She did so after squeezing herself with some difficulty into the only Marschallin costume available.

The season had begun with *Die Zauberflöte* with substantially the same cast of principals as the recording, although Tauber sang Tamino in London. Tauber had to work hard at the first performance to overcome the stuffy condescension of certain sections of the audience who regarded him merely as a singer of Lehár and popular ballads, unworthy to be performed at Covent Garden. But he won them over, and it was a matter for regret that the only other opera in which he appeared was the single *Entführung*, which Beecham conducted with zest, lightness and humour.

It was the *Elektra*, however, which proved one of the most outstanding artistic successes of the season. Rose Pauly as the tortured princess gave a superb interpretation. Kerstin Thorborg, Hilde Konetzni and Herbert Janssen supported her in a production that connoisseurs judged the best that had ever been heard in London. The sets for *Elektra, Entführung* and *Zauberflöte* had all been borrowed from Berlin, where many of the singers had established a true ensemble. The need for careful production in opera was once again being made manifest.

Beecham also conducted three performances of *Lohengrin* and of *Die Meistersinger*. Although there were changes in both casts he did have Lemnitz, Thorborg and Ralf in the first, and Lemnitz and Kullmann in the second. Lemnitz was one of the more arrogant and dedicated Nazis present in London.

It is probably true to say that this was the last really international season at Covent Garden. Singers were booked regardless of their political opinions and solely for their individual artistic integrity. There were already many refugees at the Opera House, some in the auditorium and some on the stage. Austria had been annexed by Germany in the previous March and England seemed to be one safe place in a crumbling Europe.

Beecham was well aware of all this but seldom discussed it with anybody. He did his best to help those in real trouble and unofficially backed the naturalisation of several prominent German and Austrian Jews who decided to make England their new home. Beecham had seen the conflicting aspects of Germany's totalitarian régime at first hand during the LPO's tour in 1936: on the one hand, thorough (and now possibly stifling) control and support of the opera houses and orchestras; on the other, unspeakable methods of dealing with Jews and opponents of the Nazis. Even in Italy Beniamino Gigli and a number of other prominent singers were openly toadying to Mussolini.

Beecham's tenacity of purpose was never more pronounced than at this time. If he wanted a certain soprano and tenor for an opera, he booked them – regardless of whether they might have to sing a love duet and embrace one another in spite of one being a Nazi and the other a Jew. Beecham regarded this as incidental to the needs of opera, and did not let it trouble him: music was, for the moment, seen to transcend the artificialities of politics.

Yet so much uncertainty and political conflict seem to have had an unprecedented effect on the finances of the season. Nearly £10,000 was lost and that autumn the Grand Opera Syndicate, with which Beecham had been connected since 1910, was wound up. One of the backers, M. S. ('Mossy') Myers, was Jewish, and after the 1938 season he understandably jibbed at supporting so many German singers again. However, through the enormous efforts of Lady Cunard, the 1939 season was saved; it was due to be sponsored by the London Philharmonic Orchestra of which she was president. Beecham and an accountant called Thomas Hazlem were directors. With the announcement that there would be far fewer German operas than hitherto, both Myers and rich would-be opera conductor, Sydney Beer, put up further funds.

In January 1939 Beecham wrote one of his more provocative letters to the *Daily Telegraph*. Headed 'Seasonable Thoughts' it had the sub-title 'Shall not Covent Garden stand where it did?' It was an eminently sound and shrewd mixture of politics and art, censuring politicians for their deceptive tactics and comparing the manner in which opera was regarded abroad with that in which it was disregarded in London. His main assault was on the idea of closing Covent Garden because of the international situation. 'It is seriously proposed,' he wrote, 'that because we are suffering from a temporary access of jitters and jumps that would bring discredit upon a community of elderly nuns we should discontinue an event that is as regular a feature of our yearly calendar as the Royal Academy, the Military Tattoo, or the Eton and Harrow cricket match.

'Even during the really grim days of 1914–1918 London was never without an opera at some time or another in the year. I recall with especial gratification certain performances at Drury Lane which I conducted myself to the sound of German bombs exploding within a few feet of the theatre...

'In Germany, it is hardly necessary to inform the reader that in upwards of seventy towns opera is being given practically all the year round. As for the rest of the world, I have yet to hear that at Stockholm or Prague, Budapest or Brussels or any other capital has it even been suggested that the opera houses should be closed.

'Only in London is such a proposition capable of utterance....'

Legge pressed Beecham to invite the Dresden Opera Company back to London with Strauss's latest pair of operas, *Daphne* and *Friedenstag*, but in spite of the full houses in 1936 it was politically too late to do so and these two operas have remained unperformed in Britain to this day. Plans for a visit from the Czech National Opera were well advanced when Hitler marched into Czechoslovakia in March. A few of the singers escaped to London to take part in the opera season as refugees.

A week after the German annexation of Czechoslovakia, the last pre-war gala performance took place at Covent Garden when King George VI and Queen Elizabeth welcomed the French President and Mme Lebrun to London on a state visit. Beecham was in charge of the arrangements and had collected a large quantity of excellent French tapestry and furniture from various museums and country houses with which to set off the Opera House. One especially fine tapestry, which was hung over the entrance to the royal anteroom, bore the touchingly appropriate legend *Aimez-vous, les Uns les Autres*. It had been woven for the marriage of King Charles I and Princess Henrietta Maria in 1625.

Rex Whistler designed the beautiful 'rococo' programme, and the occasion was altogether a notable one. It was also the first time that the Sadler's Wells Ballet (later the Royal Ballet) had appeared at Covent Garden. Among them was a young and nervous ballerina called Margot Fonteyn.

Beecham began the gala with rousing performances of *La Marseillaise* and *God Save the King*, and then gave Debussy's *Ibèria* with the LPO. The Ballet was conducted by Constant Lambert.

Although five weeks elapsed between the gala on 22 March and the opening of the international season on 1 May, there was now considerable public spirit and pride in Covent Garden after the part it had played in the state visit. This encouraged sales at the box office. Furtwängler was in disfavour with the Nazis, who had confiscated his passport, thus making it impossible for him to conduct in London. Flagstad was also unable to come, for contractual reasons. Beecham made himself responsible for one cycle of *Der Ring* (with Lubin and Melchior) and two *Tristans* in the German repertory; and the 76-year-old Felix Weingartner, who had studied with Liszt in Weimar and succeeded Mahler in Vienna, made his Covent Garden début conducting *Parsifal*. Later he took over *Tannhäuser*. Weingartner's appearances were welcomed by audiences and critics alike, and he agreed to return in subsequent seasons.

Beecham conducted two performances of *Aida* (the first with Gina Cigna, the second with Eva Turner, and both with Gigli) and two *Don Giovannis* with Rethberg and Tauber, and Pinza as the Don, in rather peculiar scenery borrowed from Stockholm. (Beecham had negotiated the scenery while in Stockholm during the previous year, thus making a considerable saving in production costs.) He also conducted three performances of *The Bartered Bride* – or rather *Die Verkaufte Braut* since it was sung in German, displeasing many people. It opened the season and the cast included Hilde Konetzni as Mařenka and Richard Tauber as Jenik.

At a final rehearsal of this opera Beecham was often at odds with the singers and became very angry with them. Tauber came down to the footlights and addressed him: 'Sir Thomas, we have all been singing this opera for some years, but evidently in the wrong way. We hope that you will be patient with us and allow us time to master the correct style from you.' There was general laughter in which Beecham joined. He never objected to having the tables turned on himself if it were done well.

In a previous season there had been a similar upset and Beecham had berated the offenders at close quarters. When the scene started to turn ugly the LPO decided to intervene and independently struck up with *The Blue Danube*. Very soon everybody on stage was dancing the waltz, and Beecham rushed back to the pit to take over and increase the speed to a frenzied measure. The trouble was all forgotten.

Vittorio Gui was in charge of four Italian operas, while Constant Lambert conducted two performances of *Turandot* with Eva Turner in her prime as the cruel princess and Martinelli as Calaf. Of the fifteen operas in this last season before the war there had been thirty-five performances, of which Beecham had conducted fourteen, and before it all ended with his last Covent Garden *Tristan*, a prospectus for the 1940 season appeared which advertised fifteen operas in thirty-five performances once again, including Berlioz's *Les Troyens* complete, *Boris Godunov*, Gluck's *Iphigénie en Tauride* and *La Fanciulla del West*.

Beecham was exhausted. He had carried the last four seasons and conducted fifty-seven performances in all, and he was now ordered to take a year's *complete* rest. This he could not and would not agree to, but as a compromise he announced that he would not be conducting at all in 1940. He stated that he hoped 'to place the summer season on a more permanent basis than hitherto and to establish a regular company of the most distinguished artists, with a wider and more progressive policy'.

With the declaration of war between Britain and Germany on 3 September 1939, all preparations for a 1940 international opera season at Covent Garden came to a halt. The building was closed and then leased to Mecca Cafés for use as a dance-hall. All Beecham's possessions, foremost among which was his library, had to be moved quickly, and the offices of both the LPO and Covent Garden Properties Ltd had to be evacuated.

From April 1940 Beecham was abroad, first in Australia, then in Canada and the United States. He returned to England at the beginning of October 1944, fully prepared to plan a summer season of opera at Covent Garden for 1946. He accordingly took up options on a number of singers.

The Opera House was still owned by Covent Garden Properties, its chairman the same Philip Hill who had been a member of Beecham's board from 1934 onwards. Hill was depressed at the state of the Royal Opera House, whose occupants during the war had done considerable damage to the fabric. He meant to do all he could to restore the building to its former glories and offered Boosey and Hawkes, the London music publishers, an opportunity to acquire the lease. Unless this happened Mecca would be able to renew until December 1949, which they wanted to do.

Hill's plan worked. Boosey and Hawkes bought the lease, but at first they were unable to put the House in order, and the dance-hall arrangement continued until September 1945. Boosey and Hawkes issued a statement about their future plans for Covent Garden, at which John Christie wrote a letter to *The Times*, making it clear that he wished to be associated with the House when it was reopened.

A Covent Garden Committee had been convened in 1944 with Lord

Keynes as Chairman, and Samuel Courtauld, Professor Edward Dent, Kenneth Clark, Sir Stanley Marchant, William Walton, Leslie Boosey, Ralph Hawkes and Steuart Wilson as members. The Arts Council agreed to make an annual grant of £50,000 in the first year of Covent Garden's reopening. This was to be in February 1946. The Sadler's Wells Ballet, whose continuous work throughout the war in London and the provinces had earned them a substantial following, were to become established there.

It soon became evident that the Committee (which became the Covent Garden Opera Trust) was inclined to have neither Rudolf Bing of Glyndebourne as general manager nor Sir Thomas Beecham as artistic director, musical director or any other kind of director. At once Beecham raised his voice and yelled. His letters to the newspapers were excessive in tone; he appeared to believe that the artistic directorship was his as of right. The Committee, however, regarded him as altogether the wrong man for the job. It was no longer possible for him to sponsor opera seasons, because the war had deprived most of his former subscribers of the means to continue their subscriptions; and the Opera House was now being run by a committee that was not going to be overruled by anybody. It had been appointed by the Government. Moreover, Beecham had turned sixty-six, and the fashion now was for younger men than he to be awarded the plum jobs. Worst of all, his way with money was viewed with suspicion.

Beecham's non-return to Covent Garden, terrible as it seemed to him at the time, was really providential. He was born and bred a rich man, used to treating money with disdain. Because 1946 was the first year of the reign of bureaucrats in Britain, everything had to be estimated, budgeted and strictly adhered to. Beecham would not have suffered such a régime for long, and it would have been too strong to have let him go his own way.

He carried his years comfortably (apart from his gout) and was still a Victorian in outlook. He was used to giving orders and getting others to carry them out. Many was the time between the wars when, after a musician, singer or anybody else had made repeated mistakes, he would call out 'Sack him!' Such persons never reappeared. He could never act like that again and expect the same results. What was worse, Covent Garden had virtually cried 'Sack him!' to Beecham. And he was out. *The Times* regretted this fact in a leader which discussed the announcement of an obscure Austrian-born composer and conductor, Karl Rankl, as Covent Garden's musical director.

Not only was John Christie's earlier appeal to be included in talks about the reconstitution of the Royal Opera House ignored, but Keynes was particularly unfriendly to him. Christie and Beecham, both monstrously offended, became wary allies, thrown together in the same non-cause. Beecham offered to put on a festival opera season at Glyndebourne which he would conduct without a fee. His dates were from 12 June to 13 July 1946, and he offered three operas: *The Magic Flute*, *La Bohème* and *Lucia di Lammermoor*. However, the two Italian operas gave way to *Carmen*, in French, as an opéra-comique with dialogue. Christie cast Kathleen Ferrier as Carmen before telling Beecham. He was incensed and declared that he would have no 'raw and undeveloped material'. So the two uneasy partners broke up and Beecham's season never came to pass.

The new general administrator of Covent Garden was David Webster, a canny Scot who had been one of the leading figures in Liverpool's musical life as chairman of the Philharmonic Orchestra. He was also a critic of concerts and opera performances in Liverpool and had once slated Beecham's production of *Koanga*. In righteous wrath Beecham had called: 'And who is this David Webster? I insist that all copies of the offending newspaper be burned on St George's Steps, and Mr Webster with them!' Now, about ten years later, he had every reason to ask again: 'And who is this David Webster?'

By profession Webster was general manager of the largest department store on Merseyside. During the war he had advised the Ministry of Supply on manpower, and was later a member of the Arts Council music panel. Keynes knew Webster and appreciated his firm and proven business capacity as well as his endless tact, fine social graces and profound love and understanding of music. In Webster's life business had come first and music second, although he had frequently visited Salzburg, Bayreuth and other foreign opera houses. He planned his business life in order to allow himself that sort of holiday. Webster was exactly what the committee wanted; and he was appointed.

Beecham suffered three great professional misfortunes in his life. The first was the death of his father a few hours before the moratorium on the Covent Garden Estate would have made his fortune secure; the second was the decision, by one person, to lodge an appeal to bankrupt the Beecham Opera Company, thus preventing it from becoming a National Opera; and the third was his exclusion from Covent Garden in 1945. It was the last that wounded him most deeply; his deep-seated pride never recovered from it, although it proved the least serious in the long run.

There were already two opera companies in London in 1946 and a third was in process of being formed. The Sadler's Wells Opera in

Beecham in 1942 at the time he became an associate conductor at the Met.

Beecham in Seattle, Febru[ary?]
1942, dressed as the compl[ete?]
Englishman (he was never
seen wearing a bowler at
home), during his tenure o[f?]
the Seattle Symphony
Orchestra. (*Below*) On the
film set of *The Red Shoes* i[n?]
1947. Esmond Knight hol[ds?]
forth to Marius Goring (le[ft?]
Brian Easdale, the compos[er?]
(between them), and
Beecham.

Above Beecham with Jea
Sibelius (1865–1957) in
Helsinki, 1955, and (*left*)
Carl Ebert, the German
and opera producer, at
Glyndebourne in 1960,
discussing the forthcomi
production of *Die Zaube*

Islington and the Carl Rosa Company were of long standing. Jay Pomeroy's Company, which employed Italian stars with a repertoire of exclusively Italian works, was supported by Pomeroy's own wealth. He eventually outreached himself and in 1949 suffered the same fate as Hammerstein had done, at the same theatre in Kingsway. These enterprises pulled against each other at a time when one strong company under an experienced musician might have begun to found a national opera company, as Beecham had been within an ace of doing in 1920.

Once the Glyndebourne idea had foundered Beecham decided to put on a short season at His Majesty's Theatre in direct competition to Covent Garden. He proposed *Don Giovanni, Pelléas and Mélisande* (Maggie Teyte was still singing) and *Madama Butterfly*. But two things were wrong: the successful play *Edward, My Son* starring Peggy Ashcroft and Robert Morley was firmly occupying His Majesty's, and nobody seemed at all keen to back such an enterprise. So it never happened.

This more than anything else may have convinced Beecham that he was not going to get back to opera in London by the direct route, and so he began to bombard David Webster, in the friendliest manner, with suggestions, recommendations, proposals and endless lists of suitable operas for production. 'Beecham seems fond of lists,' said Webster. On the side, though, Beecham was extremely rude about the Scotsman, and some time later he remarked: 'You know, I was walking past Covent Garden the other day and saw, to my great surprise, that they were actually announcing *The Twilight of the Sods*. It's about time.'

But if Covent Garden wouldn't have him back – yet – the BBC was keen to do so. Their opera department was under the management of the enlightened and enterprising David Harris. He and a few others, notably the Head of the Third Programme, George Barnes, knew Beecham's value to broadcasting at home and overseas. (All policy decisions were still made at Broadcasting House and not at Lime Grove or Wood Lane.)

In 1947 Beecham made BBC recordings of the complete *Les Troyens* in four sessions and for a payment to himself of £437 10s 0d for each of the two operas. While this was probably the artistic highpoint of his work with the BBC at that time, it was not the first opera he had recorded since his return from the USA. A week before the Christmas of 1945 he conducted *Prince Igor*, and also gave a talk about it for a fee of twenty guineas. Between October and December 1946 he recorded three more operas: *The Damnation of Faust* by Berlioz; *Tristan und Isolde;* and Cherubini's *The Water Carrier*. For the Berlioz opera he received only £175, for *Tristan* £250; for the Cherubini opera his fee was raised to £437 10s 0d, where it stayed. The figures are germane to later developments. These operas, it should be stressed, were BBC studio performances and not broadcasts taken from concert or stage performances.

In October 1947 Beecham arranged a festival in honour of Richard Strauss. He revelled in festivals; they reminded him of grander times when a party was a party and a gala was an event of real splendour. A festival was a good opportunity to try to recapture elegance and atmosphere among the audience, though nowadays it hardly ever did so.

Strauss had been living in Switzerland. As soon as the American Army occupied Garmisch it allowed him to go there – which the Nazis had refused to let him do. Beecham wanted to help the old man (he was eighty-three) and to let him hear a few programmes of his own works played well. Strauss flew from Switzerland and later conducted a concert himself. The operatic items were two, the first being two scenes from *Ariadne auf Naxos* staged at Drury Lane. Beecham would on no account go near Covent Garden, so he accepted 'The Lane's' stipulation that the lighting and set for their current musical, *Oklahoma!*, must not be disturbed.

The performance was on Sunday 12 October and Strauss was in the audience. The Vienna State Opera were visiting Covent Garden and Beecham borrowed Maria Cebotari for Ariadne and Karl Friedrich (who proved less than adequate) for Bacchus. The Royal Philharmonic Orchestra was in the pit, conducting and staging were by Beecham, and the set was designed by Oliver Messel. *Ariadne* had not been heard in London since a single performance by the Dresden Company which Strauss himself conducted in 1936, so it was totally unfamiliar to many in the audience.

The BBC was anxious to take some part in the Strauss Festival and Beecham opted for *Elektra*, Strauss's and his own first triumph in London in 1910. This was twice performed at the BBC's Maida Vale No.1 Studio, with the RPO before an invited audience. Erna Schlüter sang Elektra and Ljuba Welitsch, Elisabeth Hoengen and Paul Schoeffler (borrowed again from the Vienna State Opera) were respectively Chrysothemis, Klytemnestra and Orestes. After the second performance on 26 October, Strauss took a call with Beecham, whom he embraced warmly and kissed on the cheek. This performance exists on pirated records, and through the blur of more than thirty years it is possible to sense some of the atmosphere of the occasion as well as to hear how Beecham tackled this violent and angry work.

Elektra led to retribution from inside the BBC and the Furies there were soon on Beecham's track. The cost to the BBC of the two *Elektra* broadcasts was £3,704 – far above the estimate. During rehearsals

Beecham had announced that he must have two more. Already he was contracted to record *A Village Romeo and Juliet* in the studio and the BBC internal memos started to flow.

5 November 1947. SIR THOMAS BEECHAM PROBLEMS
There is real cause to suspect that Sir Thomas Beecham's additional rehearsals are only brought in when there is the possibility (as there will be in the case of Delius) of commercial recordings afterwards ...

The Victor Company of America arranged for HMV to record the closing scene from *Elektra* on 78 r.p.m. after the BBC performances were over. After much to-ing and fro-ing Beecham was informally approached over drinks and confronted with the 'rumour'. He appeared 'obviously nettled' and denied the suggestion. A memo reads: 'I feel that should there be any question of HMV recording *A Village Romeo and Juliet* after a BBC performance, Beecham will come out in the open from the very beginning.'

Beecham came back swiftly at Kenneth Wright, the man who had put the suggestion of the 'rumour' to him: 'I feel it incumbent upon me to advert to and deal with the highly unpleasant piece of information you communicated to me the other evening in respect of rehearsals and performances of Elektra last October.' Beecham declared that nobody who knew the score could ever imagine that four rehearsals were adequate for such an opera, especially as these four had been for purely orchestral purposes. Moreover, he said, extra rehearsals required for the recording had cost him £1,000 of his own money because Victor had demanded them.

George Barnes was made aware of the implied discrepancy which Beecham felt existed between a BBC recording from the studio and a commercial recording on gramophone records. He asked for estimates of the forthcoming *Village Romeo and Juliet* with Beecham and the RPO, and was told the figure. He replied: 'If the cost of £2,455 for two performances cannot be reduced we must cancel all future pencillings of Sir Thomas Beecham and the RPO and Chorus in opera broadcasts.'

The recording of *A Village Romeo and Juliet* was postponed for a while, finally taking place on two days in April 1948 at Maida Vale. It was then recorded by HMV on twenty-four 78 sides, starting on 1 May. This ambitious recording was sponsored by the Delius Fellowship and nothing was heard any more on the subject of BBC rehearsals.

The 1947 combination of *Ariadne*, Beecham and Messel bore abundant fruit at the 1950 Edinburgh Festival. This was the third annual festival which had been fathered by Rudolf Bing out of Glyndebourne, though Bing had now become manager of the Metropolitan Opera. Beecham had the co-operation of the comic actor Miles Malleson, who was a scholarly man. He made a new English translation of Hofmannsthal's play and agreed to produce it and to take the part of Monsieur Jourdain. Beecham was responsible for the production of the opera and for conducting the whole work. Messel's sets remained in use by Glyndebourne for the next fifteen years.

Beecham made some cuts in the score and allowed Ilse Hollweg, the Zerbinetta, to sing her difficult scena in a simplified form but in the key which Strauss had specified for this, the first version of the opera. Peter Anders was a successful Bacchus, possessing the ideal voice for an arduous role; while the Ariadne was the Swiss soprano, Hilde Zadek, whose mournful countenance admirably suited the suicidal heroine. This was the nearest that Beecham ever came to participating in a Glyndebourne opera, for the production was only performed in Edinburgh.

Beecham was constantly attacking Covent Garden – its administration, its policies, its performances, even its building – in the press over the years. In this he was not alone. Some of Ernest Newman's notices in the *Sunday Times,* especially those covering Wagner performances, were no less acid or vituperative. But Beecham knew as well as anybody the difficulties likely to be encountered in the early stages of a new opera company's existence. What he hated was to see every one of the mistakes being made over and over again when he felt he could have prevented many of them from his own well of experience.

In late 1949 new productions had reached an impasse under the brilliant young stage director Peter Brook, who cared less for the music than for clever tricks and 'modern' sets, costumes and lighting which the singers often had to wrestle with. Brook went back to the theatre, and Webster decided that for the Festival of Britain he would invite Beecham back to conduct one opera of Covent Garden's choice and another of Beecham's.

Beecham's first bid was for *A Village Romeo and Juliet,* which Webster vetoed although the recording was now published. Then, despite misgivings on the part of Covent Garden, the Arts Council and the City of Liverpool, who were to share the bill, the second choice became Balfe's *Bohemian Girl,* first produced exactly one hundred years before. The other opera presented no difficulties – *Die Meistersinger,* as Beecham referred to it, or *The Mastersingers* as it was billed from the outset at Covent Garden.

The Wagner opera came first in the Festival of Britain season and

Beecham insisted upon a large crowd for the final scene. It is said that the Opera House offered him a mere eighty people, but he had the figure augmented to two hundred by getting hold of students from music schools all over London. They certainly made a grand sound, and there was a tremendous ovation for Beecham each time he took his place in the orchestral pit for the four performances. The *Sunday Times* summed it up pleasantly by suggesting that Beecham's appearances were to the London public what Siegmund's assurance was to Sieglinde: 'Keiner ging doch einer kam: siehe, der Lenz lacht in den Saal' ('Nobody went, but someone came; see, Spring comes laughing into the room'). 'It is a long time since we heard a *Meistersinger* so pressed down and running over with all that makes orchestral listening a delight – ardour, passion, beauty, tenderness, thoughtfulness.' The *Observer*, on the other hand, felt that there were 'two good performances – one on the stage, the other in the orchestra – which would not quite go together ... it would have been better not to resist the conductor and to take part joyously in the unusually swift, but lovely creamy flow he gave to the music. Sir Thomas also realised ideally the beautiful golden-brown which is the predominant tone of the score.' *The Times* said that 'It was not vocally a performance of uniform excellence, but as a distillation, through the orchestra of Wagner's imaginative vision of what human sympathy is in its heights and depths, it could only be described as superlative.'

These extracts between them faithfully describe not only the achievement of these performances but also their effect on audiences and critics alike. Here was a veteran of operatic conducting presenting one of his favourite works and drawing from the press as well as from the orchestra a nobility and poetry of utterance that had not been heard for a long time.

By 1951 standards the opera was well cast. Peter Anders and Elisabeth Grümmer were the Walther and Eva; Benno Kusche was an ideal Beckmesser; and Karl Kamaan and Hans Hotter shared the role of Hans Sachs. The one singer whom Beecham knew really well and had often worked with in the past was Ludwig Weber as Pogner.

Then came 'Bo Girl', as the opera is nicknamed. Orchestral rehearsals and final stage rehearsals were held in Liverpool, where the opera was to be a centrepiece in that city's contribution to the Festival of Britain. The score had been adapted quite extensively by Beecham, and the orchestral parts often came up wet from the copyists' hands to the instrumental desks. An all-British cast supported the two first-cast principals, Roberta Peters and Anthony Marlowe; these were Americans from the Met, but there were alternate British principals. The doubling-up was necessary because the opera ran every night for a month, including full rehearsals. Sir Thomas knew the work well and knew where expert tightening-up and adjusting were needed to prevent several 1851 situations from seeming unacceptably comic to a 1951 audience. Alfred Bunn's libretto, absurd in the original, was thoroughly overhauled by Dennis Arundell, the producer, who made it into an acceptable period piece.

One cannot quite tell whether Beecham had his tongue in his cheek when he proposed moving the opera bodily to the Met afterwards. Anyway it never happened. The opera took the press mainly by surprise, but those critics who mentioned the music were highly complimentary to Beecham. Eric Blom in the *Observer* thought that 'Sir Thomas's very superior performance is most flattering to the music and makes it appear beautifully scored for the most part', while *The Times* reported that 'the cavatinas ... when played with the refinements Sir Thomas Beecham brings to them and sung in proper lyrical style exert still the charm that they have always done.'

Once more Beecham had proved that he could infect a faded work, clumsily written and composed, with such skill and finesse as to make it sound like a very good opera indeed a hundred years later. Beecham conducted eight performances in Liverpool and another eighteen in London. The remainder were capably taken care of by Beecham's first fully-qualified and totally dependable assistant conductor since Eugène Goossens – Norman Del Mar.

Shortly before Christmas 1951 Beecham returned to Covent Garden to conduct two more performances of *Die Meistersinger*. They were again sold out and had substantially the same cast as before except for the tenor, who was the less than satisfactory Hans Hopf, a wooden, unsubtle singer. Karl Kamaan sang Sachs. The first of these two performances on 14 December marked the 150th performance of *Die Meistersinger* and was also made out to be Beecham's 250th appearance in opera at Covent Garden. In fact it wasn't. Somebody had miscounted, but this did not prevent Beecham from being presented with a laurel wreath on stage afterwards. The second *Meistersinger* took place on 17 December, a date whose significance only became apparent some ten years later.

Beecham's next operatic venture in England was again with Dennis Arundell and fulfilled an ambition of many years – to produce a 'new' Delius opera. After a magical performance of Berlioz's *L'Enfance du Christ* at the 1952 Edinburgh Festival, Beecham loudly and passionately berated the audience about their lack of knowledge and interest in Delius's unperformed works as well as the performed ones. He said that he knew an opera – no, *two* operas – by Delius which had never reached the stage owing to the ignorance and apathy of the general public. He knew an opera which contained more melodies than there were in the work he had just played, and he was going to see that this opera reached the stage. Yet no one in the audience was any the wiser, for Beecham did not disclose the opera's name. *Irmelin*, Delius's earliest work for the stage, was one that he never expected to be performed. Now it achieved five representations at the New Theatre, Oxford, between 4 and 9 May 1953. The Arts Council and the Delius Trust contributed handsomely towards the production costs.

Dennis Arundell not only produced the opera but also conducted one matinée performance when Sir Thomas was incapacitated by a fall in the Mitre Hotel where he was staying. Edna Graham and Thomas Round sang the roles of the Princess Irmelin and Nils, the Prince disguised as a swineherd. Some of the words they had to sing were unbelievably naïve, but it was the music that mattered. The *Irmelin* Prelude was often included in Beecham's orchestral programmes and was considered a 'lollipop' too, but here it seemed to be extended over three acts with its principal theme used as a *leitmotif*. The *Observer*'s music critic wrote: 'The Royal Philharmonic Orchestra played the beautifully, often the very Wagnerianly, scored music with a refinement and poetry it never quite achieves under any conductor but Sir Thomas, who also showed his fine judgement by choosing a cast with hardly a known name in it and scarcely a single member who did not do remarkably well.' And *The Times* capped it all with: 'It need hardly be said that the protagonist was Sir Thomas Beecham at the head of his orchestra: he knows as no one else where Delius kept his magic. We have come to expect this, but what is astonishing is that he can, merely by taking a train to Oxford, shake out of his suitcase an unknown and exquisite opera all of a piece and without apparent effort.'

In 1955 the Bath Festival Society presented a little-known opera by an obscure eighteenth-century Belgo-French composer called André Grétry. The work, *Zémire et Azor*, contains some charming ballet music which Beecham loved, so it was not surprising that he had been invited to conduct. He insisted on – and got – a French cast, apart from Arda Mandikian, whose French was in any case perfect. The Bath authorities engaged Oliver Messel to design the opera and Anthony Besch to produce it. The story is that of Zémire the Beauty and Azor the Beast, with a small cast consisting of Zémire's father and two sisters and Ali their servant. Huguette Boulangeot was certainly beautiful; Michel Sénéchal was a timid rather than 'fearsome' Beast. However, in this production the action was dominated by Bernard Lefort as Sander,

Zémire's father, and by Ali, sung by Michel Hamel and played with great comic facility.

Such an opera was ideal for the little Sheridan Theatre Royal and Beecham threw himself into the task with a maximum of enjoyment. The Bournemouth Symphony Orchestra played handsomely for him. He had edited and arranged the score so as to avoid the orchestral banalities of which Grétry is often accused, and the result was delightful and in every respect an artistic success.

This was Beecham's last live operatic venture in England and it was right that it should have been an early French opera. There were plans for him to conduct *Les Troyens* at Covent Garden and *Die Zauberflöte* at Glyndebourne, both in 1960, but other musicians had to be found because of Beecham's poor health.

No account of Beecham in the opera house would be complete without mention of his opera recordings, which are, after all, the most tangible and lasting part of his work there. Each opera on record, priceless memento of him as it is, nevertheless represents only one facet of his interpretation. Sad to say, there are too few complete recordings available considering the enormous number of operas (roughly seventy-five) that he conducted between 1909 and 1959. Small excerpts exist on 78 records, commencing with some vocal extracts from *Hoffmann* in English made in 1910. The first complete opera was *Faust*, made for Columbia in 1929, with Miriam Licette, Heddle Nash and Robert Easton, of which an LP of extracts has been issued and later withdrawn. In 1947–8 he made a second recording of *Faust* with a French cast, just too early for LP, which made its circulation of short duration. In 1935 Beecham recorded the last act of *La Bohème*, with Lisa Perli and Heddle Nash in a performance so delicate and delightful that it is regrettable that we cannot hear the first three acts as well.

The complete *Zauberflöte*, made in Berlin in 1937–8, is a classic of Mozart recordings, as is the later *Entführung* in true stereo made in 1956. Beecham's complete *Bohème* was made by RCA in 1956. Victoria de los Angeles and Jussi Björling sang Mimi and Rodolfo respectively, with a good supporting cast. The recording has become a classic, and has been reissued in applied stereo to ensure that it remains in circulation. David Bicknell, EMI's recording manager, tells a story of Beecham in a Miami hotel the day before a concert, on another occasion. Bicknell was in the adjacent room and quite early one morning was awoken by painful howls from Beecham shouting 'No! No! No! Not even in the Fiji Islands.' Bicknell ran in, wondering what on earth had happened, to find him in bed waving away a floor waiter who had brought in the wrong breakfast – a huge ice-cream topped with chocolate sauce.

A Village Romeo and Juliet, recorded on 78 in 1947–8, has been reissued on LP and is the only complete Delius opera conducted by Beecham on record. It is thus most valuable.

The other opera with de los Angeles was the complete *Carmen* made in 1958–9 in stereo as well as mono, remarkable for its orchestral brilliance and finesse. Beecham spent a great deal of time in preparation for this *Carmen*, so much so that Lady Beecham is reported to have complained: 'Many's the night we went to bed with Carmen between us!'

The film of *The Tales of Hoffmann*, made in 1949, was a box-office success. Decca took the sound off the film and issued it on record, prefaced by a sequence not by Offenbach. This did not please Beecham, who was personally under contract to EMI and hadn't read the small print when he signed his film contract.

The commercial recordings thus add up to only seven complete operas, with one (*Faust*) duplicated. But several other performances, given at the Met during the last war, are known to exist on tape. His *Louise* has been issued on pirate discs. Others are *Le Coq d'Or*, *Mignon*, *Falstaff*, *Tristan*, *Otello* and *Fidelio*, but it must be added that the quality of some, if not all, of those would scarcely come up to 'broadcasting standards'.

The *Elektra* of 1947, recorded in Strauss's presence, has been issued several times on pirate discs, and the 1950 *Ariadne auf Naxos* from Edinburgh has also appeared in private circulation. Otherwise there are said to be tapes or discs in the BBC archive of all Beecham's operatic broadcasts, but they cannot be issued on disc because of exorbitant demands by the Musicians' Union. Were these demands to be met, the whole operation would become uneconomical to any gramophone company.

Other operas performed during the Beecham international season of 1939 are said to exist on film-sound. If so, they should include complete performances of *Aida*, *Die verkaufte Braut*, *Don Giovanni*, *Der Ring* and *Tristan und Isolde*. All this is intriguing and frustrating, especially if one adds the BBC's copies of *Bohemian Girl*, *Irmelin* and *Zémire et Azor*, not to mention their studio recording of the complete *Trojans*, *Fair Maid of Perth* – and so on. But again it is the Musicians' Union which prevents us from hearing these performances.

Even so, did Beecham want us to go on hearing them? Rebroadcasts of old material become less feasible as time goes on, and new developments like quadrophony make the sound of 1939 seem thin and unattractive by comparison.

However, let us be content that we can always listen to the complete *Zauberflöte* and the complete *Entführung*, two of the operas closest to Beecham's heart, which contain a whole world of observation, criticism and delight in mankind.

Chapter Six

BEECHAM'S WORK ABROAD

IN THE DAYS when going abroad meant crossing the English Channel by steamer or the Atlantic by liner from Liverpool the English traveller was assured of assistance, courtesy and safety. From an early age Thomas Beecham became so accustomed to foreign travel that he would often dodge off to Paris or one of the German cities that he knew well like Dresden or Berlin, where he enjoyed the change of air and of food as well as the opportunity to taste the wines that don't travel. He went to concerts and kept up to date with singers and soloists. Although he didn't bother to speak any foreign language unless it suited him to do so, he seems to have been welcome wherever he went. (In fact, despite what many people thought, his French was good and his German passable.)

His visit to the USA with his father in 1897 while on holiday from Rossall and his two visits to Dresden in 1897–8 while an undergraduate, together with many other short excursions abroad, all made him aware of the delights which existed outside the British Isles and gave him a constant desire to be on the move. In later years his penchant for travel was perhaps an indication of insecurity, but certainly in the early part of his life it was the lure of exploration and discovery which led him on.

Beecham was longing to visit Bayreuth and to hear *Der Ring* and *Tristan* under Wagner's ideal conditions. The Festivals were not held every year, and when the first opportunity came in the summer of 1899 there was no *Tristan* that year; instead there was *Die Meistersinger*, conducted by Richter, and *Parsifal*, which interested Beecham less. He prepared himself thoroughly for what he imagined would be the greatest musical experience of his life so far, but the four *Ring* performances profoundly disappointed him. His own vision of Wagner's intentions far exceeded the mundane production. Beecham criticised the singing, the staging and the orchestral playing, though the musical world considered the singing to be first-class. Anton van Rooy sang Wotan, Ellen Gulbranson was Brünnhilde, Ernst Kraus was the Siegfried and a bass called Hans Keller sang Fasolt. Siegfried Wagner conducted with his left hand. His mother, Cosima, was still in charge of the Festival and there was a strong undercurrent of unrest circulating round the 'Green Hill'. Many of the Germans in the audience felt that she was responsible for a sharp decline in the performances and that there ought to be radical changes in the administration. The more reactionary supporters would not hear of such a thing. Consequently this division of opinion was producing factions at every performance and making the festival somewhat uncomfortable for all concerned. Beecham says nothing about *Die Meistersinger* in *A Mingled Chime*, though we know that he heard it – and no doubt preferred his own interpretation.

Beecham did not go abroad again for any length of time until his protracted honeymoon in 1903, when he took Utica to Paris and on to Italy. In Paris he heard Grétry's opera *Richard Coeur de Lion*, and as a result he hunted down every Grétry score he could find; many more were unobtainable, so he went to the Bibliothèque Nationale and made copies of them in full score. By the time he left Paris in the summer of 1904 Beecham's requirements had been extended to the operas of Dalayrac, Monsigny and Isouard, all of whom lived between 1729 and 1818 and whose names are as unknown today in France as they are in the rest of the world.

Beecham was spending much of his time becoming practically acquainted with a variety of musical instruments, and he describes in his autobiography how his playing on the trombone in Lucerne was greatly objected to, first in the pension and then in a certain graveyard. So he was obliged to take a boat out into the middle of the lake, which was just about tolerable. When the time came Beecham knew he would be able to tell whether his orchestral players were doing their best. He declares that in a much later instance he demonstrated to a musician on his own instrument that a particular passage *could* be played in the way he wanted it done. So all the practice had been worthwhile.

In the spring of 1904 Beecham and his wife went to stay with Giuseppe Illica in Milan. While he had been with the Imperial Grand Opera Company in 1902, its conductor, Pizzi, had given Beecham an introduction to Illica. The resulting correspondence had provided Beecham with a libretto for his opera *Christopher Marlowe*, and now the two men were to meet. Illica was twenty-two years Beecham's senior and a great influence on modern Italian opera. Beecham spent a week of concentrated work under his guidance, which included every aspect of opera production. Illica's libretto for Puccini's *Madama Butterfly* had produced a version which, at its première in the previous February in Milan, had been a terrible disaster. He had just finished reshaping it, and

Puccini had recomposed parts of his score. He stayed with Illica while they completed the three-act revision ready for what was to be its enormously successful second première in Brescia. Thus Beecham met Puccini under domestic conditions and described his musical changes as 'marvellous, a miracle'. Yet in spite of his foreknowledge of the accepted version of *Butterfly* Beecham never conducted it.

Illica's description to Puccini of 'signor Tom Beecham, a little Englishman with a nervous facial twitch and a chronic sniff' is revealing. Beecham was introduced as a promising conductor who was composing the score of an opera about Christopher Marlowe. Puccini was not in the least interested and was barely civil, but he found Utica and her broken Italian very attractive. Beecham did not take to Puccini either, although their meeting excited him from the musical point of view.

Illica told Beecham that he found Puccini exceedingly difficult both as a man and as a colleague. He knew exactly what he wanted and was not to be budged, but was reticent at the same time. It was Puccini who devised the ending for *Manon Lescaut* because he had already composed the music and refused to let Illica's plot prevent its use. Illica was upset because, as he put it, 'nothing much happens dramatically' and of course he has been blamed since.

After leaving Utica in Lucerne with her parents and brothers to have her baby, Beecham went to Florence on his slow, solitary journey back to England. He found Florence by far the most lovely city in the whole of Europe and worked there happily, collating information from manuscripts attributed to Palestrina. He also continued to work at *Christopher Marlowe*, and records that he now had time to spare for consideration of what he could do on his return to London. He arrived in Paris in mid-December to collect the French opera scores which had been copied for him, and crossed the Channel just before Christmas 1904.

His next substantial stay abroad, after his separation from Utica, was in 1912, when he and the Beecham Symphony Orchestra accompanied Diaghilev's Ballet in Berlin. The Orchestra had become so important to the Ballet that they were booked for a month's season at the Kroll Theatre, much to the surprise of the Berliners, who had no idea that an English orchestra could even play in tune. The Beecham Orchestra and its conductor delighted them, but it was only after their first *concert* that the orchestra got a notice – in the principal Court paper, the *Vossische Zeitung*:

> The Orchestra sounded very good on the opening night of the Russian Ballet, but in the concert hall it really came into its own in a blaze of glory. The

Beecham Orchestra is, without doubt, one of the best orchestras in the world; its organisation and direction is the greatest achievement of Mr Beecham. He is a born conductor though perhaps a little like a ring-master at a circus, poised first to the left and then to the right. If this makes us want to laugh it doesn't spoil the whole effect, for he has a strong feeling for the beauty of sound, for rhythm and for contrasts. He is prudent, energetic and passionate.

The second concert at the Blüthnersaal was sold out and there could be no doubt of Beecham's personal success.

The Kaiser's interest in the Ballet promoted full houses, even when he was present incognito in a curtained side-box, getting a closer view of the barer portions of the partly-clad dancers' anatomy. And when His Majesty attended in an official capacity in the royal box at the back and in the centre of the circle, the entire audience spent the intervals staring up at him while he turned this way and that, curling the royal moustaches in the approved manner for the benefit of his subjects.

Four years later Beecham was in Rome over Christmas 1915 and New Year 1916, and he gave two concerts with the Santa Cecilia Orchestra at the Augusteo. His own musical preferences nearly ruined the first concert on Boxing Day. He played Delius's *Paris* in spite of (or perhaps even because of) the fact that the orchestra had not taken to it and rehearsals had been sticky. At the performance the audience positively hated the work and made such a noise that they brought it to a halt. Beecham put down his baton with a flourish and walked off in his most disdainful and haughty manner, to return as soon as the din had died down to conduct the Paisiello overture *Nina, o sia La pazza per amore* (whose title continues to suffer distortion in programmes over the years). This was far more acceptable to the Romans, as the applause showed at the end when *Paris* was forgotten and Beecham accepted. The second concert was a *tour de force*.

His next long visit abroad was not until 1927. In December 1926 he had announced that he was emigrating to the United States, giving as his reason a list of complaints about the way in which Britain was being governed. The press took him seriously and filled the next morning's papers with columns to that effect.

He did go to the United States, but stayed there only a few weeks. Lionel Powell's associate in New York arranged a series of concerts with three major American orchestras in the following year for him, and he then returned to London in a curious manner, via Prague and Budapest. In the Hungarian capital he was to conduct one performance of *Tristan und Isolde* at the Royal Opera on 11 February, but the rehearsals were a great trial. He did not understand a word of Hungarian and the interpreter was not beside him when he gave the downbeat for the orchestral prelude. All he could find to say was 'C'est terrible, c'est terrible, c'est terrible!' Somehow or other he persuaded the players and singers to give a creditable performance on the night.

Beecham's excuse for his premature return to England was that he could not find a single decent restaurant in the whole of the United States, where they had not the first idea about gastronomy and provided food fit only for animals. How could he possibly be expected to stay there a moment longer? But really he liked the USA. He liked Americans' energy and zest, their efficient services and their money. He would certainly go back again, and he did so in January 1928, to give twelve concerts within a month. His début was at Carnegie Hall on 12 January, when the first half of the concert ended with Tchaikovsky's First Piano Concerto played by a Russian also making his New York début. This was Vladimir Horowitz, 'an unleashed tornado from the steppes' as one newspaper described him. In the third movement he went on his own way, leaving Beecham and the New York Philharmonic to catch him up if they could. They did, and a disaster was narrowly averted; but the incident did not endear Horowitz to Beecham.

Such applause as was heard after the concerto had never been equalled in Carnegie Hall. People were standing on their seats, tearing up programmes and throwing the pieces in the air. As the majority of this ecstasy was thought to be for the pianist, Beecham was hard put to redress the balance towards himself in the second half when he played Mozart's 34th Symphony, Berlioz's *Royal Hunt and Storm* and the Overture to *Die Meistersinger*.

He went on to Boston, where Koussevitsky was in the audience; then to Philadelphia, where he met the reigning conductor, Leopold Stokowski, and where he gave what was the most substantial programme of them all. It concluded with *Ein Heldenleben*. He had tried out Delius, Mozart, Handel and Berlioz, not to mention Tchaikovsky, and spiced them with his choice little pieces by Grétry, Méhul and Paisiello.

The American musicians took warmly to Beecham in all three orchestras. They liked his wit and repartee, his droll accent and manner; they liked the idea of his title, but especially they liked the way in which he treated them, as friends, accomplices in a pleasant task, and as equals.

The 1930s were remarkable for the number of appearances Beecham made in Germany. In January 1930 the British Ambassador to Germany, Sir Horace Rumbold, gave an afternoon reception in honour of Beecham in the white and red first salon at the Embassy. There the silver bowls shone and the footmen moved quietly among the nine ambassadors and other diplomats, senior officials of the German Foreign Office and selected representatives of Berlin society. A few musicians were also present: Erich Kleiber and his wife, Max von Schillings, and a woman called Dr Berta Geissmar, representing the Berlin Philharmonic Orchestra. Furtwängler was not a party-goer.

The concert on the following evening was an enormous success and received large coverage throughout Germany. Every notice was highly complimentary to 'the brave and enterprising Sir Beecham'. The string of flattering words included 'poise', 'marvellous polish', 'elegance', 'faultless performance' and so on. 'His speaking hands shape a plastic picture of the works,' wrote one entranced critic, and Beecham was compared favourably with Hermann Scherchen, the only other conductor known in Berlin who eschewed the use of the baton – although beside Beecham Scherchen was considered to look 'heavy and awkward'. British conductors only appear in Berlin three times in ten years, said one Berlin paper, the reason being that 'the English, just as they have not a single composer of epoch-making merit, also have not Furtwängler, Munch or Toscanini, with a single exception, that is, Sir Thomas Beecham.'

> At first I imagined that this man of somewhat short stature who, in the manner of Nikisch, walked to the platform in a leisurely and dignified style and conducted without a baton, must be a little vain. More and more, however, I came to the conclusion that his conducting without a baton was not a pose or caprice, but that his entirely individual manner of conducting simply did not require the aid of a baton. He also talks to himself while conducting, probably in English.

On the following evening Beecham was due to conduct the Taube Chamber Orchestra at a concert organised by the German Society of Arts in the intimate surroundings of the Château Monbijou. But he was taken ill and it was not at all certain whether he would be able to appear. Michael Taube took charge of the first part of the programme and then, to everybody's delight, Beecham arrived and conducted the second half, consisting of works by Handel and Grétry and the Tchaikovsky Violin Concerto with Georg Kulenkampff as soloist.

In April Beecham returned to Germany, to Cologne this time, with praise for his Berlin Philharmonic concert still echoing in the press announcements. He was the first English conductor to be invited to the opera house, where he was to give one performance of *Die Meister-singer*. He had only three rehearsals and an unfamiliar Walther in a cast that was otherwise used to singing together. Again the critics were ecstatic about the performance:

> This English musician knows no German, and yet music, the super-national language of the soul, instantly gives him the key to the most German of all modern operatic creations.

> With all his thoughtfulness and calm, Sir Beecham is a passionate man; in working up a climax he jumps from his seat, leans towards the stage, then turns towards a group of instrumentalists with rounded, inviting gestures. Here was light-winged comedy, although the obviously lyrical parts were rightly unfolded with greater calm than is usual with German conductors.

> I expected to see the face of an English aristocrat and suddenly found myself looking at a decidedly French type, perhaps that of a Count from Brittany or Normandy, not unlike the great Gobineau. Perhaps there is French blood in him.

Later on Beecham was interviewed and the reporter commented on his 'well-shaped, almost delicate head, his long narrow hands, constantly occupied in one way or another, and his appearance of calm and ease. On everything he has a perfectly decided, often surprisingly original opinion. Jazz to him represents the Middle Ages. He likens it to St Vitus' Dance. "Bloody awful!" he said. "Atonal music? Bah!"'

Most of the Cologne critics stressed the important part which Beecham had played in championing German music in England, especially the music of Richard Wagner; and one stated that the invitation to Beecham to conduct in Cologne 'appears to have both a political and an artistic background'.

In the following October Beecham accepted an invitation from Wiesbaden to conduct *Lohengrin* and *Tannhäuser* at the State Opera in a cycle of Wagner's operas performed in chronological order. On 5 October he conducted *Tannhäuser* from memory, and it was especially noted that he was fully aware of the difference between the holy Elisabeth and the impure Venus: 'the sanctity had an almost complete transparency whereas the passion was reproduced in all its sensuality'; 'there was the assurance of genius in his interpretation.'

His *Lohengrin* was done four days later with very occasional references to the score. All the main dramatic and musical points were well made and the third act was declared faultless.

On 13 October Beecham conducted the Leipzig Gewandhaus Orchestra in their famous hall. The concert was a joint effort between the Orchestra and the Mid-German Broadcasting Station. 'There was a beauty of sound, particularly in the glowing melody of the strings, that definitely reminds one of the magic of Artur Nikisch. *Ein Heldenleben* had never been played with such perfection since Nikisch's death.' This was indeed a tribute to Beecham, for Nikisch had been the resident conductor in Leipzig between 1895 and 1922, and many of the players who were there still remembered him well. Beecham again conducted without a baton (he had used one for the operas) and introduced Delius's *Brigg Fair*, to a mixed reception.

Exactly a month later he was back in Berlin at the special invitation of the Philharmonic, who gave him a handsome reception when he arrived for the first rehearsal. They said how much they enjoyed playing for him and how much he inspired them. A critic wrote: 'Sir Thomas Beecham enters, bows deeply with his back to the audience, which apparently represents the English greeting. Then he commences without baton or score in a manner which shows friendliness and aplomb. His gestures are in no way comical: Beecham interests the orchestra and he interests us.'

He seemed to be tempting German taste with his programme: *The Royal Hunt and Storm*, Haydn's 97th Symphony, Tchaikovsky's *Francesca da Rimini* and César Franck's Symphony. The last work was not liked because, as one review stated, Franck's 'great themes hardly ever develop to any conclusion; in most cases they are literally devoured by the technique of their execution.' As for Beecham, his 'superior intelligence and mastery of the score was felt in the orchestra's response to him'.

While he was in Berlin Beecham was questioned about his opera performances in Wiesbaden but turned the conversation into an anecdote. This was 'an unusual story about the years when Britain and Germany were at war'. He was conducting *Tannhäuser* in a British city where there was a naval base. A few days later two German submarine officers were captured at sea, and in their pockets were ticket counterfoils of the *Tannhäuser* performance. 'Of course they weren't spies,' Beecham pointed out; 'they were good musical people who merely wished to hear their favourite opera again.'

In 1930 the Nazis were increasing their influence in the Reichstag and had gained 107 seats, half-way to becoming the largest single party there. In November Beecham again conducted the Philharmonic in Berlin and went straight on to Hamburg, where he gave a performance of *Der Rosenkavalier* from memory. This was the first time that the opera had been conducted in Germany by a non-German. As with his Wagnerian opera performances, all criticism was silenced by his vigorous yet lyrical approach to the score and by the true atmosphere which he gave of a world gone by.

When one considers Beecham's way with Mozart it seems strange that he was never invited to conduct opera in Salzburg. In August 1931 – a month which he usually devoted to holidaying – he gave a single morning concert at the Mozarteum with the Vienna Philharmonic Orchestra. The programme consisted of three symphonies: Haydn's 93rd, Mozart's 34th and Brahms's Second. For some reason, possibly musico-political, he was not invited back for some time and then he refused to go merely for one concert. He never conducted there again. Lady Cunard accompanied him on this occasion – they were otherwise holidaying together – and they met the Strausses at their house in Vienna.

If the Salzburgers did not care about hearing Beecham again the New Yorkers certainly did, and between March and April 1932 Beecham conducted their Philharmonic Orchestra for twenty appearances at $2,500 (at that time £500) a concert. This time the symphony, rather than the proliferation of short pieces as in 1928, predominated in his concert-building.

Strauss's *Don Quixote* figured as a major work and Beecham recorded it there by a new process whereby the piece was played straight through, without breaks every four minutes or so. It seems to have been a similar technique to the German micrograde system of a decade later, for the whole work was recorded on only five sides, while the conventional 78s, made simultaneously, ran to ten sides.

Beecham's twentieth and last New York concert was a huge pro-gramme of ten items which started at three o'clock on a Sunday afternoon with a new band of out-of-work players who called themselves 'The Musicians' Symphony Orchestra'. Beecham had welded those players into a most creditable ensemble, exactly in the manner of Stokowski in the film *100 Men and a Girl*, which was not made until a year later. Olin Downes, hard-boiled music critic of the *New York Times*, gave the concert a 'rave' notice. The popular José Iturbi played the Haydn D major Harpsichord Concerto, and there was also a first performance by an American called Emerson Whitehorne: his Opus 54, a Fandango.

Beecham felt that this concert, for which he accepted no fee, fully justified his late return to London and the postponement of a Royal Philharmonic concert by ten days. Nevertheless the Queen's Hall box office was thrown into great confusion.

Towards the end of July Beecham went to Munich, the heart of the Nazi movement, where he gave one concert and three opera perfor-mances. By now the Nazis were the largest party in the Reichstag and their 230 seats already constituted a threat to peace in Germany. Beecham's two performances of *Die Zauberflöte* and one of *Die Entführung* were acclaimed, and he was at once invited back for 1933 – the year Hitler became Chancellor and the Reichstag was burnt down.

The 1933 performances of *Tristan* and *Die Meistersinger* were due to Clemens von Franckenstein, the Intendant of the Bavarian State Opera whose brother Baron Georg von Franckenstein was the Austrian Ambassador to Britain, later replaced because he was not sufficiently enthusiastic about the Nazi cause. In a letter which the Intendant Franckenstein wrote from Munich about the concert, there appears the following:

> The Orchestra will gladly play *Don Quixote* under your direction but they would like our first cellist Professor Disclez to play the solo. There is a special reason for this. Professor Disclez is a Belgian and has been attacked a good deal lately by certain jingos. If he is left out on this occasion his enemies will double their crowing and say that he is not good enough, although he is an excellent musician and a very clever cellist.

Don Quixote, with Disclez as soloist, Mozart's *Prague* Symphony and Sibelius's First made up the Pension Fund concert on 14 August.

After this spate of work in Germany Beecham returned to the United States in January 1936 to give ten concerts with the New York Philharmonic at Carnegie Hall. Each of his programmes had a Mozart symphony as the centrepiece, with British works arranged round it, and each was well received.

In November 1936 Beecham took his new orchestra, the London Philharmonic, on a tour of Germany, giving eight concerts in eight different cities within nine days. This was an exchange visit with the Berlin Philharmonic, who had played in London earlier in the year. The Berlin Philharmonic were acting as agents and organisers for the London Philharmonic and made Beecham one proviso only in his programme-building: he must not play any music by Mendelssohn, who was Jewish. This directive had come from 'on high' as soon as the composer's name had been mentioned. Ironically though, Dr Geissmar, who was now working for Beecham, and several Jewish members of the orchestra were completely protected by diplomatic protocol.

On the afternoon before the concert Beecham was summoned to an interview with Hitler. The Führer was puzzled by this strange little man whose dignity and forceful manner assumed command of the conversation. Hitler told Beecham that he had intended to come to London for the Coronation in 1937 but had already decided against it, since it might inconvenience the British Government. 'Not at all,' replied Beecham, 'there would be no inconvenience. In England everybody does exactly as he likes.'

The first concert took place in Berlin and Hitler sat in the Philharmonie Box with Goebbels, his senior ministers and their wives. It was broadcast all over the Reich and relayed to Britain. The electrifying renderings of *Deutschland über Alles* and the British National Anthem were followed by Dvorak's A major Rhapsody. There was great applause, especially from the Führer's box. Beecham turned to his leader and said: 'Hm, the old bloke seems to like it.' That was broadcast. During the interval Beecham stayed in the conductor's room as was his custom. He was visited there by Goebbels, Furtwängler and Sir Eric Phipps, the British Ambassador. This wouldn't do for the editor of the *Berliner Zeitung*, who published a photograph the next day which purported to show Beecham in Hitler's box.

That night was the beginning of a round of hectic parties for the LPO. They already know their opposite numbers in the Berlin Philharmonic and the Bierabend which they attended went on until the small hours. Sir Thomas danced on a table, sang songs and told a string of stories which were quickly translated and appreciated by his hosts.

Early the next morning they were off by train to Dresden, where much the same concert took place before an audience more civic than political, though Nazi uniforms were much in evidence. Another party, another train journey, this time to Leipzig; then Munich, Stuttgart, Ludwigshaven, Frankfurt, Cologne.

The one free day of the tour was in Munich, at Beecham's request. There he met the Berlin designer, Emil Preetorius, to discuss their forthcoming production of the *Holländer* at Covent Garden. Beecham had arranged for his stage director, Charles Moor, to be present at the meeting, and they were joined by Frau Winifred Wagner, Siegfried's widow, who had come from Bayreuth to hear Beecham conducting in Munich. After their meeting a special performance of *Don Giovanni* was put on for Beecham at the Residenz Theater, with Preetorius designs. Beecham fell asleep during the first act and when asked whether he enjoyed Mozart replied that he did, very much, but only when he was conducting.

On the following day Beecham was taken to a party at Rudolf Hess's imposing house. Hess had no idea whatever about playing host: there were too few Germans present who spoke English; the Party officials kept together; and general conversation did not even begin. Beecham decided to take the situation in hand; he sat himself down at the piano and proceeded to play. Afterwards he admitted that he had been so bored that he could think of nothing better to do. While the party warmed up considerably Hess remained impassive.

During the Stuttgart banquet on the following evening Beecham decided that he was not going to be sociable in Germany any longer. He ordered a private car and drove to the next city with Dr Geissmar so that he might avoid all the setpiece reception committees and speechifyings at railway stations. He was now free to choose his own activities, and one of these was visiting cathedrals.

In Ludwigshaven the concert was recorded in its entirety by I. G. Farben (now BASF) by means of a new process called magnetic tape. These tapes still exist, and the performance of Beecham and the LPO in the Minuet from Mozart's 39th Symphony has been issued on a BASF cassette.

After the last concert in Cologne Beecham decided to go direct to Paris by train – he knew by heart the time the Nord Express left. The orchestra was returning by Ostend, so he and Dr Geissmar should have had a pleasanter journey home. She, however, appeared to be in a highly nervous state as she clutched a large paper package. 'Whatever's the matter, Doctor?' Beecham asked her. She explained that the Reichsmarks given to all members of the LPO by the Germans as daily pocket money had not been used because the players had supplies of preferential 'travel marks'. It was highly illegal to dispose of German currency, and to arrange for it to be taken out of the Reich would have entailed considerable red tape and more time than they could afford.

'I'm fed up with these rotten marks,' Beecham said; 'just give me the dam' package.' Dr Geissmar was still anxious about the customs officials at Aachen, where they were due to cross the frontier, so she arranged for special instructions about Sir Thomas and herself to be sent on ahead.

The train left Cologne punctually and the two of them sat in their comfortable first-class compartment, Beecham with his attaché case open on the seat between them and the bundle of marks prominently displayed on top of his papers. He appeared completely unconcerned, smoking his pipe and reading, while Dr Geissmar suffered tortures of apprehension and fear; after all, she thought she knew these Nazis far better than Beecham did. At Aachen the carriage door opened and a customs officer stood politely in the entrance. When Dr Geissmar, just about able to speak, told him who they were he clicked his heels, gave the Nazi salute and left. 'There you are, Doctor – you see?' said Beecham, with the air of a conjuror.

But once the Reichsmarks were in London nobody wanted them. Finding that they could only be spent in Germany Beecham took them back with him and rapidly spent the lot in Berlin. This was in the following February when he conducted two performances of *Orpheus* and one of *Die Entführung* at the Oper unter den Linden.

In November 1937 Beecham had an important assignment in Berlin. He stood on the conductor's rostrum in the Beethoven Saal to make the first wax of what was to be the most famous *Zauberflöte* ever recorded. Walter Legge was the producer, and the recording was to follow the Glyndebourne Mozart operas in the HMV Society Series. Neither Legge nor Beecham was especially sympathetic with the way in which the other Mozart operas had been produced, and they rapidly agreed as to the manner in which they were going to do this *Zauberflöte*. The first choice for Tamino had been Tauber, but he was not available. Lemnitz was the ideal Pamina and Gerhard Hüsch an excellent Papageno. Legge wanted Ludwig Weber, then only thirty-seven years old, for Sarastro, but the singer did not feel himself quite ready for it. Ultimately the choice fell on Wilhelm Strienz, who coped well with the deceptively tricky role. Legge undertook the casting almost alone and earned not only praise from Beecham but also a demand to go to Covent Garden as associate artistic director for the 1938 season. Legge prepared thoroughly for the recording, and even replaced a few members of the Berlin Philharmonic Orchestra with more appropriate musicians from the Opera.

On the first day, working his cast and orchestra like demons, Beecham made twenty-seven waxes including repeats; on the second day, twenty-four. Everybody enjoyed themselves enormously: this was music-making of the best kind, even though not everybody was completely familiar with Mozart's opera or with the way in which Beecham wanted it played and sung. His was a lighter, more Austrian touch than the usual Berlin way of conducting Mozart, and the musicians responded fully to him.

However, Beecham couldn't manage to finish recording to his satisfaction the remaining seven of the total thirty-seven sides and he had to return to Berlin in February 1938 and again in March. One side still remained but by then it was impossible to get the singer, the orchestra, the hall and the conductor together at the same time. The recording of the opera was therefore completed by another conductor, though Beecham had undeniably stamped it with his own philosophy, mischief and wisdom.

Beecham left Berlin on 3 March 1938 and only once went back to Germany, with the RPO in 1959. His job there was completed. With the outbreak of the Second World War in the following year, the financial difficulties of the LPO at home, the closure of Covent Garden and his own, overworked physical condition, Beecham gave up everything for the second time in twenty years.

In 1940 he sailed to New York, arriving on 9 May, but not immediately staying. He set off for Australia soon after and landed in Sydney on 11 June, accompanied by Dora Labbette. One old friend was there to meet them – Neville Cardus, former cricket professional, later music critic of the *Manchester Guardian* and now engaged by the *Melbourne Herald* to cover Beecham's Australian concert tour. Accompanied by the director of music of the Australian Broadcasting Corporation, Cardus waited for a long time on the quay for Beecham to disembark. At last he appeared, almost the last off, having been down in the hold extracting a box of cigars from his luggage.

He agreed to being interviewed by Cardus on the radio that night, although he had had no previous warning. Two voyages and a quiet train journey across the States had done much to restore some of the vigour which had been sapped in London over the past years, so that the fund of puckishness was well topped-up when he sat down opposite Cardus for their unscripted talk.

Cardus's opening question was: 'Do you agree with the old saying that there are no good or bad professional orchestras, only good and bad conductors?' After a long pause, a very long one in the studio and over the air, Beecham replied crossly: 'What precisely do you mean?' And so it went on. He hardly spoke at all while Cardus fumbled about, repeating himself and getting thoroughly tangled up. The next morning they were both accused of having dined too well.

This broadcast was in some ways symptomatic of the orchestral tour which followed. Beecham's first six concerts were all with the Melbourne Symphony Orchestra, and from the start the musicians took to him. Not so the audiences. As the tour progressed he became more and more unfriendly and then downright rude, stating that he had witnessed far more intelligent species in the outer, remoter parts of Bulgaria than in his Australian audiences.

By the time he returned to Sydney he had mellowed a little, possibly because he would not be there much longer. Now he stated that Australia was 'the most amiable country in the world'. In Brisbane he recalled that the coughing had been bad but well-controlled at his concerts. After the music stopped 'hundreds coughed in rhythm. I suggested to my leader that they might be pleased if I turned round and conducted them. It would have been the first time I would have conducted a coughing chorus.' But after the Sydney concert the orchestra there was favourably compared to the London Symphony Orchestra or the Hallé. Beecham said he was surprised to find the standard of playing as high as it was. 'They are painstaking and enthusiastic,' he said, 'and it augurs well for

the musical development of Australia.' He also said that he would
investigate the possibilities of giving grand opera in Australia, although
this would need thirty principal singers of high rank and between
£10,000 and £15,000 to 'fit out any of the large halls'.

Before he left Sydney the Mayor insisted upon taking Beecham on a
launch to get a close view of the famous bridge. Beecham decked himself
out in a peaked cap and a blazer with brass buttons for his short voyage in
the Mayor's launch, but when they stopped beneath the huge structure
and the Mayor asked Beecham's opinion he replied: 'I don't like it at all.
Why don't you have it removed?' Finally, when he departed the shores
amid a good deal of resentment, his parting shot to a press reporter who
asked: 'Why did you come to Australia, Sir Thomas?' was: 'Why d'you
go to a zoo?'

He left a lot of delighted Australian musicians behind him, but as a
diplomatic visit his had failed. Even so, in musical matters his criticisms
followed a consistent pattern. He made perfectly plain his dislike of
people and institutions that obstruct genuine music-making of the
highest order; and if his audiences were reactionary, stupid, ignorant or
two-faced he had great pleasure in telling them so without compromise or
flattery. It was unlike him to sting so many people without reason.

North America was a very different matter. Beecham spoke with
feeling from the concert platform and at ladies' luncheons. There his
favourite topic was the 'English' language as heard in American films. His
imitations and descriptions were far from complimentary.

His first concert was on 17 November 1940 in Toronto, and his last
was on 29 August 1944 in the Hollywood Bowl. In between he gave a
total of 113 concerts with forty different orchestras, and seventy-six
performances of opera, mostly at the Met. Beecham was in his sixty-
second year, and the thousands of miles which he was to travel during the
next four years demonstrated his stamina. After a very short time he gave
up wondering where he was on waking each morning. 'Life,' he said
somewhat wistfully, 'has become a sort of *moto perpetuo.*'

For some time he had not been alone in North America, for his liaison
with Betty Humby, begun in June 1941, had now developed into
a determination to marry as soon as each of them had obtained a
divorce.

About the same time as Beecham reached New York and put up at the
Ritz Hotel Lady Cunard and her personal maid arrived there. The Ritz
being the Ritz and one of a chain of French hotels, there was no objection
to a shared suite. Beecham told people that his friendship with Lady
Cunard was 'only that', and had been so for the past ten years. She, on the

other hand, was as painfully devoted as ever, living it up as best she could among the not-so-poor refugees such as Lady Ribblesdale, Benjamin Britten and Sir Harley Granville-Barker. She went on pretending that she didn't know anything about Betty Humby until that fateful day when the engagement was blurted out in front of her at a luncheon party. Then she was forced to accept the truth and gracefully left for London.

Relieved of the accustomed impediment of Emerald Cunard, Beecham took on a new lease of life with the lady whose apartment he was sharing most of the time, much to the delight of his American friends and of those gossipy members of the public who were in the know. But in Seattle the affaire caused a scandal, although the inhabitants took the Beechams to their hearts once they were married.

The English journalist and author Cecil Roberts was on a diplomatic mission to the US during the war and often met Beecham in New York. Roberts appeared one day looking rather dowdily dressed and Beecham broached the subject of cash. Roberts demurred, but had a personal cheque for $2,000 put in his hand. The bank dishonoured it at once, so, saying nothing and being grateful for the kind thought, Roberts forgot all about it. A few months later, Beecham introduced the subject into the conversation. 'You know that cheque I gave you?' he asked. 'Well, I find I'm just a little pressed at the moment. D'you think I might trouble you for $500 of it?'

He received about $600 a concert and much more for an opera performance when he became joint senior conductor at the Metropolitan Opera with Bruno Walter. But this was still insufficient for his needs, and his early, lucrative cooperation with Columbia Records in June 1942 came to grief when he sued them. He could have done with that contract, but he seemed to think that the figure of $600,000 he was claiming was a better bet than actually earning it. He claimed damages for his recording of Sibelius's Seventh Symphony being issued before he had passed it, saying that the records 'were imperfect and not up to the standard set by his previous recordings in England', that the company had ample notice of his complaints, and that these records were defective. He lost the case and 'adjusted his controversy with Columbia'; but not even Columbia's competitors, the Victor Company, now offered him recordings.

In 1941 he conducted nine American orchestras and also went to the Montreal and Ravinia Festivals. The Montreal concerts were all of a religious nature, performed in La Chapelle du Collège St-Laurent. Somehow Beecham's persuasive manner was able to effect a change in the following year, when in the same building he performed Prokofiev's *Pierre et le Loup* with Ludmilla Pitoëff as narrator. Two days later there was a concert performance of Gounod's *Roméo et Juliette*.

At the beginning of 1942, part-way through their 1941-2 season, Beecham joined the Metropolitan Opera at the invitation of its general manager, the Canadian tenor Edward Johnson. He made his début with his own arrangement of Bach's comic cantata *Phoebus and Pan*. The *New York Times* reminded its readers that 'Bach got in by a side door, or rather on Sir Thomas's shoulders'. *Le Coq d'Or*, which followed, contained much material that had never been heard in previous Met productions.

Several prominent critics were astonished when they found that Beecham 'was committing the heinous crime of trying to instil something like energy' into the players and singers. It took him some time to come to grips with the orchestra, the highest paid in the world and still untouched by the war. Some of the world's finest singers, a good many of them refugees from Europe, were on the Met's payroll, but performances were patchy.

An afternoon performance of *Carmen,* with Lily Djanel appearing for the first time as the heroine, produced this comment from the *New York Times*: 'There was the general impression of a conductor straining every nerve to put life into the show on the stage and also to communicate something like life to an orchestra which, as a rule, played villainously. Sir Thomas accomplished a good deal. He may well achieve more as singers and orchestra become accustomed to his wishes.'

Later, Risë Stevens took over the role of Carmen. Beecham was so familiar with the direction of the opera that he would often give cues without even looking up at the singers. At one performance he realised that Risë Stevens was seldom in the place where he expected to find her, and his face grew grimmer. In the interval he stormed into her dressing-room: 'What in heaven's name are you doing, Risë? How can I conduct this opera when you continue to improvise your stage action?' She looked him full in the face for a moment before confiding that she was pregnant. He went up and put his arms round her. 'Now, my dear, you must not do a single thing which is uncomfortable to you. Don't worry, I'll find you somehow. Just don't jeopardise the baby for this stupid old opera business.'

She told him that her doctor had advised her against making certain movements, which was why she was obliged to go against the direction so often. In Act III there came a moment when she was supposed to faint, and to her surprise she felt herself being supported by the Escamillo, Ezio Pinza, so that she didn't have to slide to the floor on her own. It was an action which Beecham had asked him to perform.

Sir Thomas Beecham

At first Beecham would not conduct any Wagner although such international season artists as Melchior, Traubel, Janssen, Thorborg and Kipnis were available. One day Bruno Walter had influenza, and Beecham agreed to deputise for him in a performance of *Tristan*. 'On the whole the most poetic and romantic interpretation of the opera that we have heard for many years,' was the opinion of Olin Downes. Beecham then recanted and went on to conduct six more performances.

His main repertoire was *Carmen, Louise* (with the redoubtable Grace Moore), *Manon, Faust, Mignon, Tales of Hoffmann* and a single *Don Giovanni*. He was very happy at the Met and the old building was much to his liking. All the same he had no time for certain sections of the audience, who often deserved his 'Australian treatment'.

In July 1944 Beecham went to Mexico City to direct a Mozart Festival which had been arranged with the financial support of the City authorities. He had previously invited Virgil Thomson to be his assistant on one of the operas but Thomson was already committed at the time and had to refuse. He always regretted having missed such an opportunity. Beecham took with him six principal singers, and was to complete and rehearse his casts locally. The orchestra was provided by Mexico City.

The operas were three: *Don Giovanni, Die Zauberflöte* and *Le Nozze di Figaro*, all sung in their original languages, with two performances of each. Because Sundays and Wednesdays were the only days allocated for performances, the Festival was to be spun out over three weeks.

When Beecham arrived in Mexico City he discovered the reason for the Sundays and Wednesdays. A spurious 'National Opera' was in occupation, conducted by Jascha Horenstein and with a cohort of Met star singers. Their *Carmen* had Rose Pauly and Kurt Baum with the celebrated dancer Argentinita and a large ballet in support; their *Tosca* starred Dusolina Giannini and Raoul Jobin with Salvatore Baccaloni as the Sacristan. The British Ambassador in Mexico City urged Beecham to resign from the whole thing in disgust, but he took it calmly and good-naturedly, only demanding that his season be put back a week. When he then announced that he would open on 26 July with *Don Giovanni*, the rival opera announced their own *Don Giovanni* for the night before Beecham's.

Beecham's rehearsals were enlivened by the behaviour of the local bass, Ignacio Rufino, who was singing the Commendatore. He wore a pistol very prominently all the time, as he had recently shot at 'an amatory rival' in a Mexico cinema and was now expecting reprisals. Although Beecham's company possessed fewer star names than Horenstein's, Beecham had John Brownlee as the Don and the splendid

Hungarian bass, Lorenzo Alvary, as Leporello. Florence Kirk (a Toscanini soprano) as Donna Anna and Barbara Troxell as Donna Elvira had good voices and appearance and, moreover, were prepared to do what Beecham asked them.

This team spirit did not apply to all the stars in the other company, whose *Don Giovanni* was a disaster. Even Salvatore Baccaloni, the Leporello, admitted as much: 'Though I say it myself, it stank.' The cast was not outstanding except, perhaps, for the Donna Elvira of Regina Resnik, but what let it down was a complete absence of cohesion, let alone of style. The critic of one of the leading Mexican papers had to leave the performance to file his review before midnight and gave it the benefit of the doubt. But he had not seen and heard the worst. By the time Horenstein's *Don* had dragged itself to a conclusion at 2.15 a.m., it was clear how awful the whole thing had been.

Beecham had already found undesirable evidence of his predecessor with the orchestra. 'You know what we do with a musician like him in England?' he asked. 'We clap him in the Tower!' On the Sunday night it indeed sounded like a different orchestra. Beecham's performance of *Don Giovanni* was described as 'some of the most warmly polished Mozart that Mexicans had ever heard'.

Another performance of *Don Giovanni* was followed by two of *Die Zauberflöte*, with Mimi Benzell as a very good Queen of the Night, Brownlee as Papageno and Alvary as a noble Sarastro. At a rehearsal of Act I of *Figaro*, Beecham had put down his baton at the end and stated very firmly that they were not ready to go on. Consequently there had to be two extra performances of the *Don* and the *Zauberflöte*, and after some intensive rehearsal in between, mainly for style and timing, *Figaro* reached the stage for two performances after the 'National Opera' had left. Beecham, so often right in his strategy, had fully indicated his decision to stay put and see it through, to the extent of having achieved two extra performances because of the delay in mounting *Figaro*. He conducted all the eight performances.

Beecham visited every part of the United States during his stay there, always travelling by train and always taking a keen delight in the more unusual places. He liked Salt Lake City with its Mormon temple and Brigham Young's house with its fifty-seven bedrooms, which greatly amused him. He was constantly assaulted by newspaper and radio reporters, who sometimes asked the most ingenuous questions and got unexpected answers:

Q. What is the right way to learn opera?

Beecham: Begin at the beginning and go through it efficiently.
Q. Can one sing and smoke?
Beecham: It is extremely difficult both to sing and smoke at the same time.
Q. Do you know parts other than your own?
Beecham (eyes grown wide): Not being a *singer* myself, I have no parts.

He was once persuaded to conduct his stepson's school orchestra at Eaglebrook, Massachusetts. The opening piece was Schubert's *Marche Militaire,* but for once Beecham's downbeat failed him. Three times the baton came crashing down. Silence. A terrified music master came running up and whispered in Beecham's ear: 'It's no good like that, Sir Thomas, you have to go "A-one, a-two, a-three!" '

Beecham enjoyed himself in the States apart from the attacks of gout which had been worsening since his first bouts in the early 1930s. He was meant to be on a diet; though he never ceased to reprove his hosts for having no decent restaurants and poured scorn on pre-packed food, he still went on ordering the most lavish meals with champagne. 'Why do I go on doing this?' he said. 'Because it's nice to look at.'

In 1941 he was appointed conductor for two seasons of the Seattle Symphony Orchestra, which he championed against the rival claims of nearby San Francisco. Most of it was familiar Beecham programme material, although he did include one or two unfamiliar works like Virgil Thomson's *Second Symphony* and his *Filling Station* and *The River.*

Virgil Thomson was the much-feared music critic of the *New York Herald Tribune.* He and Beecham became good friends and Beecham much admired his opera *Four Saints in Three Acts* and *The Mother of Us All,* both set to fragmentary and surrealist libretti by Gertrude Stein. Beecham said he considered *Four Saints* to be 'the finest vocal music in English since Elizabethan times'. His admiration for Thomson was such that he used to say: 'Virgil is the only man in the world who can keep me up until four.'

Whenever a piano concerto appeared in a programme, Betty Humby played it: Mozart and Delius especially. She and Beecham were exceedingly happy in the States and sure of a demand for their return once they had left for England. This they did at the end of September 1944.

But they spent only four months in drab, ration-racked London. Covent Garden was still closed, the London Philharmonic would only have Beecham back on their own terms, and there didn't seem anything for him to do. It was remarked that he had not changed during his absence in America, whereas Britons had become more serious-minded and disinclined to approve his flippancy.

Three months and eleven concerts back in the States seemed far more like living again. In San Francisco in May 1945 a new orchestra called the People's Symphony Orchestra announced three concerts with seats at a flat rate of fifty cents (plus a ten-cent tax). All 4,000 seats were taken on the opening night when Beecham conducted. The eighty-five members of the orchestra had had little rehearsal, had never played together before, and were trying to rival the city's established orchestra with its high prices. The San Francisco Symphony Orchestra reacted to their appearance with alarm.

This was just the kind of challenge that Beecham enjoyed, and in spite of a bad attack of gout he took on the venture without a fee either for himself or for Betty. 'I've been preaching popular concerts for thirty-five years,' he said, 'and just the idea of a millionaire seated next to the crossing-sweeper has always appealed to me.' And in answer to a question: 'No, I do not feel that in conducting a fifty-cent symphony I have lowered my colours. Quite the contrary.' But in spite of good attendances, publicity, playing and reviews the enterprise collapsed three months later.

The Beechams were back in London in May 1945 and stayed there for the rest of the year. He conducted every orchestra that would have him – six of them in all – then back to North America for three months at the beginning of 1946.

Thereafter a concentration on BBC orchestras once again belied the fact that Beecham was about to form the Royal Philharmonic Orchestra, which he did in September. He took it proudly round Britain, showing off its versatility; sometimes he conducted the BBC Symphony; and he made many studio broadcasts and gramophone records.

Beecham's agent suggested he take the Royal Philharmonic to the USA, and plans were at once put in hand for the earliest possible date: 1950. Meanwhile Beecham had been invited to conduct in South Africa. People in this dominion felt that they had been left out of his itineraries; after all, he had conducted in Australia, and more frequently in Canada. He liked the idea.

On 13 August 1948 Sir Thomas and Lady Beecham, with the cellist Michael Cherniavsky, arrived in the *Warwick Castle* at Cape Town. Waiting for Sir Thomas in some trepidation was the largest orchestra ever assembled in South Africa. The Cape Municipal Orchestra was reinforced by the South African Broadcasting Corporation's studio orchestras from Cape Town, Durban and Johannesburg. Their total strength was ninety-five players of both sexes, and they had all read with some misgivings of Beecham's rages and furies in London about all the things he disapproved of, principally the closing of Covent Garden's doors to him.

He was suffering from a bad attack of sciatica in the right leg and was carried off the ship in a wheel-chair. Later, in his hotel, he dominated the press conference. 'I invite specific questions. To each specific question I will give an equally specific answer. What's that? "What's specific?" A question that is not specific is "What do you think of South Africa?" I haven't seen South Africa yet.' And glaring round he continued: 'And if you were to ask whether I like being photographed, the answer would not be quite so specific.' And so he went on, his angry – or mock angry – countenance soon softening as humour and sarcasm melted into one another. It was all a game to him, as the press was quick to recognise.

He gave nine concerts in all. The broadcasting contingent moved round with Beecham to join the Johannesburg and Durban orchestras in turn, thus forming a nucleus of continuity. The programmes were chosen so as not to be unduly demanding on the players, who had only minimum rehearsal time.

The tour was considered a great success. Beecham told his audience at the first concert that if they wanted encores he would expect a crate of bananas to be sent to Britain for the 'Hungry Children Fund'. Press cartoons showing Beecham with bananas helped his campaign and the audiences got their encores. At the last concert the orchestra subscribed £5 as a personal present for him – a touching tribute from virtual strangers.

Beecham conducted from the moment he got back to England in October for the next twelve months, without going abroad again. He safely negotiated his seventieth birthday celebrations, persuaded the BBC to let him record works which he wanted to do more than they did, though they refused him *The Mother of Us All* (Thomson Stein), and got away in October in time for the Montreal Festival. He and Betty then went on to Dallas, where he gave a lecture on Mozart accompanied by himself at the piano and a concert three days later, which unexpectedly included not a single Mozart work.

From January to early August 1950 the Beechams were in London. Immediately before leaving for the USA he gave four Mozart concerts at Glyndebourne. Now came the great American tour with the RPO.

The orchestra disembarked from the *Queen Mary* in New York on 12 October and gave fifty-two concerts in sixty-four days, mainly one-night stands, throughout the length and breadth of the USA. They had to face snow, blizzards, torrential rain, and centrally heated buildings which they weren't accustomed to. They discovered all kinds of new inventions

Above Beecham batting for fun. He had injured his hand playing cricket at Rossall, and never played seriously again. *Right* Being greeted on arrival at Nice (c. 1956) by the town's chief *gendarme*.

Lady Shirley Beecham and Sir Thomas, shortly after their marriage in 1959.

Beecham's 80th birthday dinner at the Dorchester Hotel, London, on 1 May 1959. To his left are David Webster, General Administrator of the Royal Opera House, and Sir Malcolm Sargent. *Below* The RPO at the special luncheon given by Beecham on 7 May 1960 in Portsmouth. They all watched the Cup Final on television during the afternoon, and what proved to be Beecham's last concert took place there that evening.

Beecham in about 1960. The face is that of an elderly man, but the strength is unmistakable.

such as washing-machines and drip-dry shirts. The orchestra was under the management of Sol Hurok, but Sir Thomas employed another manager, which set an edge on all the arrangements.

The programmes were fairly conservative and allowed a maximum of shuffling so as to avoid too enormous a repertoire. The orchestra knew the works intimately, having played them at home since their formation. Weather conditions meant that sometimes the orchestra arrived only just in time to give a concert and that sometimes they had to leave far earlier than expected the morning after. Their coach-drivers were ever-cheerful.

At one date the RPO was welcomed, to their surprise, with a sign saying 'Greetings to Sir Thomas Beecham and the London Philharmonic Orchestra'. In New Orleans, during mid-November, Beecham was walking about the railway station waiting for his train to Jackson, Mississippi, when a little black girl took his hand and said she wanted to go on the train with him. The picture caused a sensation. Indeed, the whole tour was a sensation; Beecham and the Royal Philharmonic Orchestra were seen as a superb exercise in waving the flag. Moreover the tour was a financial success as well as an artistic one. 'And not a penny of taxpayers' money has gone into it!' boasted Beecham, always looking for chances to take pot-shots at the BBC.

On 16 December an exhausted RPO finally tumbled back into the *Queen Mary* after their marathon trip. Beecham alone emerged fresh and debonair as though he had only just arrived.

1951 was the year of the Festival of Britain, and although Beecham was not invited to the Royal Festival Hall (or perhaps he refused the invitation because of all the uncomplimentary things he had been saying about the building), he took the RPO on a major tour of the UK and remained in the country for the whole year.

From 1952 a new pattern of concert-giving emerged. In accordance with new tax laws imposed by Attlee's government in 1951, a British citizen might avoid payment of full income-tax and super-tax if he lived abroad and only entered the land of his birth for 180 days in the year (with a maximum of ninety days at a time). For the rest of his life Beecham took advantage of this law, so that the number of his concerts in Britain was reduced considerably.

Beecham and Betty spent much of their exile in the south of France and in Italy, although for the first two months of 1952 and a month between March and April 1955 Beecham had concert engagements in North America. In 1956 this was extended to fourteen concerts between the end of January and the third week in March. The pattern repeated itself in 1957, with television concerts, interviews and discussions (like the one between himself, Maria Callas and Victor Borge in New York).

Beecham's diary entries in these years reflected the care with which he watched his stays in London: 'Must be away in 3 weeks'; 'MUST be AWAY in 6 days'; 'LAST DAY'. This meant that he was separated from his beloved RPO for too long, but in October 1957 he took them on a two-week European tour that started in Paris, included six Swiss cities and ended with two concerts in Vienna. He was recording more and more in Paris, where the acoustic of the wooden Salle Wagram suited him perfectly and where he was sometimes able to record with his own orchestra.

During the summer of 1958 Beecham had fixed himself up with the wonderful prospect of conducting five of his favourite operas at the Teatro Colón in Buenos Aires. They were (as billed locally) *Otello, Carmen, Sanson y Dalila, La Flauta mágica* and *Fidelio*. But what was going to be a treat turned out to be the most unhappy tour he had ever undertaken, for Betty died in Buenos Aires three days before the opening night of the *Flute*. Stricken as he was, Beecham refused to let her death interrupt the season, and apart from cancelling two rehearsals he carried out the scheduled programme as well as a concert with the Buenos Aires Orchestra.

He returned to London alone and by air, weary, lonely and hampered by both sciatica and gout. But by the beginning of 1959 he was fit to resume his normal January–February commitments, this time with the Philadelphia and Chicago Orchestras.

He sailed from Britain for New York on 16 December 1959 to begin what turned out to be his last American tour. It was a farewell to the usual cities: Pittsburgh, San Francisco, his old Seattle Orchestra, Chicago and Washington. In between were two concerts in Vancouver.

Beecham always kept in touch with London by telephone and he was looking forward to conducting – at last – *Les Troyens* at Covent Garden in 1960. Although he and David Webster had buried the hatchet, there were still some aspects of Covent Garden's policies that irritated him. Consequently he telephoned the Royal Opera House one April morning from Toronto to say that under no circumstances would he have anything to do with an English version of the two Berlioz operas.

When he came down to breakfast the next morning, David Webster was in the hotel foyer waiting to see him. He had dropped everything and had flown over to pacify Beecham. But it was all in vain; Beecham never conducted *Les Troyens* at Covent Garden.

He flew back to London for the last time on 12 April and thereafter never left England. He overstayed the permitted days to die, but the taxman was relentless. Foreign orchestras had gained enormously from his need to keep on the move and away from home, and his seemingly endless travelling gradually ate up his reserves of strength and fire. Perhaps Dame Ethel Smyth summed it up best: 'I have watched him draw flames, sighs, dreams, laughter out of them, and it is as though his spirit were reflected in a mirror that gives back his essence in thousand-fold strength.'

Chapter Seven

BEECHAM'S MUSIC

In November 1906, when Beecham stood alone in front of his orchestra in the Bechstein Hall to face the London public and critics, he knew that he must make an instant impression upon them or else go down. If he went down, the climb back would be intolerable. He faced the established conductors – Henry Wood, Nikisch, Richter, Elgar – as well as other, lesser fry, each with his devoted following. He was setting himself against them all.

Beecham's musical background had been supported by large sound. The orchestrion and his father's other musical boxes, whose tunes he had begun to absorb from the age of four, poured out the noisier, bigger selections from operas and symphonies. Unlike that of the conventionally musical child, his own experience came least of all from the piano stool. When he had objected to piano exercises and asked his master to tell him the stories of the operas instead, he was pursuing the course that his father had inadvertently set him on. Now, in 1906, this background proved one of his strongest weapons.

Having a small orchestra he considered the possibilities open to him. He might give either a concert of popular works of the kind that the public could hear almost anywhere or else a carefully selected programme of the most interesting unknown works that he could devise. In the first instance, the public would come and listen more for the sake of the old favourites than for the sake of Beecham. At this stage in his career the public mattered less than the critics and musicians. If he could tempt *them* into liking his programmes he was more than half-way there. The public believe the critics, and musicians pay heed to other musicians.

Beecham's trunk, which he had brought back from his travels in France and Italy, contained copies of ancient manuscripts of French scores made by him and his hirelings in the Bibliothèque Nationale, as well as choice Italian opera scores which had not been heard in England for a generation at least – if at all. So he built programmes from mainly his own resources; but he had the wisdom to commence his first concert with Mozart's *Prague* Symphony.

The result of the three concerts is well-known. The public stayed away, but the critics praised Beecham and his orchestra highly, particularly Beecham. They were excited by the fresh sounds and the delicacy of the playing. Beecham included a lot of Méhul (born 1763) as well as overtures, entr'actes and arias – indeed his preference for overtures ran to a total of ten in the three concerts, one of which still looks very odd in print: 'Méhul – Overture Henry Cockles'. In France they spell it 'Coclès'. Järnefelt's *Praeludium*, which ended the first concert, was encored; C. P .E. Bach's Symphony in D, which opened the second, was considered a most interesting (if not an odd) work, and Haydn's Symphony in E flat (No. 99) was admired. Beecham allowed one English work in the second concert: Charles Wood's Prelude to *Iphigenia in Tauris*. Wood was a musical don who later became professor of music at Cambridge. Beecham already knew him.

As an immediate result of the Bechstein Hall concerts Beecham and the committee of the orchestra brought themselves up to full symphonic strength as the New Symphony Orchestra and booked nine dates at Queen's Hall for the following season. It was at the second of these nine concerts that the momentous meeting between Delius and Beecham occurred.

If ever a composer was in need of a strong and sympathetic interpreter of his works it was surely Delius, and Beecham performed the task lovingly and in an entirely dedicated manner for the rest of his life. When people told him that they found nothing in a Delius score, Beecham replied that he found it 'as alluring as a wayward woman and was determined to tame it!' Among the three main composers whom Beecham took up Delius was the closest friend, and Beecham succeeded in capturing every nuance in the output of his most elusive music, with the exception of one composition, the *Requiem*. It was the kind of partnership in which Beecham edited the scores and then gave them a shape and meaning for the listener by bringing out the hidden melodies and achieving a proper instrumental balance. Delius ignored these considerations when committing to paper the sounds which he heard so clearly in his head.

Beecham's enthusiasm for Delius's music was immediate. He played *Paris* and *Brigg Fair*; he then engaged the North Staffs Choral Society ('because there isn't a decent choir in London') and performed *Appalachia*, *Sea Drift* and then *A Mass of Life* for the first time. All this greatly astonished the critics, who had not yet got to grips with Delius's voice but were absolutely certain that Beecham had.

Henry Wood had given a few of Delius's compositions in London but without any special *éclat*. Here was Beecham positively hurling it at the public and proclaiming it as the most important English music in living memory. By degrees some members of the audiences for these works became convinced too, and the Delius cult was established in Britain. In Germany it had a vogue as long as conductors like Haym and Cassirer promoted it, but not otherwise, while in France and Italy it has never caught on.

Over Delius's grave in Limpsfield in 1935 Beecham called him 'a great Englishman'. Perhaps Delius's nationality does not matter, for arguments about it still go on; but Beecham found that Delius's 'arrival' encouraged a number of British composers to try and compete against him. Now at last there seemed to be a champion of English music – someone who would give them a proper hearing.

Among these composers struggling against antipathy towards British music were Arnold Bax, Vaughan Williams, Cyril Scott, Frank Bridge and others. Beecham considered that Bax 'revealed an all-round technical accomplishment of the highest order'; Vaughan Williams 'was already striking out that individual line which was eventually to mark him as the most essentially English composer of his time'; and 'the rare and charming personality of Cyril Scott' was fully present in his smaller pieces.

However, it was Josef Holbrooke more than any of these who struck Beecham as 'the most picturesque and singular figure of the hour', tall and gaunt with piercing blue eyes behind steel-rimmed spectacles. His was an electric talent best suited to fantastic subjects. He urged Beecham to become his collaborator in two performances of his Second Symphony, subtitled *Apollo and the Seaman*. (The whole question of Beecham's conducting the work was contradicted by Holbrooke many years later.)

Holbrooke was compounded of contradictions and eccentricities, and it may have been these which attracted Beecham towards him. Holbrooke was outspoken, self-confident, amazingly industrious and blessed with a large and sprawling talent entirely lacking in any form of self-criticism. He modelled his compositions largely on Liszt and Richard Strauss.

Beecham was always game for something out of the ordinary, something that offered a challenge, and *Apollo and the Seaman*, with its important magic lantern that gave a new dimension to the entertainment, its large orchestra and its split-second timing, certainly needed all Beecham's skill, and basically serious frame of mind, comical though the whole enterprise seemed to him. Despite its failure (from Holbrooke's point of view) at both performances and despite his indignation at the way in which Beecham took it so lightly, the fact that it had reached performance at all was greatly to the conductor's credit.

Holbrooke had Beecham to thank again in 1914 when he staged his opera *Dylan*; and in between Beecham gave a fair selection of his shorter pieces at concerts. Bearing in mind how hard-up Beecham was during the years 1907–8 one cannot help wondering whether Holbrooke's influential and rich backers, who included Lord Howard de Walden, were not a major reason for Beecham's interest and willingness to play Holbrooke's music.

In the year before he strode so confidently into the orchestral arena, Beecham had become closely associated with the Oriana Madrigal Society in London. It was an amateur organisation, founded in 1906 by Charles Kennedy Scott, and Beecham sang principal bass at their first concert. Thereafter his name did not appear as a singer (which will not surprise anybody who ever heard his method of vocalisation) but as a writer of programme notes. These were something out of the ordinary in scholarship and conciseness. The names of John Mundy, Thomas Tomkins, Thomas Vautor and John Bennet, as well as their styles and their compositions, seemed to be as familiar to him as those of the more celebrated Byrd, Dowland and Orlando Gibbons; his familiarity with them and their music sounded almost as though he had lived among these Elizabethan masters. Here, then, lay a true feeling for English vocal music which later events tended to obscure. The Oriana remained very close to Beecham's heart up to the end of his life.

Beecham continued to sponsor the works of Granville Bantock, and during the First World War he also played new compositions by Delius, Sterndale Bennett, Frank Bridge and Frederic Austin, keeping the national music flag flying. But it was not until the Leeds Triennial Festivals of 1928–37, of which he was musical director and Malcolm Sargent his assistant conductor from 1931, that Beecham seriously took his compatriots into account.

He had to cater for the splendid Leeds Choral Society, which allowed him to indulge his fondness for Handel, but he also included compositions by Frederic Austin, Lord Berners and Cyril Scott, as well as two large-scale works by Elgar, then Master of the King's Music. Beecham's attitude to Elgar's music, which was by then well and truly established, remained ambivalent. On the whole he found it too German by half, although he played *Cockaigne* and found it went down well abroad. He played the *Enigma Variations* infrequently, conducted the

Cello Concerto only once, and cut the First Symphony to pieces at a Hallé concert because he found it far too long-winded. Elgar protested in a mild fashion, so one day when the symphony was again down for rehearsal Beecham said to the orchestra: 'Gentlemen, the composer of the immortal masterpiece we are now about to rehearse again, has written insisting that we play it as written, in its entirety. So now, gentlemen, if you please, we'll play it *with all the repeats.*'

In 1931, for the first time, Beecham found himself at Leeds, required to play a Vaughan Williams symphony, the *Pastoral.* At the end of the last movement a single soprano voice fades away to silence. Beecham placed the singer in a gallery in the farthest corner of Leeds Town Hall. At the rehearsal, in front of a fair number of people who had come to listen, Beecham went on beating after the soprano had finished. He turned to his leader and asked: 'Why aren't you playing?' The astonished man looked up and whispered: 'There's nothing more to play, Sir Thomas.'

'What?' shouted Beecham.

'It's over, that's all, it's finished, Sir Thomas.' To which Beecham replied 'Thank God.'

Vaughan Williams probably heard about this, because he turned antagonistic towards Beecham. At the end of his life a friend whom he met going up in the lift at the Royal Festival Hall asked the old man whether he was going to the Beecham concert. 'I am not,' he replied, 'and I don't propose to attend any of his concerts until he learns to play my music.'

Beecham occasionally gave one work by that 'ultra-modern' of the late 1920s and the 1930s, William Walton. He conducted the ballet *Façade* for the Camargo Society in 1932, and thereafter played the Suite at festivals and in the United States. But he never undertook any of Walton's major works or even his overtures – although who resembles *Scapino* more than Beecham? On one occasion he played the 1937 Coronation March.

Beecham definitely did not like the compositions of Benjamin Britten. During an orchestral exchange with the French in 1945 Beecham was persuaded to include the *Four Sea Interludes* from *Peter Grimes* in his progamme, and murdered them. When asked some time later what he thought of Britten and his fast-increasing output, he replied: 'I never comment upon the works of struggling young musicians.'

Possibly his attitude to his fellow-countrymen's music has never been better shown than in his series of concerts at Carnegie Hall in 1936. There he set a Mozart symphony at the centre of six out of the seven programmes and surrounded it with Boyce, Elgar, Vaughan Williams, Delius, Bax, Walton, Berners, Bantock and Holst. It was a clever idea and it worked. The only programme grossly out of balance (by today's standards) was the first, which began with Mozart's *Paris* Symphony hotly pursued by Vaughan Williams's *London*. After the interval came Ethel Smyth's Overture to *The Wreckers,* the *Calinda* and *Hassan Serenade* by Delius and Elgar's *Cockaigne* Overture.

Much later Beecham took up William Alwyn's Third Symphony, and he helped Richard Arnell considerably, recording his *Punch and the Child*. He was generally sympathetic to young composers and looked at many of their works in manuscript; but it seems that he only found in Arnell the pulse and melody which inspired him to play it. The new schools of serialists (and worse) were incomprehensible to Beecham and he poured scorn and disgust on them, for he found no melody there.

Beecham was utterly at home with French composers, except for Ravel. He evidently agreed with Ernest Newman's opinion – 'Scratch Ravel and you will find Chaminade' – but nevertheless he gave a wonderful performance of the left-hand concerto with Jacques Février for the BBC after the last war and a performance of the *Daphnis and Chloë* Suite during the First World War. After some persuasion he agreed to play the Suite again at the Royal Festival Hall in 1956: he did it from memory and came to grief after the huge climax in the *Danse générale*. Dennis Brain and Jack Brymer held it together over the ostinato side-drum beats until Frederick Riddle came in with his signpost on the viola, thus taking Beecham and the whole orchestra safely home. And that was the last time that he included anything by Ravel in his programmes.

Beecham conducted Debussy's *Petite Suite* very early on and also arranged his cantata *L'Enfant Prodigue* as an opera. Of course he gave *Images, La Mer* and *Nocturnes. L'Après-midi d'un Faune* was one of those works which he had learned from watching the Russian Ballet, and his reading was delicate and magical. He recorded it twice.

Beecham quoted Hans Richter as saying that there is no such thing as French music merely to show what an ass he thought Richter was. Berlioz is so French that he transcends nationality; Beecham realised this at the turn of the century through reading 'dozens of text books, histories and biographies' and knowing by heart the *Grand Traité* by Berlioz (his treatise on orchestration). The great Byronic figure is still largely unrecognised in his native France, and most of the gramophone records of his music available there have been made elsewhere. The manner in which Beecham expounded Berlioz's music seemed like a ferocious vindication of its creator, and Beecham is responsible for the strong following which Berlioz still has in Britain.

His choice of the *Carnaval Romain* Overture to launch both the

Beecham Symphony Orchestra and the London Philharmonic was a brilliant stroke; the *Hungarian March* from *The Damnation of Faust* – in the words of one spectator – caused 'the walls of Covent Garden to dissolve' at a later LPO concert there and seemed to transport the furious Beecham at the head of an army seeking death or glory. All the famous Berlioz overtures received this swashbuckling treatment, except for the *Beatrice and Benedict,* which was a lesson in elegance and tip-toeing daintiness. He made *Harold in Italy* a luscious, dreamy affair, while the *Te Deum* and the *Grande Messe des Morts* were both sonorous, serious calls to account. His rare performances of these huge works were red-letter days in the musical calendar. Few conductors could approach, let alone equal, that much-played work the *Symphonie Fantastique* as Beecham did it. He gave a moody impression of the artist's drug-laden mind such as nobody else has quite succeeded in bringing off since; the changes of scene from the lilting *Ballroom* to the *Scène aux Champs* and onwards to the terrifying finale was done with a maximum of surprise to emphasise the unreality, and left the listener completely exhausted.

Among the lesser French composers should be mentioned Chabrier and his 'circus music' such as *España* and the *Marche Joyeuse* which Beecham tackled with relish and abandon.

César Franck, of course, stands with his Symphony as a kind of half-way house between French and German music. Beecham recorded this work twice, with its laborious chromatic ascents and descents taken boldly for what they are worth – although some other conductors make them sound to be worth very little. But the Franck tone-poem, *Le Chasseur Maudit,* was played in a truly French manner, striking a chill to the listener with its dramatic, almost Gothic message.

It would not be running true to form if Beecham did not introduce a few eccentric choices from time to time. In the orchestral field perhaps the most vacuous were both French: Godard's *Concerto Romantique* and Lalo's G minor Symphony; while Goldmark's *Rustic Wedding* Symphony, in Beecham's view a perfect example of true Austrian music, sounded amazingly fresh and beautiful under his hand but perfectly hopeless under any other.

Among the German composers, Beecham championed Strauss in Britain and was devoted to *Ein Heldenleben,* which he first played as a prelude (and what a prelude!) to the New Year's Eve end-of-season *Salome* in 1910. Thereafter it figured quite often in his programmes, more often than *Don Quixote* to which he held the secret of light and shade, zany comedy and heart-rending tragedy. Never was there a more lovely ending to this work than at the Edinburgh Festival of 1956 when John

Kennedy's cello solo of the dying Don, under Beecham's inspired hand, closed a superb performance. *Till Eulenspiegel* and *Don Juan* (both more suitable characters to represent Beecham than their intended master, Strauss) were in his repertoire, but not the sprawling *Also Sprach Zarathustra* or the doleful *Tod und Verklärung*. The *Bourgeois Gentil-homme* incidental music was a Beecham favourite, for it showed off the virtuoso qualities of his musicians.

Among the classical German symphonists, Beecham was choosy. He seemed to hold Beethoven in some awe; his strength and character were rather too straightforward and granitic, or else too obvious. He conducted the First Symphony once only, it seems, in 1899; and the Ninth he did as infrequently as possible – he considered that Beethoven, because of his deafness, had made an error of balance in the last movement. His favourite symphony by far was the Second. He brought it out all fresh and sparkling in 1926 and made it sound quite different from any previous performance by anybody else. He recorded it three times; and he recorded the others with the exception of the First, Fifth and Ninth. He eventually came round to playing the two Beethoven Masses and, of course, *Fidelio*, whose structure, one might say, is almost symphonic. He accompanied the Fourth Piano Concerto with pleasure, finding it nearest Mozart in spirit; but the *Emperor* he played only rarely, for he considered it to be an irritating work, reminiscent in its aggressive insistence of the Seventh Symphony.

Beecham never played Brahms's Fourth Symphony, and he gave the First only once or twice at the most. The Second, his favourite, he played far more often than the Third. He is known to have accompanied the Second Piano Concerto on three occasions, once with Schnabel in New York, once at the Royal College of Music with the student orchestra and the young Norman Tucker as soloist, and then much later with the RPO.

He played all Schubert's symphonies with the exception of the Fourth (*Trauer*); Mendelssohn's last three and the Violin Concerto often; but of Schumann's symphonies only the third.

Haydn, the down-to-earth wheelwright's son with a twinkle in his eye and an endless invention to go with it, was in a sense Beecham's counterpart. He matched Haydn's jokes, pretended solemnity and fertile imagination in his own life as well as in his playing of the old Austrian's works, so natural and simple in their good humour.

Beecham recorded the twelve *Salomon* Symphonies (between 1957 and 1959) but only about half of their number ever figured prominently in his concerts, notably Nos. 93, 97, 99, 100 and 101. There was then no alternative to the nineteenth-century Peters scores, which the pedants now deride because they differ in detail from the composer's autographs. Not that this made a ha'porth of difference to Beecham's performances, or that anybody since has been able to rival his interpretations, even with the 'authentic' scores before him. Beecham was always agreeable to altering the values of the printed notes so long as the result justified it, and the result, in his case, meant a clarity and refinement in the musical texture, phrasing and subtlety in nuance.

The Seasons was the only Haydn oratorio that Beecham played regularly, although he came round to *The Creation* in 1944 after his return from the USA. To both he gave his sure touch; and although he always performed them in English the general effect was of warmth, tenderness and complete integrity.

Whether Beecham regarded George Frederick Handel as German or English made no difference to his devotion towards his music. In *A Mingled Chime* he gave a pleasing and persuasive account of the reason why Handel's music was so important for amateur choirs and choral bodies in England. Elsewhere he stresses the fact that much of Handel's scoring was left in a sketchy state, with figured bass only, so that executants might improvise over his guidance. What Handel really intended, with the small and rawly constituted orchestras of his time, is anybody's guess.

In 1926 Beecham edited and reproduced a radically new version of the *Messiah*. Gerald Abraham has stated that 'his racy tempos not only caused the hair to stand upright on some thousands of elderly heads; they did remind us that *Messiah* is a musical masterpiece and not a religious monument.' In 1959 Beecham commissioned Eugene Goossens to make another realisation and again horrified a great many people. Both versions were recorded and still demonstrate Beecham's intention to bring the work up to date and prove it to be a work for any age. Meanwhile the 'professors, pedants, pedagogues – bah!' failed to remember that Mozart, Mendelssohn and Robert Franz all found the autograph score of *Messiah* quite impossible to perform as it stood, and each edited it to suit his own particular requirements. Beecham carried on this tradition.

Such was his understanding and knowledge of Handel's works that he was able to make arrangements for two ballets, *The Gods go a' Begging* and *The Origin of Design*, the chosen movements being entirely new music to all but Handel scholars. Beecham's three suites, *The Faithful Shepherd*, *Amaryllis* and *Love in Bath*, continued this scholarship and brought a freshness and vitality to the numbers in much the same way as they must have done to their first audiences. He then fashioned a piano concerto for Betty from utterly appropriate sources.

Among the oratorios he had a preference for *Israel in Egypt* and *Solomon;* and he gave several of the *Chandos Anthems* when he had the right singers. Beecham's knowledge of Handel was great enough for him to have given a Festival and entertained the public night after night with the treasures he had discovered. Perhaps, since Beecham, we have returned to a state of ignorance and apathy about the jewels still concealed in the old scores, similar to that which existed in Britain before *Messiah* was first given by Beecham in 1916.

The last composer whom Beecham championed for all he was worth was Jean Sibelius, who wrote music of a totally personal and unusual texture and sound in remote Finland. His First Symphony was composed in the nineteenth century, his Seventh in 1924. Then there was symphonic silence until his death in 1957. Beecham learnt these works gradually until he gave his Festival of Sibelius in London in 1938, showing that his works were conventional in construction insofar as he kept to the rules of nineteenth-century symphonic composition. Sibelius's other works, the Violin Concerto and symphonic poems, all gleamed and shimmered with an undertone of iron strength in Beecham's interpretations, urging people to take him seriously for what he is: a classicist of today, son of the north wind, fathered by Brahms.

Beecham probably learnt the First Symphony in 1932 and by 1938, a year without special significance in Sibelius's life (he was seventy-three that December), Beecham knew them all. A Festival seemed like the answer.

Once again this upset Henry Wood. He wrote to Sibelius saying that he considered it 'very extraordinary that the London newspapers are announcing "in large letters" that Sir Thomas Beecham is giving a so-called SIBELIUS FESTIVAL. It seems to have been unaccountably overlooked that during the Proms of 1937 I gave what was indeed a Sibelius Festival and through the season did your seven symphonies. But because it was during the Proms it passed unnoticed and unrecognised. This has hurt your friend extremely.' It was bad luck, of course, but superfluous of Wood to have complained, for Beecham's publicity, whether for himself, his orchestra or his festivals was of hereditary excellence.

He gave four concerts of Sibelius's music at Queen's Hall and two at the Aeolian Hall between 27 October and 12 November. Among the names of those connected with the Sibelius Festival occurs that of Walter Legge. This talented young man had been at HMV for some years and had attracted attention by his invention, production and editing of the Society Volumes of 78 r.p.m. gramophone records that began with six volumes of Hugo Wolf lieder sung by over a dozen eminent singers. This was such a success that further volumes followed and then *Die Zauberflöte* from Berlin which Beecham conducted. Now the series was being augmented by the Sibelius Society Volumes, of which three had already been published by 1938.

It was undoubtedly Beecham's Sibelius Festival and the records which were made round it, including two volumes by Beecham and the LPO and Heifetz playing the Violin Concerto, which crystallised the public's interest in, and knowledge of, this very individually flavoured music.

But even Beecham's festivals devoted to Sibelius and Delius and his fondness for Handel could not replace the pre-eminent position which Mozart held in his estimation. He described him as a bridge between the ancient and the modern worlds of music, but a bridge which had upon it 'many lovely structures of his own'. Beecham never ceased to revere these structures and his love and knowledge of Mozart's works surpassed every other. Mozart was apart, god-like in his absolute command of every form of composition yet at the same time a real man whose occasional personal (though never musical) vulgarities delighted Beecham.

He often reminded people that whereas Haydn 'invented' the early symphony it was Mozart who, from the *Paris* to the *Jupiter*, ennobled and perfected its form, leaving the pattern for Haydn to use in his own finished examples after Mozart was dead. Mozart was 'the central point of European music' and in his short life of only thirty-five years he showed those who came after the importance and the place of 'increased grandeur, resonance, tragedy'. Indeed, he cleared away the rubble and laid firm foundations for successive composers.

Beecham produced a sound in Mozart that was at once familiar, confident and perfectly easy to grasp. He negotiated all the so-called danger-spots with cleanness, accuracy and total disregard for his colleagues' apprehension and uncertainty. With this subconscious affinity with Mozart, Beecham began a new phase in the playing of the master's works and in the public's understanding of him in Britain or wherever Beecham played. Not only this, but he made English translations of at least two of the great operas and edited the (incomplete) *Requiem*. He considered that about eleven of the piano concertos were 'the most beautiful compositions of their kind in the world' and played them many times with Betty.

Beecham discovered, quite late in life, the importance of finishing a concert with a short composition of an entirely different character from that of the last advertised one in the programme. He was in the United States when he discussed this with Betty. Generally, after a symphony, a soft and gentle work was required, something even a little sweet and sickly. 'Lollipop!' said Betty, and the name was born in musical parlance. Beecham describes it himself as 'of an essentially syrupy, soapy, soothing and even soporific nature, and the effect upon the audience has been that its emotional temperature, raised to a high point at the conclusion of the actual programme, is gradually reduced to the normal, so that everyone walks out happy and comfortable.'

Chapter Eight

CODA

In his *Jupiter* Symphony Mozart wrote a magnificent coda to the last movement which seemed to say that, had he been allowed more time on earth, he could have gone on composing symphonies *ad infinitum*. Beecham refused to allow himself the merest thought that he wasn't going to fulfil all the plans he had made for the future; only very rarely was there a hint of the weariness of age or a disinclination to carry on. A formidable programme awaited his return from South America and *work* was the only remedy.

Thirteen public concerts (one to be televised) and four BBC studio recordings filled in the whole time between the first concert on 15 October 1958 and Christmas Day. Then he had to fly back to America for six weeks with the Philadelphia and Chicago Orchestras.

The first London concert after Betty's death was at the Royal Festival Hall, and immediately before it Beecham uttered these uncharacteristic words: 'I'd give £10,000 not to have to conduct tonight.' Yet in this mood he gave a heavy programme; Schubert's Third and Mendelssohn's Fourth Symphonies, and *Ein Heldenleben*. This was for the Royal Philharmonic Society. Four days later he was back there for one of his own promotions.

Three somewhat unusual concerts took place on 23 October at the Sheldonian Theatre, Oxford, on 30 October for the Bar Musical Society (televised), and on 15 November at Eton College. By Christmas Day, when he took the RPO into the BBC Studio on double pay to pre-record a concert, Beecham was back in the old routine and on top of his form again.

After the American concerts and television he had to stay abroad until shortly before 29 April and his eightieth birthday. This was celebrated twice in London. On the actual day he entertained about sixteen of his closest friends (and one relative) in a suite at Brown's Hotel. They included Beverley Baxter and his wife, Lord Boothby, Neville Cardus and Shirley Hudson, the RPO's administrator.

By contrast, on 1 May there was a 'public' birthday party at the

Dorchester Hotel which was attended by a great number of professional friends and hangers-on. It was rather like a jamboree. Among the telegrams was a most charming one from Beecham's Pamina of 1914 at Drury Lane: 'Heartiest congratulations to my youngest musical friend with warmest greetings and many more happy returns of the day your ever devoted and grateful friend. Claire Dux.' After all the telegrams had been read out Beecham observed aloud: 'What? Nothing from Mozart?'

Beecham went to Lucerne in September to conduct the Philharmonia Orchestra at the Festival. He gave a performance of a newly scored version of the *Messiah*, done at his instigation by Eugène Goossens. It caused a stir and was regarded as disgraceful in some quarters on account of its rich and shining colours and 'modern' effects. Beecham declared that it was meant to be in the grand manner whatever the age in which it was performed, and that the work had never interested him before. But this was far from so: as far back as his first Leeds Festival, in 1928, he had given it at the opening concert. At rehearsals he had observed the mincing way in which a cohort of elderly ladies had been singing 'For unto us a Child is born, unto us a Son is given'.

'Now come along ladies,' he urged them, 'a little more joy please, and not quite so much astonishment.'

At Lucerne, too, there was another event which surprised the world. Beecham took Shirley Hudson off to Zürich and married her at the town hall in a civil ceremony on 10 August. Although he was a widower (up to this point), he took great care once again to convince himself that his divorce from Utica was in order, for she was still alive.

The new Lady Beecham was twenty-seven, Sir Thomas a little over eighty. Their being so often together in the office, at concert halls and on journeys had inevitably brought a deeper relationship. They had, nevertheless, managed to keep it a close secret, something that is almost impossible to do in orchestral life.

After Lucerne, Beecham took the RPO to the Coventry Festival for two concerts, on a short German tour, and then up to Huddersfield, Manchester and Leeds.

On 27 November he made his first appearance at the Free Trade Hall with the RPO, and the critic of the *Manchester Evening News* wrote in glowing terms: 'To judge by the reception given to Sir Thomas Beecham and the RPO last night, anyone would think that Manchester was cut off in the wilds and the Hallé Orchestra and Sir John Barbirolli had never been heard of.' After doubting the real depth of feeling in Tchaikovsky's Fourth Symphony and regretting the demonstration of audience hysteria after it, the critic ended with these words: 'The performance of Mozart's

39th made one feel that the gods had come down among us. Nowhere else on earth last night could there have been such music-making.'

Then, after three months of concerts in the USA between January and March 1960, Beecham came back to England for what were to be his last two concerts.

On 24 April (five days before his eighty-first birthday) he gave a typically Beechamesque concert at the Royal Festival Hall: Haydn's Symphony No. 100, Schubert's Fifth, Goldmark's Violin Concerto, *On the River* from the *Florida Suite* by Delius, and finally the Bacchanale from *Samson and Delilah*. Then, after a few 'tidying-up' sessions for EMI, he had a date in Portsmouth. The day was a special one in several senses.

Because he and the orchestra had not been about together for nearly a year, owing to his being in America and to his being ill, Beecham took the musicians to lunch in the city's banqueting rooms. Afterwards they strolled across to Portsmouth Guildhall, that uninviting building below the mainline railway station, at the time surrounded by bomb damage. It was the day of the 1960 Cup Final.

Beecham's fondness for football had sometimes been a reason for fast tempi at the end of a concert so that all the players might get away in time for the match on the following day; his jokes about rival loyalties to teams and parading of colours was an old gambit to cheer up the orchestra during a cold morning's rehearsal. But for this particular rehearsal he merely checked openings and endings of Schubert's Fifth and Haydn's *Military*, and caressed a few phrases of Delius's *Florida Suite* for balance.

'And now, gentlemen,' he said, laying down his baton with a sigh of pleasure, 'to the important business of the day.'

A television set was brought out and placed on the platform; the orchestra sat back and watched the match. The concert that night ended in a furore – the audience seemed to want him to stay all night. Such was the last concert he ever gave.

The virus pneumonia which had brought Beecham back prematurely from America was still lurking about. He was keenly looking forward to conducting *Die Zauberflöte* at Glyndebourne, and to restore his health he and Shirley went to Montreux for a holiday beforehand.

On 21 June he suffered a thrombosis and was forced to give up all thoughts of Glyndebourne. The best place for him was in bed in London, but he had to watch his 'allowed number of days in Britain'. These looked like being exceeded and so he went into hiding. Shirley had a flat in the Marylebone Road where they both lived. He had plenty to read and to think about; she made him happy and confortable and was an admirable nurse. She also had the knowledge and the personality to negotiate on his behalf. One of the few people in London who knew where he was and who visited him in hiding was Malcolm Sargent.

From time to time Beecham emerged to lunch at the Mayfair or the Connaught Hotel, or at the 'Compleat Angler' in Marlow. Muffled to the point of disguise, he was carried into a car and conveyed to a corner table under the watchful eye of a head waiter who always expressed great concern for his customer.

This kind of treatment helped to improve Beecham's health. He greatly enjoyed the game, and by the beginning of 1961 he felt well enough to plan a number of recordings and to consider giving half a concert, with Sargent conducting the other half – just like the old days at the Leeds Festivals.

But these plans were not for this lifetime. A second attack took him away at 3 a.m. on 8 March 1961.

There was never any question of a resting-place in Westminster Abbey, although it was talked about. Although Handel is buried there Beecham did not want such a roof over him – he preferred the sky. He loved the deep countryside where wild birds fly unhindered by traffic or people. So on a very rainy 10 March he was taken on his last, short journey to Brookwood cemetery, Surrey, thirty miles south-west of London. Rhododendrons and fir trees grow round the crossing of paths where the modest white stone bears these words by that prince of dramatists, John Fletcher:

NOTHING CAN COVER
HIS HIGH FAME BUT
HEAVEN; NO PYRAMIDS
SET OFF HIS MEMORIES
BUT THE ETERNAL
SUBSTANCE OF HIS
GREATNESS

BIBLIOGRAPHY

BEAUMONT, CYRIL. *The Diaghilev Ballet in London*. Putnam, 1940.

BEECHAM, SIR THOMAS. *A Mingled Chime*. Hutchinson, 1944.

BEECHAM, SIR THOMAS. *Delius*. Hutchinson, 1959.

BEECHAM, SIR THOMAS. *Romanes Lecture*. Oxford University Press, 1956.

BEECHAM, UTICA. *Our Baby*. Leopold B. Hill, 1920.

BING, RUDOLPH. *5,000 Nights at the Opera*. Hamish Hamilton, 1972.

BIRKENHEAD, EARL OF. *F. E.* Eyre & Spottiswoode, 1960.

BIRKET FOSTER, M. *History of the Philharmonic Society of London*. John Lane, 1912.

BLISS, SIR ARTHUR. *As I Remember*. Faber & Faber, 1970.

BROOK, DONALD. *Conductor's Gallery*. Rockliff, 1945.

BUCKLE, RICHARD (ed.). *Dancing for Diaghilev*. John Murray, 1960.

CARDUS, NEVILLE. *Sir Thomas Beecham*. Collins, 1961.

COOPER, LADY DIANA. *The Rainbird Comes and Goes*. Rupert Hart-Davis, 1958.

DEL MAR, NORMAN. *Richard Strauss* (Vol. I). Barrie & Rockliff, 1962.

ELKINS, ROBERT. *Queen's Hall*. Rider & Co., 1944.

ELKINS, ROBERT. *Royal Philharmonic*. Rider & Co., 1946.

FIELDING, DAPHNE. *Emerald and Nancy*. Eyre & Spottiswoode, 1968.

FRANCIS, ANNE. *A Guinea a Box*. Robert Hale, 1968.

FRY, C. B. *Life Worth Living*. Eyre & Spottiswoode, 1939.

GAISBERG, FRED W. *Music on Record*. Robert Hale, 1946.

GEISSMAR, BERTA. *The Baton and the Jackboot*. Hamish Hamilton, 1944.

GILMOUR, J. D. (ed.). *Sir Thomas Beecham – The Seattle Years*. World Press, Aberdeen, Washington, 1978.

GOLLANCZ, VICTOR. *Journey towards Music*. Gollancz, 1964.

GROVE, SIR GEORGE. *Dictionary of Music and Musicians*. First Edition, Macmillan, 1899.

GROVE, SIR GEORGE. *Dictionary of Music and Musicians*. Fifth edition, ed. Eric Blom. Macmillan, 1954.

HALTRECHT, M. *The Quiet Showman*. Collins, 1975.

HESELTINE, PHILIP. *Delius*. Bodley Head, 1923 (revised ed. 1952).

HOWES, FRANK. *Full Orchestra*. Martin Secker & Warburg, 1944.

HUGHES, SPIKE. *Glyndebourne*. Methuen, 1965.

JACKSON, GERALD. *First Flute*. Dent, 1968.

JACKSON, STANLEY. *Monsieur Butterfly*. W. H. Allen, 1974.

JEFFERSON, ALAN. *Delius*. Dent, 1972.

JEFFERSON, ALAN. *Inside the Orchestra*. Reid, 1974.

JEFFERSON, ALAN. *The Operas of Richard Strauss in Great Britain*. Putnam, 1963.

KENNEDY, MICHAEL. *The Hallé Tradition*. Manchester University Press, 1960.

KENNEDY, MICHAEL. *Barbirolli*. Macgibbon & Kegan Paul, 1971.

KESSLER, COUNT HARRY. *Diaries of a Cosmopolitan*. Weidenfield & Nicolson, 1971.

KOCHNO, BORIS. *Le Ballet en France*. Hachette, Paris, 1954.

KOCHNO, BORIS. *Diaghilev and the Ballets Russes*. Harper & Row, 1970.

LASSIMONE, DENISE. *Myra Hess*. Hamish Hamilton, 1966.

LEHMANN, LOTTE. *On Wings of Song*. Kegan Paul, 1938.

MACDONALD, NESTA. *Diaghilev Observed*. Dance Horizons, 1975.

MOORE, GEORGE. *Letters to Lady Cunard*. Rupert Hart-Davis, 1957.

PEARSON, HESKETH. *Pilgrim Daughters*. Heinemann, 1961.

PEARTON, MAURICE. *The LSO at 70*. Gollancz, 1974.

PERCIVAL, JOHN. *The World of Diaghilev*. Studio Vista, 1971.

PROCTER–GREGG, H. *Beecham Remembered*. Duckworth, 1976.

REID, CHARLES. *John Barbirolli*. Hamish Hamilton, 1971.

REID, CHARLES. *Malcolm Sargent*. Hamish Hamilton, 1968.

REID, CHARLES. *Thomas Beecham*. Gollancz, 1961.

ROBERTS, CECIL. *Sunshine and Shadows*. Hodder & Stoughton, 1972.

ROBERTS, CECIL. *Years of Promise*. Hodder & Stoughton, 1968.

ROSENTHAL, H. D. *Two Centuries of Opera at Covent Garden*. Putnam, 1958.

RUSSELL, THOMAS. *Philharmonic Decade*. Hutchinson, 1945.

SHORE, BERNARD. *The Orchestra Speaks*. Longmans Green, 1942.

SITWELL, OSBERT. *Great Morning*. Macmillan, 1948.

SMYTH, ETHEL. *Beecham and Pharaoh*. Chapman & Hall, 1935.

SMYTH, ETHEL. *Female Pipings in Eden*. Chapman & Hall, 1934.

SMYTH, ETHEL. *Streaks of Life*. Longmans Green, 1920.

SPENCER, CHARLES. *The World of Serge Diaghilev*. Elek, 1974.

STRAVINSKY, IGOR. *Themes and Conclusions*. Faber & Faber, 1972.

TERTIS, LIONEL. *My Viola and I*. Elek, 1974.

THOMSON, VIRGIL. *Virgil Thomson*. Da Capo, New York, 1966.

TUCHMAN, BARBARA. *The Proud Tower.* Hamish Hamilton, 1966.
WEBBER, R. *Covent Garden – Mud Salad Market.* Dent, 1969.
WHITE, ERIC W. *The Rise of English Opera.* John Lehmann, 1951.

A Beecham Discography. The Sir Thomas Beecham Society, New York, 1975.

Index